SELF-MANAGED WORK TEAMS IN HEALTH CARE ORGANIZATIONS

ELIZABETH D. BECKER-REEMS

AHA

AHA books are published by
American Hospital Publishing, Inc.,
an American Hospital Association company

The views expressed in this publication are strictly those of the author and do not necessarily represent official positions of the American Hospital Association.

Library of Congress Cataloging-in-Publication Data

Becker-Reems, Elizabeth D.

    Self-managed work teams in health care organizations / Elizabeth D. Becker-Reems.
        p.   cm.
    Includes bibliographic references.
    ISBN 1-55648-122-5 (pbk.)
    1. Health services administration. 2. Self-directed work groups.
3. Health care teams. 4. Total quality management. I. Title.
    [DNLM: 1. Personnel Administration, Hospital—methods.
    2. Institutional Management Teams. 3. Total Quality Management.
    4. Patient Care Team—organization & administration.   WX 159 B396s 1994]
    RA971.B343 1994
    362.1'068—dc20
    DNLM/DLC   94-21253
    for Library of Congress   CIP

Catalog no. 169109

©1994 by American Hospital Publishing, Inc.,
an American Hospital Association company

All rights reserved. The reproduction or use of this book in any form or in any information storage or retrieval system is forbidden without the express written permission of the publisher.

Printed in the USA

AHA is a service mark of the American Hospital Association used under license by American Hospital Publishing, Inc.

Text set in English Times
2.5M—9/94—0376
3M—4/95—0412

Audrey Kaufman, Acquisitions/Development Editor
Anne Hermann, Production Editor
Peggy DuMais, Production Coordinator
Cheryl Kusek, Cover Designer
Marcia Bottoms, Books Division Assistant Director
Brian Schenk, Books Division Director

Contents

List of Figures v

List of Tables vii

About the Author viii

Preface ix

Acknowledgments xii

Part One. The Advantages of Teams

Chapter   1.   Introduction to Self-Managed Work Teams 3

Chapter   2.   Team Performance in Health Care 11

Chapter   3.   Employee Responses to the Team Concept 21

Chapter   4.   Critical Success Factors 33

Part Two. Team Design

Chapter   5.   Organizational Structure 41

Chapter   6.   Team Roles, Responsibilities, and Personalities 61

Chapter   7.   The Role of Supervisor 83

Chapter   8.   Work Redesign 95

Part Three. Team Development

Chapter   9.   Introduction of the Team Concept
              to the Organization 113

Chapter 10.   Skills Acquisition 127

Chapter 11.   Team Training 141

Chapter 12.   Team Development 153

Part Four.	**Compensation and Rewards**	
Chapter 13.	Pay Systems	165
Chapter 14.	Reward and Recognition Systems	177
Part Five.	**Making Self-Managed Teams Work**	
Chapter 15.	Readiness Assessment	187
Chapter 16.	Change Management	195
Chapter 17.	Unsuccessful Teams	209
Chapter 18.	Team Improvement Strategies	219

List of Figures

Figure 2-1. Health Care Model for Self-Managed Work Teams 16
Figure 4-1. Team Communication System 36
Figure 5-1. The Functional Structure 43
Figure 5-2. A Typical Department 45
Figure 5-3. The Laboratory 46
Figure 5-4. The Nursing Unit 47
Figure 5-5. Matrix Structure 49
Figure 5-6. Self-Managed Teams 59
Figure 6-1. Team Leader Options 64
Figure 6-2. Team Coach 67
Figure 6-3. The Five-Point Star 75
Figure 6-4. The Ten-Point Star 76
Figure 6-5. Same Point Teams 77
Figure 7-1. Management Roles in the Self-Managed Environment 90
Figure 8-1. The Communication Game 100
Figure 8-2. Sample Comparison Question 102
Figure 9-1. Opinion Leader Assessment 116
Figure 9-2. Force-Field Analysis 117
Figure 11-1. The Five Phases of Team Education 143

Figure 12-1.	Team Development Stages	155
Figure 13-1.	Employee Tasks of a Patient Care Assistant before and after Multiskilling	169
Figure 13-2.	Traditional versus Banded Pay Structure	171
Figure 13-3.	Flattening the Organization and Broadbanding	171
Figure 15-1.	The Self-Managed Teams Readiness Assessment	189
Figure 16-1.	Management Commitment Quadrant	201
Figure 16-2.	Stages of Change	203
Figure 18-1.	Process Flow Diagram for Role Clarification	222
Figure 18-2.	Team Assessment	225
Figure 18-3.	Team Assessment Score Sheet	227
Figure 18-4.	Self-Assessment	228
Figure 18-5.	Self-Assessment Score Sheet	230

List of Tables

Table 2-1. Sample Implementation Plan 19

Table 7-1. Example of Number of Management Positions Needed as Self-Managed Teams Are Implemented 87

Table 9-1. The Communication Plan 124

Table 13-1. Gainsharing 167

Table 13-2. Traditional versus Skill-Based Pay for Patient Care Assistant 170

Table 18-1. Sample of Improvement Goals 231

About the Author

Elizabeth D. Becker-Reems is the director of human resource development at Memorial Mission Hospital in Asheville, North Carolina. With 20 years of experience in personnel management and human resource development in health care, Ms. Becker-Reems provides internal consultation to nursing and ancillary departments in the areas of organizational effectiveness, process consultation, training, team development, and leadership development. She is also the organization's coordinator for the total quality management and customer relations programs and a frequent speaker on the subjects of workforce preparedness, leadership, total quality management, and work teams. Ms. Becker-Reems holds a bachelor's degree in political science and Spanish from Michigan State University and a master's degree in human resource development from Western North Carolina University.

Preface

Self-managed work teams are becoming common in American industry. Health care organizations are just beginning to try team structures in their work environments. Will teams work in health care? Are there advantages to self-managed teams that will help health care organizations succeed as they face the massive changes that health care reform will entail? This book addresses these questions and provides a simple system for the development and implementation of self-managed teams in health care organizations.

The book is designed for senior and middle managers as well as supervisors and employees who are interested in self-managed teams. It presents both sides of the many issues surrounding the question of the feasibility of self-managed teams while clearly advocating the benefits of teams.

Although health care organizations have long endorsed the value of teamwork, few have implemented self-management along with the team concept. Because an organization implementing self-managed teams undergoes tremendous structural change, it should only embark on the self-managed team process if supported by a strong business justification to do so. Even though the implementation of self-managed teams improves employee morale, teams should not be implemented solely for this reason. Self-managed teams should be implemented to increase the efficiency and effectiveness of the organization and to optimize the organization's most valuable health care resources—its employees.

The book comprises five sections, each focusing on a specific aspect of self-managed teams. The first section provides an introduction to teams; the second reviews the elements of team design; the third focuses on the training and development processes of teams; the fourth explores team compensation and rewards; and the fifth final section offers tools and techniques for helping teams achieve high levels of performance.

Part 1 discusses the advantages of teams. Chapter 1 introduces and defines self-managed work teams. It gives a brief history of self-managed work teams and identifies forces within the health care environment that are encouraging health care organizations to try new methods of work improvement. Chapter 2 reviews team performance in health care. It briefly describes self-managed work teams in three health care organizations and provides a model for self-managed work team development. Chapter 3 looks at the responses of employees to the team concept. It describes ways to deal with both negative and positive responses to the concept of self-managed work teams. Chapter 4 focuses on critical success factors. In it, the five critical success factors for team performance are reviewed: senior management support, emphasis on performance, work systems that support teams, employee training, and communication. The chapter also identifies problems that can occur when these critical success factors are not addressed.

Part 2 provides information on team design. It begins with chapter 5's focus on organizational structure, in which functional and matrix structures and their applications in health care organizations are described. This chapter also reveals the advantages and disadvantages of the functional and matrix structures, identifies the benefits of the team structure, and explores the types of health care teams and team roles. Chapter 6 looks at the different roles of team members, clarifies the role of the team coach, and discusses team personality and team behaviors. In chapter 7, the role of the supervisor is reviewed. In addition, guidelines covering the transition from the traditional supervisor's role are provided, as is a discussion of the transition's impact on the manager. Chapter 8 concentrates on work redesign. It identifies work redesign options, describes necessary systems redesign, and reviews three basic rules for work redesign.

Part 3 focuses on team development, outlining a method for obtaining organizational support and providing extensive information on team training and development. Chapter 9 discusses how to introduce the team concept to the organization. It provides a communication plan, describes methods for overcoming barriers within the organization, and includes a helpful opinion leader assessment tool. Chapter 10 explores skills acquisition and development in the technical, interpersonal, teamwork, and supervisory areas—all needed in successful teams. Chapter 11 discusses the team training plan in five phases: preparation, assessment, selection, connection, and education. Chapter 12 covers the five stages of team development from "preteam" through "fully autonomous team."

In part 4, compensation and rewards systems are addressed. Chapter 13 explores pay systems, providing a brief overview of gainsharing, discussing the advantages and disadvantages of skill-based pay, and looking at the benefits and drawbacks of broadbanding. Chapter 14 examines reward and recognition systems—both cash awards and a variety of noncash awards and various recognition programs.

Part 5, the final section of the book, provides information, tools, and strategies to help keep strong teams performing and to improve the performance of developing teams. Chapter 15 offers a readiness assessment tool that can be used by senior management, specific departments, or groups of interested employees to assess the difficulties that will be encountered in implementing self-managed teams in their particular organization. Chapter 16 discusses change management, introducing effective change strategies on the organizational level and describing change strategies on the personal level. Chapter 17 addresses unsuccessful teams: why some teams fail, what the warning signs of failure are, and what team-saving strategies can be used. Finally, chapter 18 focuses on team improvement strategies. It lists the characteristics of effective teams and includes an assessment tool for teams and a self-assessment tool for individual team members.

Acknowledgments

It is not often that the housekeeping staff is the first group to implement a dramatic change in the work environment of an organization. Nonetheless, the housekeeping employees, team leaders, and supervisors at Memorial Mission Hospital deserve recognition and thanks for their willingness to embark on an experiment with self-managed work teams. Particular recognition goes to Martha Ballard and her team, the "6th Floor Sharpies," for being the pilot team that proved and improved the concept and structure for other teams in the department and the hospital.

My special thanks also go to Cliff Carlin, the retired director of the department, who made this project his final legacy to his employees, and to his successor, Bill Morgan, who continued and expanded on self-managed teams to make them the success they are today. Without these leaders' firm belief in the capacity of their employees to learn and their trust in their employees to serve the needs of the organization first, the experiment in self-managed work teams would not have worked.

Recognition also goes to the housekeeping supervisors and team leaders who took the concept of self-managed work teams and adjusted it to fit the special needs of their individual employees and work areas—supervisors like A. J. Ward, Ruth Wells, Ruth Owenby, Decie Sherlin, and Linda Lunsford, who devoted hours to the planning, design, and implementation of self-managed teams while knowing that their jobs would change drastically in the process. And recognition goes to team leaders like Devolia Chambers, Jamie Myers, Nellie Williams, Charles Woody, Charles Bishop, Larry Gault, and Annie Autry, who took this major change in their roles and work life and gave 100 percent to make it work.

I would also like to acknowledge the help and support of Betty Smathers, Gwen Marvels, Jenny Crook, and Gina Kirkland in the human resource development department, who encouraged me to write this book and who worked extra hard to ensure that I had the opportunity to learn and experiment with self-managed work teams in our organization. And thanks to my boss, Doug Geister, who, regardless of his reservations, allowed me to pursue this new way of working with a sizable and valuable group of employees within the hospital.

Loretta Klassen at Hartford Memorial Hospital, William B. Newkirk with Alliant Health System, and Sylvia Swarner at Sutter General Hospital deserve my gratitude for generously sharing information on their organizations' self-managed team, shared governance, and patient-focused care efforts.

Finally, I would like to thank Wendy Leebov—author, consultant, and inspiration—who through a single phone call gave me the opportunity to write this book.

The book itself was improved and enhanced by the efforts of the Books staff at American Hospital Publishing, Inc.

Part One

The Advantages of Teams

Chapter 1

Introduction to Self-Managed Work Teams

Throughout the United States, manufacturing and service industries are implementing a new organizational structure and culture called self-managed work teams. More than 20 percent of the *Fortune 1000* companies indicate that they are now using these teams and plan to increase their use of them in the future.[1] This movement toward self-managed work teams is in response to pressures in the marketplace that are causing many companies to examine and cast off old ways of doing things in order to implement more successful methods of operation. The success of self-managed work teams does not depend on an assembly line structure; rather, it depends on an organization's willingness and ability to create an environment in which employees can work interdependently.

This chapter provides a definition of a self-managed work team and discusses the impact its utilization has had on the manufacturing and service industries. It also discusses some of the various innovative approaches to managing cost and quality currently being considered by health care organizations that increase employee involvement and have the potential to lead to the implementation of self-managed work teams.

• The Evolution of Self-Managed Work Teams

Although there are many definitions of the term *self-managed work team*, the simplest one is this: It is a permanent, self-managed group of employees who work together to produce a product or service. A self-managed work team differs from a task force, quality circle, and quality improvement team in that it is a permanent work group, rather than a group of employees temporarily assigned to work together to solve a specific problem(s). Additionally, although self-managed work teams operate within the policies and procedures established by the organization (just as any of its departments or sections do), unlike their departmental counterparts, team members are empowered to make many "operations" decisions without deferring to a supervisor or other manager. Under the guidance of a coach, team members schedule work, make work assignments, solve problems, improve quality, and communicate directly with customers and other departments in the organization.

Generally, a self-managed work team is composed of 5 to 18 employees who possess the knowledge and skills to complete an entire work process or segment. With additional training, they often are then able to perform management functions as well as support functions.

Self-managed work teams had their beginnings in England in the early 1950s. Working with Eric Trist, a noted British social scientist, The Tavistock Institute of Human Relations observed and reported on the implementation of autonomous teams in the coal industry. Their experiments showed that the utilization of teams resulted in improvements in productivity, work systems, and employee satisfaction.[2] In the United States, although they were initiated at General Electric in 1968, self-managed work teams did not begin to find favor with many manufacturing and service organizations until the mid-1980s.

The movement toward self-managed work teams frequently is associated with the implementation of total quality management (TQM) and other employee involvement practices (although companies initially did not implement self-managed teams in order to get employees more involved). However, the principal reason companies implement self-managed work teams is to effect a positive impact on the bottom line.[3] In attempting to respond to increased competition from abroad, the need to downsize, and the need to reduce cycle time, industries have found that the use of self-managed work teams consistently increases productivity, reduces cost, and enhances quality and service. Many companies have reported as much as a 20 to 40 percent increase in productivity.[4]

At the same time, industries that have implemented self-managed work teams have been able to reduce their total number of employees. Most often, self-managed teams lead to a reorganization of work that (1) reduces the need for high-cost management positions and (2) consolidates professional and support functions, reducing process time. In some instances, organizations have been able to eliminate entire management layers and numbers of support positions.

• The Health Care Environment

Across the country, health care institutions are attempting to cope with growing pressure to reduce cost and improve productivity and yet maintain high levels of quality and service. Faced with declining census figures, some institutions are downsizing in order to achieve a break-even bottom line. Others, needing to be among the low-cost providers in their market area, are negotiating managed care contracts. Whatever the reason and whatever the method, the need to change is critical.

To respond to pressures from the external environment, health care organizations have begun to experiment with new ways of doing business. Many of these new methods are actually phases of increased employee involvement that, if carried to their logical conclusion, would result in self-managed work teams and the benefits they can bring. These methods include:

- Total quality management
- Self-governance
- Patient-centered care
- Management engineering and benchmarking

Total Quality Management

Like manufacturers and other industries, health care organizations have been using total quality management (TQM) approaches to improve quality and customer satisfaction. *Total quality management* is a method of increasing employee involvement in problem solving to achieve those goals and, ultimately, to reduce cost. It involves employees in temporary problem-solving teams but does not carry the team approach through to the extent that it becomes a permanent organizational structure. As employees participate in problem solving, their level of empowerment increases: They are given access to previously unavailable information and data, access to customers, and greater freedom to make decisions.

However, their participation in this process lasts only as long as they serve on the problem-solving team. When the problem is solved, the team is dissolved and team members return to their normal work environments where their input is limited and channeled through a supervisor or other manager.

If the organization that has success with quality improvement teams were to extend the team structure throughout its operation, it would carry the TQM team concept to its logical extension—the self-managed work team. The organization would then realize the benefits of improved productivity and reduced cost that result from teamwork and the elimination of a number of management and support positions.

Self-Governance

Some health care organizations (primarily in their nursing units) are implementing a concept called unit-based self-governance. *Self-governance* is a method by which certain management functions are transferred to employees who serve on "councils" within the department, most often the nursing unit. These councils may be responsible for work schedules, employee relations, problem solving, the quality improvement process, and training and development.

The benefit of self-governance is that it enables employees to participate in nursing management decisions, thus increasing their satisfaction and enhancing the quality of the decision-making process. In so doing, this method resembles the self-managed team concept. However, self-governance does not include work redesign, access to customers, and self-management. If these missing elements were incorporated into this method, the organization would reduce cost, increase productivity, and ensure employee commitment to, and ownership of, their work.

Patient-Centered Care

A third method for improving quality and customer satisfaction while reducing cost is that of patient-centered care. *Patient-centered care* is a back-to-basics system in which the needs of the patient are paramount. It frequently is accomplished through a structural change in the organization in which support employees are incorporated in a nursing unit team to provide consistent care to a group of patients. The idea is that (1) patients will interact with fewer staff, (2) staff will be cross-trained to provide a number of support services, (3) the organization will need fewer support staff, and (4) excellent quality and service will be achieved, while costs are either maintained at current levels or reduced.

One advantage to patient-centered care is that it restructures the organization to improve the patient experience. Another advantage is that reductions in staff are a direct result of redesigning the work of the unit and permitting employees to be cross-trained to provide care.

In contrast to self-managed teams, patient-centered care does not reduce or eliminate higher-paid management positions. It also does not inspire the increased commitment to performance that a self-managed approach does. The psychological difference between employees who report to a direct supervisor and those who are given responsibility for their work is apparent in the attention and commitment they give to responsibilities such as cost control and customer relations. Employees who believe that the success of their work rests entirely with them have a stronger purpose and clearer goals.

Management Engineering and Benchmarking

A fourth method being used by health care organizations to respond to today's changing environment is management engineering. *Management engineering* involves the study and analysis of work systems with an eye toward improving efficiency. Although management engineers have worked in health care for years, recent demands for cost reduction have stimulated renewed interest in this approach.

Management engineers frequently have access to databases and networks from which they can gather comparative data. As a result, health care organizations can "benchmark" off the data, meaning they can determine standards that can be used to identify opportunities for improvement. In addition, through work studies management engineers can make recommendations on productivity standards and staffing levels, which, if followed, could reduce cost and improve productivity.

When management engineers make recommendations about increasing employees' workloads, reducing staff, or changing the work process, their recommendations are based on facts and data gathered from observations and interviews. Frequently, these data and justifications for subsequent changes are not accepted or are resisted by the department's managers or employees because management engineering fails to transfer "thinking" to employees. However, when employees on a self-managed work team perform similar studies, gather data, and suggest opportunities to make changes, those changes are implemented with enthusiasm because they come from the employees.

The work redesign that management engineers do is a step toward improved efficiency but, because it is a one-time event rather than an ongoing effort, it is inferior to the self-managed concept of continuous improvement. In addition, it rarely results in a reduction in the number of management jobs.

Moving an organization to self-managed teams is a planned process in which the people who are doing the work and who know the work best are empowered to make decisions regarding their work. This system incorporates thinking *with* doing, rather than assigning these two processes to separate entities—manager (thinking) and employee (doing).

• Resistance to Self-Managed Work Teams

Resistance to self-managed work teams comes primarily from management. This is because not only will managers have to give up authority, control, and traditional roles and responsibilities, but management will have to change a number of organizational systems in order to support a team environment. Communication and information-sharing systems must change, along with job design, job evaluation, job description, performance appraisal, job classification, compensation, reward, recognition, planning, budgeting, reporting, quality control, and inspection systems.

For example, if a group of employees in a department were to become self-managed, the first change would be to redesign their work to incorporate tasks that produce an entire service. These tasks could come from other jobs in the department, including the supervisor's. This change would necessitate rewriting the supervisor's job description and performance appraisal form. If this work group were to do team or peer evaluations, the performance appraisal system would need to change. With the addition of other duties and responsibilities, the job could be reviewed for appropriate classification. It might warrant movement to a higher pay grade. In addition, if the organization pays employees based on individual merit, employees who depend on team members for performance achievement could not be compensated. Likewise, recognition would have to be given to the team, rather than the individual. Employee-of-the-month programs would need to be changed to team-of-the-month programs.

In many health care organizations, supervisors and managers are the only members of the department who participate in planning for the future. If the supervisor position were not to exist, the team would need to be involved in planning. Additionally, because communication to front-line employees comes from the supervisor, the system would need to be revised to permit communication directly to the team.

Because teams manage budgets, they would need to be included in the budget development, monitoring, and reporting process. And in organizations in which quality control and inspection functions are performed by supervisors, directors, or quality assurance personnel, these systems would all need to change to be performed by the team.

• Conclusion

Two primary ingredients must be present in an organization considering implementation of self-managed work teams: a strong impetus to change, and a work force composed of employees whose work relationships are interdependent. Health care is facing a stronger impetus to change today than it has in recent memory, and it is composed of job functions that are highly interdependent. Thus, self-managed teams will work in health care. In fact, there currently are several examples of successful self-managed teams functioning in health care organizations today, including teams at Memorial Mission Hospital in Asheville, North Carolina, and the Alliant Health System in Louisville, Kentucky.

Is a self-managed team system the answer to all the problems that health care organizations face today? Of course not. However, just as they are doing in the manufacturing and service industries, self-managed teams can make long-lasting improvements in the cost and marketplace position of a health care organization's products and services. Self-managed teams can increase quality and customer satisfaction, as well as create a positive work environment that raises employee morale, encourages commitment, and reduces absenteeism and turnover.

References

1. Lawler, E., Mohrman, S., and Ledford, G. *Employee Involvement and Total Quality Management.* San Francisco: Jossey-Bass, 1992, p. 3.
2. Weisbord, M. R. *Productive Workplaces: Organizing and Managing for Dignity, Meaning, and Community.* San Francisco: Jossey-Bass, 1987, pp. 150–52.
3. Lawler, Mohrman, and Ledford, p. 9.
4. Orsburn, J., Moran, L., Musselwhite, E., and Zenger, J. *Self-Directed Work Teams: The New American Challenge.* Homewood, IL: Business One Irwin, 1990, p. 15.

Chapter 2

Team Performance in Health Care

Self-managed work teams are beginning to find acceptance in large and small health care organizations throughout the United States, ranging from health care systems to freestanding hospitals to clinics. Their implementation seems to come about for one of two reasons: Either the organization is experiencing strong pressure to change, or it has already implemented TQM.

Self-managed work teams can work in almost any area of the health care organization—the pharmacy, the laboratory, housekeeping, food service, cardiology, respiratory therapy, rehabilitation services, business and accounting offices, general and critical care nursing units, and so on. The only restrictions seem to be whether the work requires interdependence and whether it involves a sufficient number of employees (at least five) to form a team.

This chapter describes the performance of self-managed work teams in three different hospitals or systems in different parts of the country. It also explains a simple model that has been developed for the systematic implementation of self-managed work teams in health care.

• Examples of Self-Managed Team Performance

Self-managed work teams generally start after total quality management has been initiated. Impetus for implementation of self-management may come from management in response to either a specific organizational need or an overall cultural change, or from employees looking for a model to support increased participation and involvement. Whatever the reason for the desire to change to self-management, team success (in either large or small organizations) depends on the organization's culture and readiness and, perhaps more important, on management and staff education. Every hospital that has implemented teams reports that teams do not and cannot just happen; they need guidance and support as they develop and mature.

Accordingly, all self-managed work teams have structured guidelines and expectations, and some have bylaws.

Overall, employee response to team implementation has been enthusiastic. Employees find the opportunities for growth and development a rewarding part of self-direction. They also appreciate the control and influence that increased involvement and participation give them, and feel a greater sense of ownership and commitment to the work. Generally, the concerns that have emerged relate to the scope of responsibilities assumed by teams. For example, some employees want to move cautiously before assuming discipline and firing responsibilities.

Following are three examples of hospitals and health systems in which self-managed work teams have proved successful: Mission Hospital in Asheville, North Carolina; the Alliant Health System, in Louisville, Kentucky; and Hartford Memorial Hospital, in Hartford, Wisconsin. The teams in these health care organizations have achieved improvements in efficiency, budget performance, quality, customer satisfaction, and employee satisfaction. In addition, team implementation has resulted in reductions in management positions (although in some cases the new responsibilities that teams take on require adding full-time equivalents [FTEs] when supervisory positions have been removed).

Memorial Mission Hospital

Located in Asheville, North Carolina, Memorial Mission Hospital is a private, non-for-profit, acute care, regional referral hospital. It was established in 1885 and is licensed for 503 beds. The hospital began implementation of TQM in 1990, and the emphasis on teams and employee empowerment started shortly thereafter. Although teams have been tried and are undergoing implementation elsewhere in the hospital, it is the housekeeping teams that will be described in this chapter. These teams have existed longer than others in the hospital and have been quite successful.

Housekeeping decided to divide into self-managed work teams in the spring of 1992. The director, assistant director, and supervisors met to discuss their concerns and the changes they wanted to implement. Working with the director of human resource development, they decided that a potential solution to their concerns, and a way to achieve their desires to implement change, lay in the development of self-managed work teams. They designed their self-managed teams to accomplish these management expectations:[1]

- To meet or exceed standards for quality
- To improve productivity
- To enhance customer satisfaction with work and service
- To satisfy team members and improve morale

- To improve the department's image
- To ensure that teams function effectively

For six months, the housekeeping management team met to design the work, structures, job descriptions, and systems that would be needed to support the teams. Meanwhile, human resource development designed training programs to support the implementation process. Housekeeping also chose to implement a team-incentive program along with the self-managed teams. Part of the six months was spent in developing the incentive plan and its corresponding team rating system.

The teams were developed around geographical areas of the hospital. They were responsible for cleanliness, equipment and supplies, record keeping, and customer relations. One group of employees was selected to be a pilot team and worked for a month before other teams were implemented. Due to limited training resources, not all teams could be implemented at once. The pilot team, named the "6th Floor Sharpies," was a tremendous success. It surpassed the expectations set for the teams and identified 23 changes that were needed to help make the team process more effective.

Since implementation of the housekeeping teams at Memorial Mission Hospital, the average rating of quality (cleanliness) has improved from 72 to 90 percent. The nursing units and departments that the teams serve give them high ratings for responsiveness, cleanliness, and courtesy. Additionally, with only a few exceptions, employees report a much higher degree of job satisfaction than in the past.

The only group in this process that was not universally pleased was that of the housekeeping supervisors. Although they had been an integral part of the development of the team concept, once the teams were implemented, the supervisors experienced a dramatic change in their everyday duties and responsibilities. They no longer were troubleshooters and problem solvers for the employees and the departments they served. Because their role had been assumed by the teams, they suddenly found themselves underutilized. They needed to be assigned more challenging work.

The answer was to form the supervisors into a self-managed management team, and they have been receiving training in advanced management skills and team coaching skills. With the hospital expanding, the supervisors will be needed to establish and coach teams in two new buildings as well as to focus on the continuous improvement of the teams in the current building.

The success of these self-managed work teams has caused housekeeping to withdraw its request for two new supervisory positions, one for each new building. Though now functioning as team facilitators, the existing supervisors will be able to oversee the new buildings and also support the housekeeping teams assigned to keep them clean.

The Alliant Health System

According to William B. Newkirk, coordinator of education and development at the Alliant Health System in Louisville, Kentucky, self-managed work teams have been in place in the Alliant System since the first team was started by Shirley Powers, administrator of Norton Hospital, in 1990.[2] Since then, the Alliant System has had as many as 34 teams functioning at one time. An early goal was to establish 10 new teams per year within the system.

Although teams at the Alliant System are given a template for creation, no two teams are created exactly alike. Teams write their own job descriptions for the team leader role, team size varies, and at least one team—geriatric psychiatry—spans three shifts. Additionally, although teams within the system do not receive additional compensation for their work, each one is eligible for a one-time certification bonus when it has successfully met the organization's criteria for self-management.

With an objective in place to provide every team member with 40 hours of training, an extensive training program has been designed for teams. For example, teams learn about the Hannaford Star concept.[3] In this system, team members are trained and assigned responsibility for up to 10 roles designated on the points of the star. *High-task roles* consume more time than *low-task roles*. Team members may rotate through the star assignments so that no one team member is permanently assigned a role that consumes an extensive amount of time.

Initially when teams were implemented at Alliant, employee reaction was enthusiastic. However, as teams proliferated, they did not always receive the resources they needed to perform the additional responsibilities they were assigned. Some employees felt "dumped on" and eventually requested that the supervisor position be reinstated.

Even though no one group was required to be a team, many were interested in the concept. And vice presidents were given incentives to establish teams, which may account for their rapid growth. On the other hand, supervisors were apprehensive and uncertain about what the change to teams would mean to them.

For the most part, teams within the Alliant System have been effective. A number of management positions have been eliminated, and cost savings and quality improvement have been significant outcomes of the system's change to teams.

Hartford Memorial Hospital

Located in Hartford, Wisconsin, the 71-bed Hartford Memorial Hospital is part of the Aurora system. It was established in 1916 as an 8-bed infirmary, and has grown and advanced to become a strong community-focused hospital. The hospital has worked to achieve a culture that supports "creativity, risk-taking, and openness for change and growth."[4]

A tremendous amount of change was initiated at Hartford Memorial in the early 1990s. First, TQM was implemented in 1991. This was followed by shared governance and the first self-managed team in January and August 1992, respectively. The change to self-governance and self-management was initiated by hospital staff. Although enthusiastic about the concept, at the same time the staff was cautious about how much self-management it wanted to assume. Supervisors initially were concerned by the change in roles, but their concerns diminished as the role of coach was expanded.

As of this writing, Hartford Memorial has self-managed work teams in the intensive care unit, obstetrics, diagnostic imaging, emergency department, and accounts payable. It has reduced its management staff by 22 positions and has implemented a modified matrix organizational structure. The goals of the new structure are to improve budget performance, staff retention, productivity, and customer satisfaction. As part of the overall system, Hartford Memorial has initiated an incentive compensation system related to these goals that focuses on self-managed team development, quality, and budget performance.

• Model for Self-Managed Team Development

A model for self-managed team development emerged from discussions with health care organizations that have implemented teams. The model (see figure 2-1) contains these components:

- Strategy
- Awareness and education
- Work design
- Systems revision
- Training programs
- Pilot team
- Implementation plan
- Evaluation

The organization needs to address certain elements within each component part to be well prepared to implement self-managed teams. The following subsections describe the different components in more detail.

Strategy

At the outset, the health care organization needs to identify the business reasons for implementing self-managed work teams. For example, the

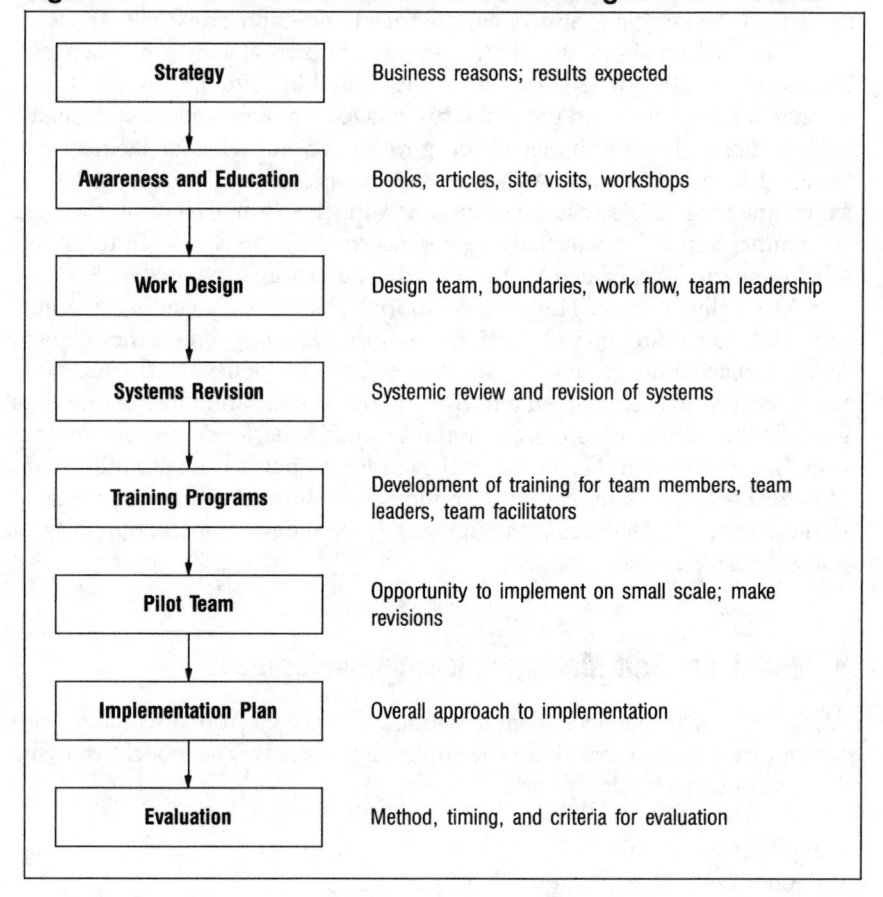

Figure 2-1. Health Care Model for Self-Managed Work Teams

Strategy	Business reasons; results expected
Awareness and Education	Books, articles, site visits, workshops
Work Design	Design team, boundaries, work flow, team leadership
Systems Revision	Systemic review and revision of systems
Training Programs	Development of training for team members, team leaders, team facilitators
Pilot Team	Opportunity to implement on small scale; make revisions
Implementation Plan	Overall approach to implementation
Evaluation	Method, timing, and criteria for evaluation

organization may want to reduce cost, increase the contribution that each employee makes to the organization, reduce the need for high-paid management positions, increase quality, improve customer satisfaction, and so on.

If there has been a history of increasing employee participation, the organization might view self-managed work teams as a natural extension of a strategy to expand employee involvement. For example, a number of organizations have implemented TQM and some elements of shared governance. Self-management takes increased participation several steps further than most forms of self-governance. It certainly reduces the need for hands-on management and may eliminate the need for many supervisory-level or middle management positions.

Awareness and Education

The group that is making the decision about self-managed work teams needs to become educated about team structures and systems in order to make appropriate decisions about team implementation. Methods of education include reading magazines, journals, and books; going on site visits to other health care organizations or local industries; and attending workshops.

Work Design

Some health care organizations use a design team, others do not. Regardless of whether a formally trained design team will be used, the process of work design (or redesign) needs to occur. The design team will need to determine which parts of the work will be transferred to the self-managed work team and will need to look at the whole work process, including the functions performed by support positions and supervisors. In addition, it will need to consider which parts of the work currently being done can be eliminated or assigned elsewhere.

In some instances, other departments may be doing work that should logically fall within the purview of the team. In these cases, negotiations with other departments must be initiated to begin the process of transferring that work (and possible FTEs) to the team. If the supervisor position is going to be eliminated, the transition must be planned. Consideration also must be given to other opportunities within the organization for supervisors who are displaced by the change to teams.

Another decision that must be made is that of establishing the roles of team leader and team facilitator. Both positions should be given a job description and clear expectations for performance. Job descriptions for team members also need to be developed. Additionally, if the organization has a job classification system, the jobs may need to be reviewed for compensation impact.

The design team also needs to evaluate the team's physical location. Team members should be located as close together as possible. They also need easy access to a meeting room or meeting space.

Systems Revision

Each department or organizational unit depends on internal systems to accomplish its work and manage its resources. Self-managed work teams are no different. They, too, depend on planning, financial, personnel, communication, and work systems in order to function. In most health care organizations, these systems are designed to support the established hierarchy and individual workers, not teams and team members. All major organizational systems need to be modified to support the concept of teams.

Training Programs

The implementation of self-managed work teams requires extensive training. Management needs to be trained to understand the concepts, changing roles, and the changing culture. Team members need to be trained to understand why teams are being implemented and how they function, how to perform newly assigned supervisory work, and how to perform other jobs on the team as the need arises. Team members need improved interpersonal skills as they coach and counsel each other and deal directly with customers.

The team leader needs to learn how to assume the responsibilities associated with team leadership, how to communicate with the organization, obtain and monitor resources, and ensure that the team continues to improve its effectiveness. The team coach or facilitator needs advance training to help with team implementation and support. Employees in support departments need training or awareness education to enable them to incorporate working with teams as well as individuals into their daily work patterns.

Pilot Team

When possible, the organization should implement a pilot team to give all the thoughts, programs, policies, and procedures a test run before using them on a number of teams. With every program of this magnitude, some errors in conception or implementation will need to be corrected before the program is carried forward.

Implementation Plan

When the organization undertakes a change as large as the implementation of self-managed work teams, an implementation plan is a very beneficial support tool. It serves to define the sequencing of events, roles and responsibilities, and expected completion dates. Implementation should be managed by a task force. See table 2-1 for a sample of a typical implementation plan.

Evaluation

The organization has invested a considerable amount of time and effort in self-managed work teams in order to implement them. At some point following implementation, it is important to take time to look at the teams' accomplishments. Were the business objectives established at the outset achieved? Is progress being made toward the expected results? The evaluation process will help keep the team implementation process on track, as well as identify areas for improvement.

• Conclusion

Self-managed work teams represent a way of working that is dramatically different from traditional methods in health care and one that will change

Team Performance in Health Care

Table 2-1. Sample Implementation Plan

Tasks	Month 1	Month 2	Month 3	Month 4	Month 5	Month 6	Month 7	Month 8
	1 2 3 4	1 2 3 4	1 2 3 4	1 2 3 4	1 2 3 4	1 2 3 4	1 2 3 4	1 2 3 4
Establish business reasons								
Develop awareness								
Select pilot								
Establish design team								
Perform work redesign								
Assess systems								
Implement systems revisions								
Develop team training								
Train managers								
Train coaches								
Train team members								
Implement pilot								
Evaluate effectiveness								
Make revisions								
Implement next teams								

19

both the organization's structure and culture. However, the self-managed work team concept can work in almost any area of the hospital, depending primarily on whether the work to be performed requires interdependence and whether there are enough employees in the area to form a team.

To provide an implementation guideline for health care, a model for team implementation has evolved from the experiences of a number of organizations. Three health care institutions in particular—Memorial Mission Hospital in Asheville, North Carolina; the Alliant Health System in Louisville, Kentucky; and Hartford Memorial Hospital in Hartford, Wisconsin—have reported successful performance outcomes. The model outlines eight components that organizations need to address in order to be prepared to make the change to self-managed work teams.

It is important to remember, however, that although self-management promises a number of positive outcomes, it is not a step to be taken without sound reasons. Because of its potential impact on organizational structure and culture, the practical health care organization must take whatever time is necessary to investigate, study, and plan for the process prior to beginning implementation.

References

1. A proposal for self-managed work teams and incentive pay in the housekeeping department, prepared by the housekeeping department, Memorial Mission Hospital, Asheville, NC, Aug. 26, 1992.
2. Telephone interview with William B. Newkirk, coordinator of education and development, the Alliant Health System, Louisville, KY, Aug. 13, 1993.
3. Wellins, R. S., Byham, W. C., and Wilson, J. M. *Empowered Teams: Creating Self-Directed Work Groups That Improve Quality, Productivity and Participation.* San Francisco: Jossey-Bass, 1991, p. 114.
4. Telephone survey and report from Loretta Klassen, vice president of patient care, Hartford Memorial Hospital, Hartford, WI, Jan. 12, 1994.

Chapter 3

Employee Responses to the Team Concept

Although the vast majority of employees are interested in and excited by the concept of teamwork, a few resist it. For some employees, working on a team will never be a desirable alternative to working on their own. For others, a good team experience will bring home the concept's advantages. And for still others, initial acceptance of the team concept may change to disappointment in a relatively short period of time.

To some extent, employee responses to team participation depend on individual personalities and work goals. However, to a larger degree, employee responses to working on teams are directly related to how management communicates, structures, and maintains the team concept.

When employees express negative feelings about working on teams, managers need to listen closely to try to identify the causes of their responses. It is possible that a negative response is in fact a misdirected reaction to some other, unwanted change in their work life, such as a change in job status, compensation, schedule or shift, or daily assignment.

Individual employees can help make teams effective through enthusiasm and cooperation, or they can undermine and destroy the experience for the entire team through negativism and uncooperativeness. The fact is that once management has made the decision to implement teams, employees have few choices. It is the responsibility of the team leader or facilitator to observe group dynamics closely and to work with those employees who are having difficulty making the adjustment.

This chapter illustrates some of the common reactions, negative and positive, that employees have to participation in the self-managed team concept. It also identifies strategies that some health care organizations have used to work with unhappy and negative team members.

- ## Individual Responses

Some employees will immediately embrace the idea of teams, others will adopt a wait-and-see attitude, and still others will resist the concept altogether.

For the most part, the reasons for their different responses fall into three categories: past experience, personality type, and personal perception of gain or loss.

Past Experience

Some employees have no experience working with others in a team setting. Through either circumstance or choice, they have structured their lives to exclude team and group activities. Employees in this category often approach the team concept with a wait-and-see attitude. They may need more information, time to study and reflect on the change, and time to experience what it is like to work on a team. Their eventual impression about teams will depend in large part on how the concept is presented to them, how quickly they must make the transition to teamwork, and what they experience during their first weeks as a team member.

Other employees, who have played on teams, are involved in group activities at work and/or during their leisure time, or follow team sports, wholeheartedly endorse the team concept. They instantly perceive the advantages to teamwork in their immediate environment and are eager to get started. Although an enthusiastic supporter usually is a positive force within the employee group, an individual who is too enthusiastic sometimes can irritate the group's wait-and-see members and possibly irrevocably alienate those team members who openly resist the concept of teams.

Other employees may resist the concept because of previous negative experiences with working on teams. Although they may reserve their negative opinions in front of management, often these employees regale their coworkers with stories of previous experiences when the facilitator is not present. By so doing, they can undermine management's positive introduction to teams by swaying those who are undecided about the concept.

Personality Type

An individual employee's personality can play a significant part in his or her interest and willingness to serve on a team. Employees who are outgoing and extroverted frequently see team participation as desirable. They typically are energized by working in groups, interacting with others, and exchanging ideas in problem-solving sessions.

Employees who are introverted prefer to avoid the increased communication, involvement, and confrontation that are part of successful team behavior. They prefer to work alone, look inward for answers to problems, and avoid the disruption that group interaction can bring to the work environment.

Perception of Gain or Loss

Another aspect of the employee response to teams is the way the individual perceives the change that teamwork will bring about. If he or she sees teamwork as an opportunity to learn new skills, assume a larger role in the organization, and have greater control over his or her destiny, the change will be perceived as a gain and the team experience as positive.

Other employees, however, may not perceive the change in a positive manner. Some may perceive it as a loss of personal prestige, position, and power, as well as the loss of opportunity for advancement. For example, employees who are recognized within the organization for their special role, skills, or accomplishments are likely to perceive participation on a team as a diminution of their unique position. They will see themselves as having to give up too much that is important to them in order to help the team succeed.

• Negative Responses

Employees who respond negatively to the team concept do so for a number of reasons. Generally, these individuals oppose the concept's implementation because they (1) distrust management, (2) have a natural resistance to imposed change, and/or (3) do not trust working with others. Following are examples of these negative responses to teamwork and management strategies that may be used to address them.

Distrust of Management

Employees who distrust management do so for a variety of reasons. For example, either because they are naturally cynical or because of past experience, they may distrust management's motivations or even its ability to make appropriate decisions. The following comments illustrate the employee perception that team implementation is just *another* management mistake.

"It's Just a Management Fad"

Employees who express their cynicism by calling the change to teams a management fad often are open in their criticism, desirous of letting everyone know that they are not fooled by a management ploy and that they will not waste their time on a management fad. Their public stand on the issue makes these employees difficult to convert, even when they in fact have a positive team experience, because an admission that they were wrong would be embarrassing.

This type of response is difficult to prevent. One strategy is to head off the degree of commitment to the notion that team implementation is a management fad by discussing this possible interpretation before a negative employee has the opportunity to verbalize it. If the organization communicates its awareness that there will be skepticism to its plan and that some people will see it as a fad, the heat with which those sentiments are expressed will be minimized. This approach gives the organization an opportunity to ask employees to hold off their criticism until they have given teams a chance. Another way to reduce skepticism is to invite employees to participate in the design and implementation process.

"We're Only Doing This So the Vice Presidents Can Get Their Bonuses"

The organization may have communicated that team start-ups will net vice presidents a nice bonus. This approach catches the attention of the vice presidents, but it also sends a message to the employees. What they hear is that, regardless of its merits in their situation, the team concept will be implemented so that someone at a higher organizational level can receive a financial reward. This is particularly aggravating to employees who will not be receiving a financial reward for their participation in the implementation process.

This perception is easy to remedy. The organization can either implement teams without giving bonuses to vice presidents or give bonuses to everyone involved in the implementation process.

"We Have to Cut Back, and Management Is Only Doing This to Save Money"

Frequently, teams are implemented as part of a cost-reduction strategy. Although this may not be the only reason for implementation, it often is the one most talked about, and teams that generate the greatest savings seem to receive the most recognition. Employees chafe at changes that make their life more difficult, particularly if upper management does not appear to be making a similar effort. The employees' perception is that their world is being turned upside down, whereas upper management is continuing as before.

To reduce cynicism, the benefits of teamwork to employees and customers should be communicated with as much enthusiasm as the benefits of cost reduction. Additionally, it would help if upper managers were implementing a team design within their own structure or were involved in cost-reduction strategies that likewise visibly affected their work life.

"This Is Management's Job; Let the Managers Do What They're Paid to Do"

When a team is formed and management responsibilities are added to the work that the team members already do, some team members may feel "dumped on." This perception will produce a negative response to the team concept. Team members may not want to take on duties they see as "management's job," or they may not want the headaches without similar remuneration.

If this complaint surfaces, it generally is because the employees were not included in the design and timing of the transition to management work. However, this complaint also may surface when employees truly do not either have the time to or see the benefit of performing management functions. Perhaps they have not received the training they need to perform the management tasks they have been given responsibility for.

To prevent or reduce the frequency of this response, the organization should involve employees from the start in the redesign of their work. If employees are involved in determining when management tasks should be transferred to them, they will be less likely to feel dumped on. In addition, as mentioned previously, the advantages of teams to employees and patients should be communicated at the outset and employees should be provided the training they need so that they can assume their new management-level assignments. If team members truly are so understaffed that they cannot handle the scope of their assignment, they should be given support with their workload. If this issue is handled appropriately, few employees will balk at having to do management-level work.

"Our Managers Don't Work as a Team, So Why Should We Have To?"

Whenever a cultural change is initiated in an organization, employees look to management for role modeling. They will commit to the change to the extent that they see managers demonstrate changed behaviors. If managers are not "walking the talk," employees will be unwilling to go through the agonies of change. If employees perceive the change as neither permanent nor important to management, they will not want to waste their energy on making it work.

Managers should be trained in teamwork and should be expected to function as a team before they implement teams with employees. In that way, the desired behaviors will be modeled by managers and employees will be unable to use management behavior as justification for noncooperation.

"If We Make the Decisions, We Can't Blame Anyone But Ourselves If They Don't Turn Out Right"

It is interesting to see this reaction of employees to self-management. For the first time, employees have to face an important reality of self-management—that the team is accountable for its decisions. Management can no longer be used as the scapegoat if something goes wrong in the department. For many employees, this reality gives them a valuable sense of freedom and self-control. For others, it confers a burdensome amount of responsibility.

To alleviate this fear in employees, management can provide employees the training and information they need to make good decisions. Additionally, the staging of the transfer of responsibility can move slowly so that employees gain confidence in their skills and abilities before they receive new assignments. Management can also provide teams the services of a team facilitator to offer the support and encouragement the team needs as it makes decisions.

"We're Working Harder Than We Ever Have Before, But We Aren't Getting Paid Any More"

Employees have the right to expect that management has taken their current workload into consideration before assigning more work. Generally, when employees begin to work as teams, they become more productive and are able to take on more work. However, they also can reach a point of overload.

To deal with the problem of workload, management needs to evaluate the quantity of work assigned to the team. If the workload is excessive, some of it should be assigned elsewhere or eliminated. If the workload is not excessive, then management needs to look at underlying reasons for the complaint and work to fix those hidden problems.

If employees are expressing concern with pay, there may be a pay inequity that needs to be addressed. Employees frequently complain about pay when they are really feeling like they are undervalued or not appreciated. Again, management needs to look below the surface to identify what is really of concern to the employees.

Resistance to Imposed Change

Many negative employee responses are directly related to the natural human resistance to imposed change. Following are examples of these responses and management strategies for counteracting or preventing them.

"Self-Management at Work Is Not Right or Natural; I Like My Job the Way It Is"

Employees who feel this way are strongly committed to past stability. Generally, they respect the traditional ways of doing their work. To the extent possible, these employees avoid change, do not seek to initiate it, and are slow to accept it when it is forced on them.

The best way to work with these employees is to involve them early on in the process, soliciting their suggestions on needed changes. Involving them in developing implementation plans will help ensure that change occurs in a planned and structured sequence and at a pace that is reasonable for them. A forced change that is rapidly implemented will be the least acceptable to this type of employee.

"I Like to Be in Control of My Work, Do It Myself, and Get Credit for It; It'll Take Longer and Won't Be as Good If Someone Else Is Working with Me"

Employees who have this response may be perfectionists whose self-esteem is wrapped closely in the work they produce. They may have had past experience working with other employees whose work habits were not at the same level. In addition, these types of individuals generally have a strong need to receive credit for their work, rather than share it with others.

To cope with this attitude, when implementing teams, the organization needs to ensure that team effort and team success achieve the highest levels of recognition. When this type of employee becomes aware that individual success is not valued as highly as team success, he or she will be less focused on receiving personal recognition. In addition, this employee needs to experience the benefits of working with several minds to improve work processes and results. Regardless of bad past experiences, a successful teamwork experience will go a long way toward changing the perception that individual work produces the best results.

"I'm Not Sure I Can Do This Teamwork"

This response illustrates a fear of failure. Employees who feel this way recognize that the team concept represents a different way of working that requires new skills, and they question their ability to acquire these skills.

Management can do several things to prevent or reduce the strength of this response. First and foremost, management can ensure that employees are trained before they are assigned new tasks to perform. Because employees cannot absorb too many changes and too much learning at one time, training and new task acquisition need to be spaced over time. Otherwise, gun-shy employees may become frustrated and question their ability and willingness to succeed.

"I Like to Know Exactly What I'm Going to Do Each Day; All This Teamwork and Changing Assignments Is Driving Me Crazy"

Some employees like to work in a highly structured environment, in which their day-to-day work is predetermined by management and rarely changes. They find comfort in being able to go to a manager for direction at any point, to leave all decisions to management, and to abstain from involvement in problem solving.

There is no clear strategy on how to deal with this response. Because of their work style preferences, these employees may never be comfortable in a self-managed team environment. Although they can adapt to self-management when it permits them to spend the major portion of their workday on routine matters, they will likely never adjust to an environment in which the work has a lot of variety. Self-managed teams that are cross-functional and involve frequent changes in job duties based on workload fluctuations will not appeal to these employees.

Distrust of Working with Others

When employees work together on teams, they must be able to trust each other. Without trust, teams cannot achieve high levels of performance, nor will they present heightened job satisfaction to their members. Some negative responses to the team concept relate to problems with trust. Following are examples of these employee responses and management strategies that can be used to address them.

"I Don't Like (or Trust) My Team Members"

Employees who make statements such as this one have either had bad experiences with a specific team member or heard and believed negative comments about a team member. These employees may not object to the team concept but, rather, to the particular team members with whom they will have to work.

The remedy to this response is to educate team members on the importance of trust to team effectiveness. The process should include discussion of any barriers to trust, as well as exercises that suggest ways to overcome those barriers. The exercises should lead to actions that team members can agree to take in order to begin to support each other. If the process is successful, trust will be reestablished. However, if one member betrays the newly established trust, the team may never regain its momentum. In this case, the only alternative is to remove the offending individual from the team.

"This Would Work Except for X; She's Not a Team Player"

This response represents yet another barrier to team effectiveness that must be addressed. The reason for this sentiment may be based on one employee's past experience with the individual or on knowledge of the individual's current work habits.

If just two employees are involved, they may need to confront each other about the trust or work habit issue. Confrontation and an attempt to bury past grudges can work together to alleviate the problem. However, the effectiveness of this solution depends on the reliability of the employees' future behavior. If the problem does not resurface, it can be considered resolved. On the other hand, if it does resurface, trust may never be possible between these individuals and the employee who violated the trust may never be an appropriate member of any team.

"Two of Us Do All the Work, and We Don't Like Carrying All the 'Free Riders' on This Team"

This complaint commonly surfaces after the team has been in existence for a while. Teams frequently have aggressive members who assume a greater leadership role and sometimes take on a larger share of the workload. These individuals tend to be highly competent and action-oriented, and often are perfectionists. Initially, they take on the additional work willingly, and the other team members, out of pique or relief, let them. However, a team that has a few members doing most of the work is a situation that needs to be corrected. The whole team needs the opportunity to grow and share in the workload. If there is dissension about who is working harder, the team will not be as productive.

A remedy for this complaint is to involve the entire group in determining work assignments and workload. A reassessment and reassignment of work may need to be done each quarter, because initial assignments can become lost in the pressure of daily activity and work change.

Another way to address workload inequality is to assign employees to work with "buddies." A buddy system will divide the workload into teams of two, and it will become obvious if the workload is being unequally shouldered.

A third suggestion is to do a role clarification exercise with the entire team. Once roles are understood and role expectations are clarified, confusion over responsibility no longer should exist.

• Positive Responses

As mentioned previously, the vast majority of employees will see real benefits to team membership. They will likely view membership in a self-managed team as an opportunity for great personal liberation that will allow them to flourish, and their pleasure will result in heightened job satisfaction and high morale. Following are examples of positive responses to team membership.

"I'm Finally Responsible for My Own Work"

This comment is made by employees who are able to decide how to do their work without following a procedure developed by management. It expresses the feeling of ownership that employees have when they can make their own decisions, and it meets a need they have to be in control of their work environment.

"We've Been Able to Make Changes We've Always Wanted to Make"

Many teams make changes to the work structure early in their development. Often members have had ideas about how the work should be done before they became a team but believed that no one either listened to their ideas or gave them the chance to make changes. Once they have the chance, they take tremendous pride in seeing how effective their changes are.

"I Really Feel I'm Making an Important Contribution"

When employees can make decisions about their work and actually implement them, they have a greater sense of their personal contribution to the organization. They can see the impact of their decisions and know that they, and not their supervisors, are responsible for those results or improvements. This ownership of the results of the work gives employees a strong sense of accomplishment.

"I Love It When a Customer Says 'Thank-you' Directly to Me for Something I Was Able to Do on My Own"

This comment reflects the employee's gratification at being able to receive feedback on his or her work directly from the person who uses and/or benefits from it. In the work structure before teams, employees typically heard through their supervisors when they had done something well. Thus, teams offer members a way to satisfy their need for feedback on their efforts.

"I Really Look Forward to Coming to Work Each Day"

When employees feel in control of their destiny, their outlook about work improves. They have a sense of ownership and responsibility that enhances their self-image and self-esteem. They are proud to be able to produce results that reflect well on their efforts and decision-making ability. Team membership satisfies their need for achievement and control.

"I've Never Been So Challenged"

The one constant in self-managed work teams is the emphasis on continued growth and development for all team members. Teams are asked to focus on continuous improvement, which means continuous change. This opportunity to grow and learn is one of the greatest gifts that the organization can give its employees.

"I Feel a Real Closeness to My Team Members"

Some team members like working on teams because the camaraderie and closeness that teamwork requires fills a human need. These employees perceive real value in having a supportive relationship with a group of people at work.

• Conclusion

Employees introduced to the concept of self-managed work teams have many individual responses to participation. Some employees are immediately delighted, others assume a wait-and-see attitude, and still others are decidedly negative to the idea. Their responses depend in large part on their past experience, personality type, and perception of what they have to gain or lose. The method that management uses to introduce teams also has an impact on employee response.

Employees who respond negatively to the prospect of working on teams generally do so for one of three reasons: (1) They distrust management, (2) they harbor a natural resistance to imposed change, or (3) they distrust the people who will be working with them. Management can work with a number of strategies to reduce either the number of negative employee responses or their intensity.

However, the vast majority of employees accept self-managed teams as a positive change. Teams give them the ability to take control of their destiny, to obtain direct feedback on their efforts, to enhance their self-esteem, and to form closer relationships with their coworkers.

Chapter 4

Critical Success Factors

Critical success factors are key performance elements that are specific to an organization. They help focus attention on those areas in which performance must be excellent in order for the organization to succeed—for example, productivity, economic health, innovation, quality, and customer satisfaction. Using critical success factors in planning and assessment can help an organization avoid problems and increase the likelihood of positive performance.

Like other service-focused industries, health care organizations are highly likely to be successful when they implement self-managed work teams. The principal reason for this is that work in health care is built on a system of interdependency, in which one department or health care employee depends on another for information or services in the process of providing patients with high-quality care. Yet, despite the existence of this interdependency, most health care organizations are designed with strong barriers to horizontal cooperation and collaboration.

In order for self-managed work teams to succeed in any type of organization, the organization needs to focus on critical success factors that are specific to team performance. These factors include:

- Senior management support
- Emphasis on performance
- Work systems that support teams
- Employee training
- Communication

The organization can plan for team success by emphasizing these critical success factors during team implementation. It is important to note that the organization must place emphasis on *all* five factors; emphasizing only certain factors and ignoring others will seriously hinder performance. After teams have been in existence for a while, the organization can assess how well they are doing by evaluating their performance in these areas.

This chapter discusses the critical success factors for teams and outlines their characteristics. In addition, it identifies problems that can occur when one of the critical success factors does not receive its share of emphasis.

• Senior Management Support

From the outset, self-managed work teams need senior management support in order to succeed. Because the entire organization generally looks to senior management to provide direction on how to behave, employees will look to senior management to discern the level of its commitment to this new organizational structure and will pattern their behavior accordingly.

Senior management behavior can be an inspiration to teams that are struggling to perform in an entirely different setting and work environment. It can provide positive feedback and recognition that will be communicated throughout the organization. Additionally, it is senior managers who allocate resources to help smooth the way for teams and their allocations reflect how they value the team concept.

Ideally, senior managers will model team behaviors, making it clear to everyone exactly what the behavioral expectations are. One strategy is for senior managers to use consensus decision making. They can involve others in decisions that affect them, focus on teamwork rather than individual work, and recognize team accomplishment over individual accomplishment. If senior managers model these team behaviors, they will be perceived as sincerely committed to the team concept.

Another element of senior management commitment is support for team ideas and suggestions. Because the team structure is new to most health care organizations, few have learned which approaches are effective. Thus, senior management needs to show support for risk takers. If a team wants to try something new, senior management needs to provide opportunities for experimentation, reflection, and learning. If the experiment is successful, senior management can help the team celebrate and share the results with the rest of the organization. However, if the experiment is a failure, senior management needs to have created an environment in which team members are encouraged to accept and learn from their mistakes.

Because the team concept represents such a different way of working and requires so many resources and so much attention to get started, it relies heavily on senior management support. Without it, self-managed work teams will face an extremely difficult, if not impossible, challenge.

• Emphasis on Performance

Employees serving on teams need to understand that the purpose of teamwork is to improve organizational performance and to better meet the needs of customers. Consequently, for the team structure to be effective, it must be designed to focus on accomplishing goals that will achieve those ends. Indeed, teams may have a variety of goals, including quality improvement, enhanced customer satisfaction, greater productivity, and/or cost reduction. However, whatever the goal, it must have organizational significance. Both employees and senior managers will invest in the team concept if they can see that it is helping the organization accomplish important goals.

The team concept is a work structure designed to give the organization a competitive edge. It is a means of involving the minds of all employees, not just managers, in the work. Teams are effective because of the focus they can bring to the work of the organization.

Teams also can improve employee morale, although this element of the team concept should be viewed as a side benefit. Because teamwork gives employees greater control over their work, they approach their work with a sense of ownership. Additionally, teams offer employees the opportunity to continuously grow and develop, gradually building their self-esteem. Thus, when teams are implemented effectively, employees benefit as much as the organization. In the long term, employee participation on teams helps ensure the organization's continuation and the employees' job security.

It should be noted that in organizations as sensitive to people as health care organizations are, it is tempting to develop teams merely to improve employee morale. However, development of self-managed work teams for that purpose alone would be a mistake. Teams developed primarily to improve employee morale tend to be inwardly focused, working on interpersonal skills and group dynamics rather than working to move the organization forward. Additionally, establishing teams for a lesser, although valuable purpose diminishes their importance and effectiveness in the eyes of both management and employees.

• Work Systems That Support Teams

When self-managed work teams are implemented in an organization, they are struggling to survive in an environment that is structured to support individual work rather than teamwork. Most of the organization's systems will need to be modified to support the new structure. Examples of systems that will need to change are:

- Budgeting
- Communication
- Compensation
- Customer relations
- Decision making
- Discipline

- Hiring
- Information access
- Performance appraisal
- Planning
- Problem solving
- Purchasing
- Recognition
- Reporting
- Training
- Work (how work is assigned and accomplished)

Without changes in these systems, employees will continue to run into organizational roadblocks to effectiveness and will have to work twice as hard to succeed. For instance, in most organizations communication travels in a vertical path, from individual to individual. If an employee in one department has a problem or concern related to an employee in another department, he or she shares it with the department supervisor, who in turn discusses it with his or her director. The department director then relates the problem to the director of the other department, who passes it on to the supervisor of the employee in question, who then discusses it with that employee. However, in a team setting, if an employee in one department has a problem or concern with an employee in another department, he or she shares it with the team. The team then contacts the team in the next department and the two teams try to resolve the problem (see figure 4-1). A change in the communication system that would permit teams to communicate directly, without going through a management hierarchy, would improve the quality and efficiency of communication within the organization.

Figure 4-1. Team Communication System

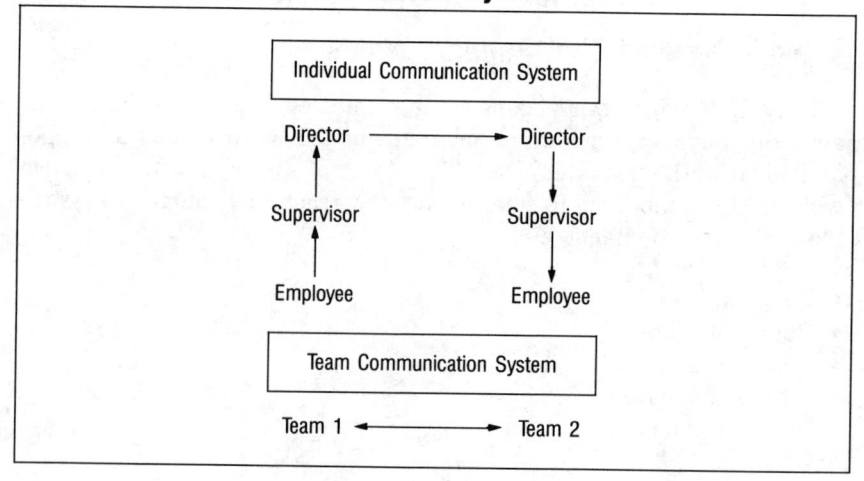

• Employee Training

In addition to requiring the organization to change its structure and systems, implementation of self-managed work teams will require employees to learn new skills — technical, interpersonal, team, and supervisory. For example, an employee who serves on a cross-functional team will be expected to perform some of the *technical skills* of other team members. In addition, he or she will need to learn the skills that go along with changes in systems and procedures. Team members may need to learn how to purchase, keep records, and make reports.

Interpersonal skills will teach employees how to: ask for help; clarify issues or problems; confront a coworker when there is a problem; praise team members' accomplishments in specific useful terms; and listen to feelings as well as the spoken word. *Team skills* will enable employees to generate ideas through brainstorming, make decisions, and solve problems and resolve conflicts in a team environment. Finally, *supervisory skills* will help employees learn how to set goals, order supplies, provide performance feedback, train and coach new team members, and budget and allocate resources. (See chapters 10 and 11 for further discussion of skill acquisitions.)

Without appropriate training, the new set of expectations that employees must meet will be beyond their experience, knowledge, and skill, and they will struggle, flounder, and eventually fail. The single most effective way to deliberately sabotage implementation of self-managed work teams would be to withhold employee training.

• Communication

Successful implementation of the team concept, even if only as a pilot program, will depend in large part on a system of open communication with management. Initially, the employees' new work environment will be chaotic: They will be working harder than they have ever worked before, and they will be solving problems and implementing change at a rapid rate. Consequently, the team will need all the reinforcement, feedback, and recognition the organization can provide.

Managers who are most closely involved with employees on newly implemented self-managed work teams will need to bring to bear all their coaching and training skills to help guide the teams through this period of dramatic adjustment, keeping team members motivated and on track through regular feedback. Additionally, teams will need direct feedback from their customers in order to know that their efforts are working and are appreciated.

Communication must not only be open, but it also must be ongoing. Often the first team that is started receives a great deal of management attention, but as the number of teams increases and they demonstrate their ability to operate on their own, management withdraws its support too quickly. If an organization ignores its teams, failing to provide regular communication and feedback, they may begin to feel "dumped on," reasoning that they have been given all the problems to solve but without support or recognition for doing the work. As a result, they may feel abandoned and begin to exhibit negative behaviors to regain management's attention.

It is important to remember that few employees in health care receive additional compensation for their participation on self-managed work teams. Their reward for service is mainly intrinsic—a personal sense of accomplishment and pride in what has been achieved. Whether additional compensation is given or not, the organization has an obligation to provide the extrinsic rewards of communication and positive feedback.

• Conclusion

Critical success factors are key areas in which an organization's performance must be excellent in order to achieve overall success. These factors can be used in planning as well as performance assessment. As discussed in this chapter, there are five critical success factors for self-managed work teams: senior management support, emphasis on performance, work systems that support teams, employee training, and communication. If self-managed work teams are to succeed, the organization must place emphasis on all five critical success factors. Organizations that ignore one or more factors risk poor results and possibly failure.

Part Two
Team Design

Chapter 5

Organizational Structure

Health care organizations are conservative in the way they are structured. Although there has been some movement away from the traditional hierarchical structure based on function to the matrix structure based on product (ultimately, the customer), the hierarchical structure is still largely predominant.

In an organization that supports teams, the structure is quite different from the hierarchical structure. It is flatter, less rigid, and more fluid. There are fewer management layers and fewer barriers to horizontal movement. Employees communicate across department and function lines with ease. They quickly adjust to changes in work activity and move to areas where work demand is heavy, rather than remain in areas regardless of the level of work activity.

A relative newcomer to health care is the matrix organizational structure. This structure combines product and functional structures, is less rigid than the functional structure, and opens horizontal barriers that a strictly functional structure imposes.

Team structures can be implemented in either a functional or a matrix-structured organization. They also can form an organizational structure that is entirely a team structure.

This chapter reviews the traditional functional organization structure as well as the newer matrix structure, and compares both structures with the team structure. It also describes the benefits of these structures as well as the barriers they present to efficiency and effectiveness.

- ## Functional Structure

Over the past 100 years, the majority of health care organizations have existed with a functional organization structure, in which departments are organized into functions that report up the hierarchy to the top-level function—the

CEO. (See figure 5-1.) Generally, the hierarchy is steep. In comparison to team-structured organizations, the functional organization structure is rigid and restrictive. Boundaries between functions are adhered to, and employees are restricted to following the chain of command vertically through the chart.

The functions represented within the hierarchy include departments such as nursing, ancillary services, finance, human resources, and purchasing. Within these functions the hierarchy of president, vice president, director, supervisor, and employee occurs. The functional organization structure has clearly defined roles, responsibilities, chain of command, span of control, and boundaries.

This organizational design has been effective in health care for years and is particularly effective in industries where there is little change, or where change and the response to change can take a long time to occur. Drawbacks to the functional structure exist in industries where innovation is rapid, product life cycles short, and departments interdependent. There is a sense of permanence about the way resources are allocated in a functional structure. The feeling is that change either will not occur or will occur so gradually that resources can shift gradually. When innovation does occur and resources no longer needed in one area are in high demand in another, the functional organization has difficulty freeing them up. Thus, innovations and the opportunities they present will be passed by, or resources will be added to the area of need but not removed from the area of lesser need.

Other problems with this structure arise when an organization has a number of departments that must work together to provide a service. The hierarchy and the boundaries created by the functional structure retard an organization's ability to work effectively in a horizontal mode. The bureaucracy creates roadblocks to communication, delays in response from one functional area to another, and an inability to understand the problems presented by one functional area to another. The rigidity and its problems are seen easily when ancillary departments provide services to nursing.

For example, a patient used to eating breakfast at home at 6:00 a.m. may have to wait until 8:00 a.m. to eat at the hospital because that is when dietary serves breakfast on the patient's floor. Or, a patient's lab work may be drawn at 5:00 a.m. even though the results will not be needed until afternoon because that is when the lab draws blood on that particular floor.

Health care organizations are beginning to recognize the problems with the functional organization structure and are experimenting with a matrix structure in an attempt to improve coordination of functions to provide services to specific patient populations.

Within these organizationwide structures is the microstructure of the department. Because departments tend to mirror their organization's structure, the typical department in a functional structure reflects the organization's hierarchical form. Generally, it is headed by a director who oversees a supervisory level of direct reports to whom the employees report.

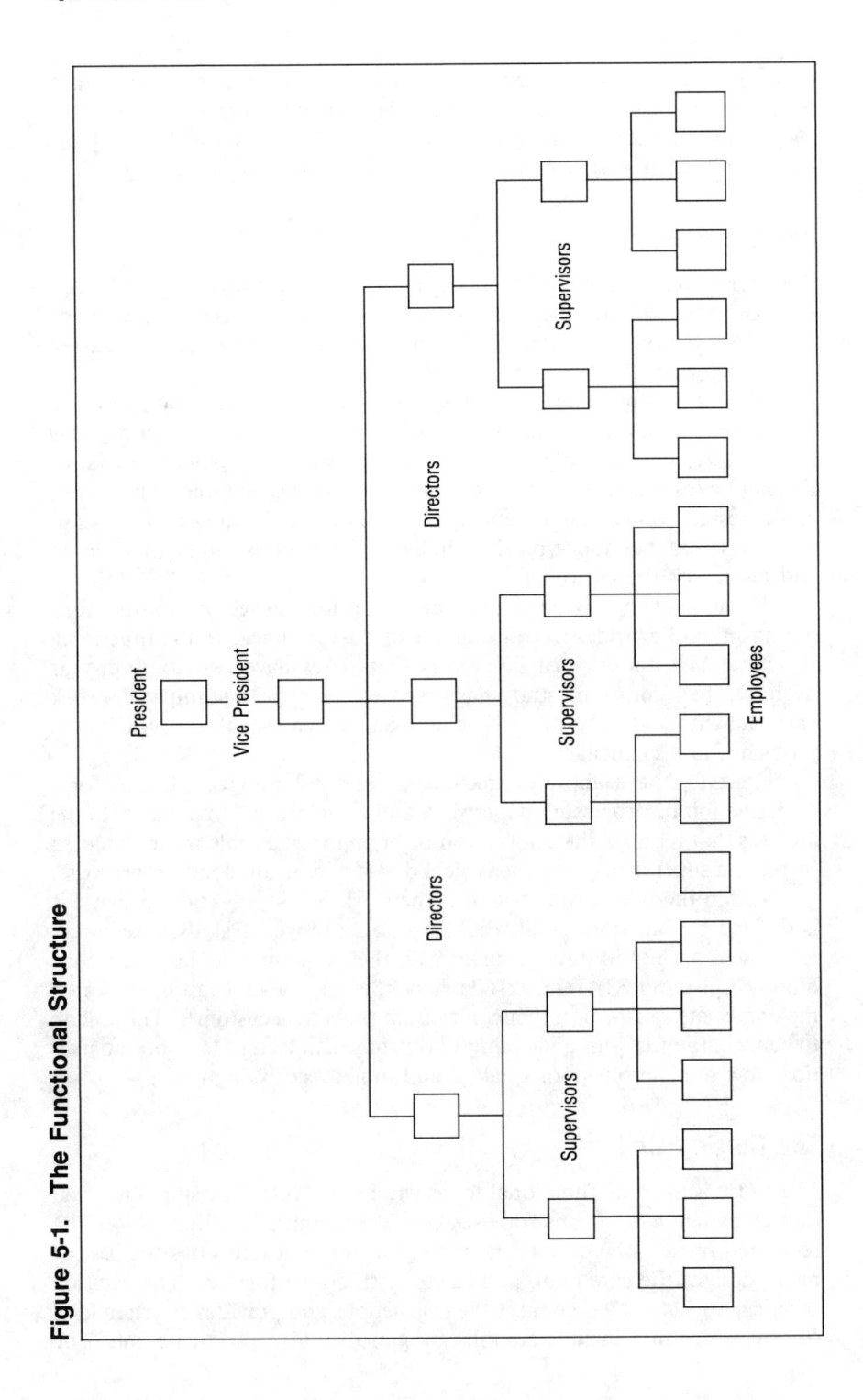

Organizational Structure

Figure 5-1. The Functional Structure

(See figure 5-2.) The departments may span one, two, or three shifts. Employees in these departments work independently on specific tasks, even though their work may be interrelated. Following are examples of the functional organization structure within the laboratory and a nursing unit.

The Laboratory

The laboratory is designed in functional sections, as follows: microbiology, chemistry, blood bank, hematology, phlebotomy, and clerical. (See figure 5-3.) Each section has a section chief or supervisor who reports to an assistant director or director.

When a patient comes to the hospital, he or she may need blood drawn, microbiology tests, and chemistry tests. Each section of the laboratory may be *separately* involved in providing these services to the patient. Although the employees are performing interrelated tasks (draw sample, test sample, report results) on the same patient, they are not performing their tasks as a team. Thus, they focus on their individual functions rather than on an end result—or the customer.

The laboratory has been an ideal setting for the segregation of work into tasks, and provides a clear example of the drawbacks to the functional structure. The majority of laboratory employees have two- or four-year degrees. Their course of study has prepared them for a stimulating work environment, and they are well equipped to deal with complex issues, problems, and challenges.

However, in the laboratory technicians and technologists alike perform a routine job of processing paperwork and tests in which machines do the analysis that requires the application of brainpower. Problems are handled by section supervisors, and the typical day is one of unrelenting sameness.

Within the laboratory structure, the work has little variety because it is divided by function. As a result, a narrow range of skills is required. Employees are not in direct contact with their customers unless they draw blood or give out STAT results. They neither see the end result nor enjoy the immediate satisfaction that comes from pleasing a customer. This failure to connect the job with a meaningful outcome can lead to low job satisfaction, low motivation, poor quality, and unnecessarily high cost.

The Nursing Unit

There also is a strong functional focus within the typical nursing unit, even though patient care "teams" do exist on nursing units. (See figure 5-4.) The registered nurse (RN) admits the patient to the unit and does the assessment, designs the care plan, and leaves instructions for care. The licensed practical nurse (LPN) then takes the instructions and provides a certain level of care, which may include administering medications and treatments. The

Figure 5-2. A Typical Department

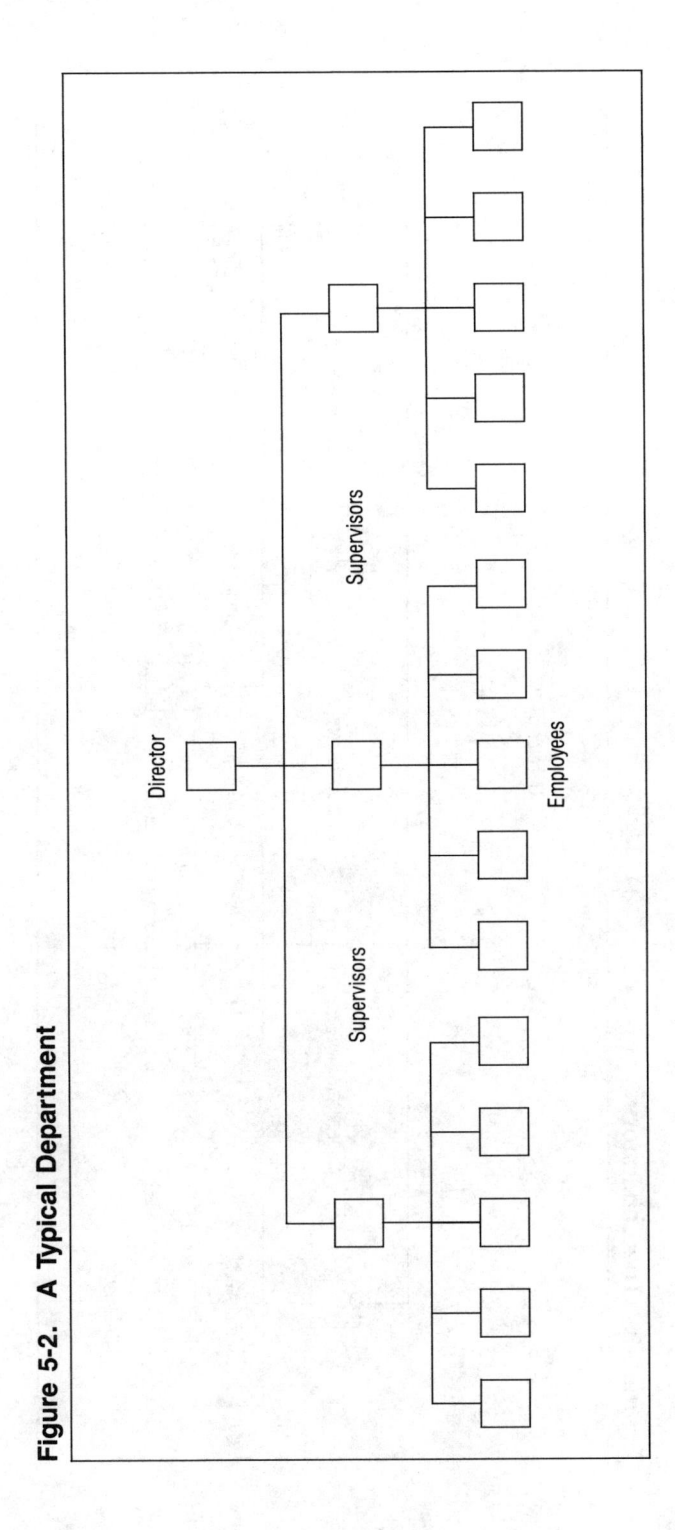

Figure 5-3. The Laboratory

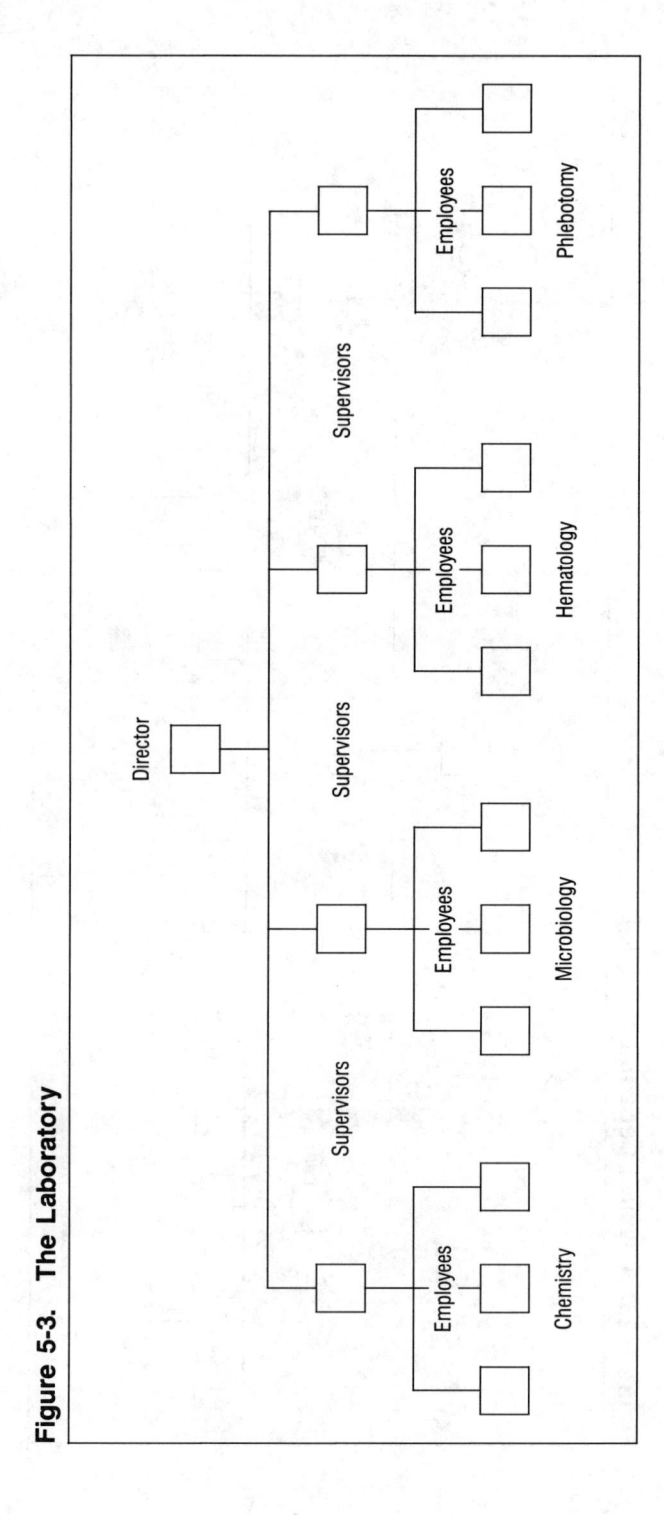

Organizational Structure

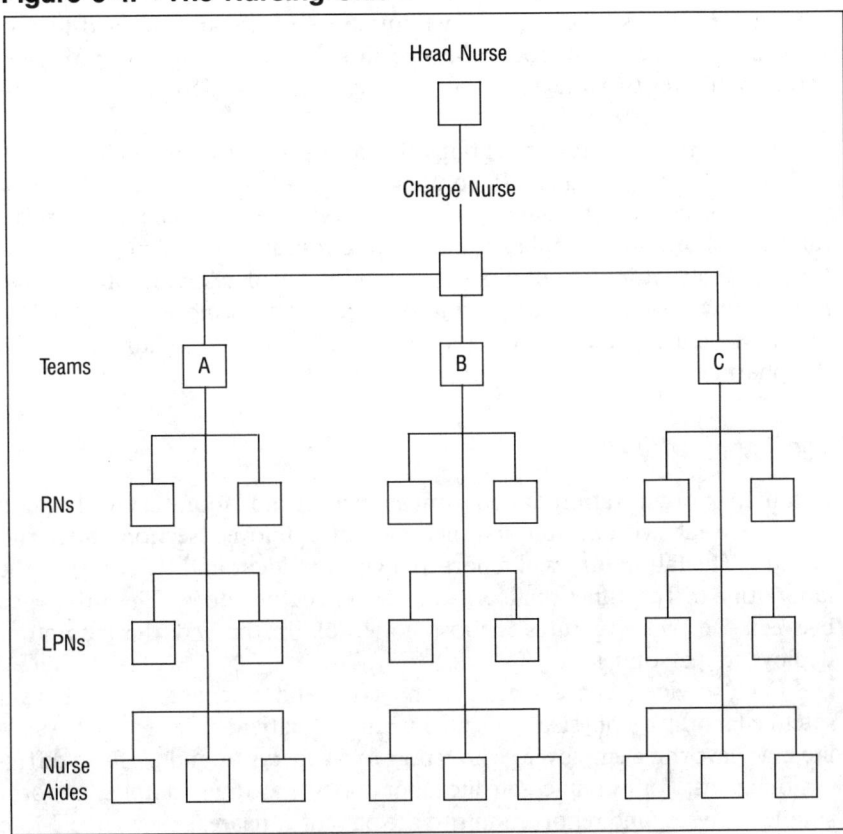

Figure 5-4. The Nursing Unit

nurse assistant provides yet another level of care, such as taking vital signs, bathing the patient, changing sheets, emptying bedpans, and answering call bells. If the patient needs to be admitted or discharged from the unit, he or she must wait for the RN. If the patient needs medicine, he or she must wait for the medicine nurse. If the patient needs to have a bedpan removed, he or she may have to wait for the nurse who has that responsibility. If the physician needs to speak to someone, he or she must wait for the RN. This segregated, task-focused system was designed to create greater efficiency. Instead, it leads to delays in care, lower productivity, inefficiency, reduced customer satisfaction, and lower employee satisfaction, commitment, and motivation.

- ### Matrix Structure

As mentioned previously, the matrix structure combines products/services and functions in a matrix arrangement, with both vertical and horizontal integration. (See figure 5-5.) Although the functional hierarchy is retained, sections or groups of employees within departments are assigned to provide direct service to the product/service lines. In such a structure, the organization promotes two allegiances: one to the functional department and one to the product/service line.

The matrix structure maintains the controls of the hierarchy and yet is an effective way to focus the organization's attention on the main purpose of business—high-quality product or service delivery. The matrix structure has a horizontal emphasis and is more responsive to change than the functional structure. It permits easier movement of resources in response to the growth or decline of products/services. Following are examples of matrix structure implementation in two different areas: the laboratory and the pharmacy.

The Laboratory

In a matrix organization, a department such as the laboratory will have a centralized lab with an internal hierarchy of employee, section chief, and director. The laboratory will report to a vice president and CEO just as the laboratory in the functional organization structure does. The difference between the two structures is most noticeable in the way the laboratory deploys its personnel.

Each service (such as cardiac, oncology, and emergency) may have a satellite laboratory physically located within its patient care area. The satellite may have three employees who report to a supervisor and perform different functions. For example, satellite laboratories may draw samples, perform simple analyses, and report results to the patient care areas they serve. More complex tests will still be drawn by the satellite laboratory but sent to the central laboratory for analysis and results reporting. The satellite laboratory will be staffed on the day shift; evening and night shift laboratory requests will be sent to the central laboratory.

Employees who work in these satellites have a closer relationship with the departments and types of patients they serve. They may become more knowledgeable about specific tests and results parameters. They can more easily recognize the urgency of the requests that come from the units they serve. And they have an allegiance to their particular service, as well as to their functional department.

Additionally, the satellite can easily adjust its activities to the needs of the service area. For example, it may be able to perform a larger quantity of tests for one unit than for another. The units that it serves generally are understanding about the satellite's priorities because they all see themselves as part of the same matrix service line.

The satellite laboratory may be able to institute a new test more quickly than a general laboratory, because the medical technologists who serve the

Organizational Structure 49

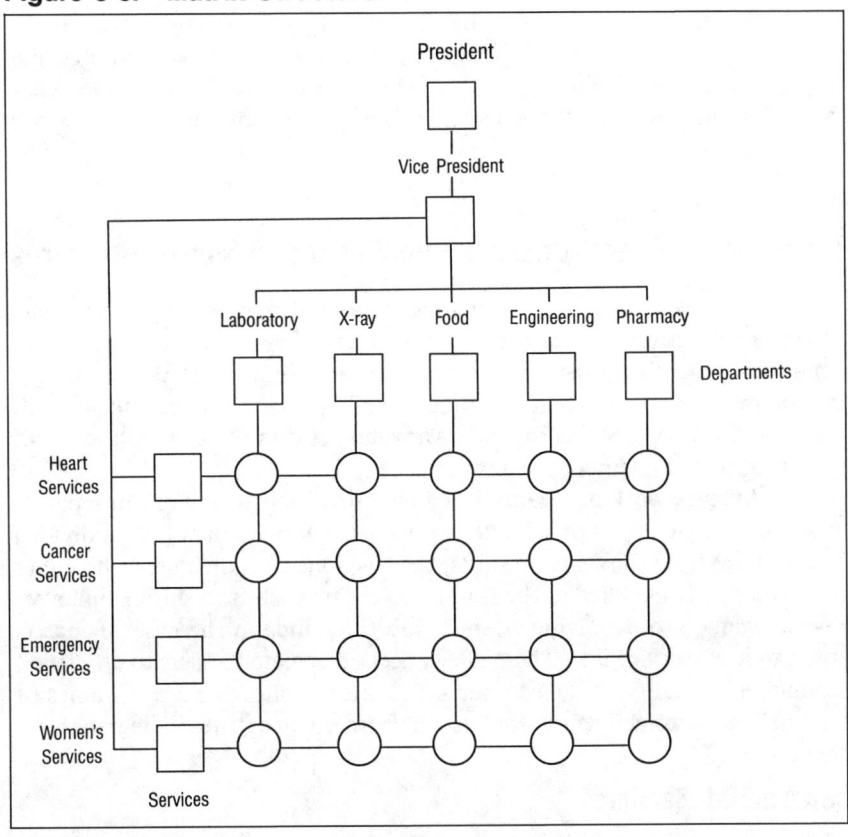

Figure 5-5. Matrix Structure

nursing units have more contact with the physicians and nurses, and become more knowledgeable about the special needs of the patient population they serve.

The Pharmacy

The pharmacy in a matrix organization would be centrally located and have several satellites, or deployed pharmacists. Pharmacies typically have a satellite in the operating room and may have one in critical care units. Although not all services will have satellites, most will know the name of the pharmacist assigned to serve their needs.

The pharmacy meets its matrix obligations by having its pharmacists learn more about the drugs that are available and/or typically used by the individual service lines. A pharmacist in a matrix organization may be centrally located but makes rounds on the units he or she serves.

In the pharmacy, the advantage of the matrix structure over the functional structure is that the level of service and support it provides to the nursing units is increased. The satellite pharmacy, or the assigned pharmacist, is more responsive to the needs of the nursing units it serves. The pharmacist is more available and accessible to staff, physicians, and patients when questions arise.

• Barriers to Effectiveness in Functional and Matrix Structures

As practiced in health care, both functional and matrix structures create barriers to effectiveness. Some barriers are created by adherence to the functional structure that exists in both matrix and functional organizations. Others are created by reliance on individual work rather than teamwork. The cross-functional structure and its advantages do not occur in an organization until it implements teamwork.

Health care work is accomplished by individuals who work in separate functional departments or satellites, which in turn frequently are subdivided into shifts. Within the separate shifts, work is done by individuals who either are permanently assigned to the shift or rotate from shift to shift. Employees have allegiance to department, shift, job title, and, in the case of matrix organizations, service line. These allegiances can create barriers to efficiency, productivity, quality, and customer satisfaction. Following are examples of the barriers to effectiveness that result from each of these allegiances.

Department Barriers

Department barriers work in two ways. First, employees operate as if their responsibilities end at the line drawn between the work of their department and the work of any other department in the organization. For example, when a visitor to the hospital asks an employee at the information desk for a patient's location, that information is readily given. It is the information desk's responsibility to provide that information. However, if a visitor were to request that information on the fifth floor, he or she is likely to be directed to the information desk on the main floor, even though a telephone call or a glance at a computer screen would provide an answer. Employees reason that taking time to provide a service that is another department's responsibility infringes on the time they have to spend on their own work and thus reduces their productivity.

The second way in which the department barrier works is when employees could offer a service that is outside their department's role but do not because the responsible department would be incensed that they had crossed its functional boundaries. Employees recognize that the hassle from the other department would create more problems than would their failure to offer assistance. For example, housekeeping employees are instructed to enter a patient's room only to clean it. If the patient asks for a bedpan or to be handed his or her glass of water, housekeepers must leave the room and summon a nursing employee because they are not allowed to provide these simple services. Nursing anticipates potentially serious problems for its patients if people from other departments provide nursing services, even though employees in other departments could easily be trained to provide those services.

Shift Barriers

Animosity and barriers to productivity also can occur between shifts within a department, regardless of whether the organization has a functional or matrix structure. Inevitably, day-shift employees believe they have the most work to do, evening-shift employees believe they inherit the day shift's unwanted work, and night-shift employees believe they never get the attention or resources they need to function effectively.

If day-shift employees had the opportunity to do work reserved for the evening shift, they would hesitate, reasoning that the evening shift might come to expect them to perform that work. Even though it is unrealistic to assume that work occurs only according to the arbitrary times by which shifts are scheduled, most health care employees stick rigidly to their shift assignments, thus losing opportunities to enhance service and increase productivity.

Job Title Barriers

The most restrictive barrier is the one that exists among employees working for the same department and service line and on the same shift, but functioning within different job titles. Departments that employ both professionals and support personnel often develop a "caste" system within which the professionals perform one set of duties and the support personnel perform another. It is highly unlikely that a professional will "condescend" to perform the work of a support person and equally unlikely that a support person will risk censure and possible termination for trying to perform work normally done by a professional.

Job title barriers to productivity, effectiveness, and customer satisfaction are inherent in the current organizational structures, where allegiance is to function, task, job title, or service line rather than to customer or end result. Implementation of self-managed work teams can eliminate many of these barriers.

Service Line

When employees develop an allegiance to one service line, they may neglect to provide services to all other service lines, or they may not provide them at the same level of quality. For example, a nurse who is assigned to the heart service line may be highly irritated if she has to fill in for an absent nurse in the medicine service line. Whereas her technical skill may not diminish, her attitude will project her dissatisfaction to the extent that she will not be as efficient or productive as she would be working in a heart unit.

Employees who form strong ties to their service lines may be highly competitive for resources, services, and esteem. They may not be as willing to share resources and support each other if they work in different service lines.

• Team Structure

When successful, self-managed work teams address many of the barriers to efficiency and effectiveness that exist in an organization with a functional or matrix structure. In addition, they move the organization toward increased service to its customers while reducing cost. Although self-managed work teams are not a panacea, they do offer solutions to many of the problems resulting from organizational structure.

Benefits of Team Structure

The team structure accomplishes a number of things for the organization. It can flatten the organization, increase employee job satisfaction and flexibility, increase commitment to the work, and help reduce cost while improving the quality of service provided.

Flattened Structure

When teams do the work of the organization, the organization flattens: The numbers and levels of managers decrease and boundaries between people are reduced, thus lowering the cost of doing business. Teams also provide greater flexibility in the way work is done. They are able to shift from areas of low work volume to areas of high work volume more easily than individuals can. Because team members frequently are cross-trained, they can provide the type of work in the volume needed without the added expense of additional personnel.

Increased Employee Job Satisfaction and Flexibility

The idea behind self-managed work teams is to combine interrelated tasks into a natural cluster of jobs needed to provide a complete segment of work or to produce a complete product or service. This produces jobs of greater variety, requiring a wider range of knowledge and skills. Increasing the variety of work is integral to increasing employee job satisfaction. From management's perspective, it also increases flexibility and productivity, and reduces downtime.

Increased Commitment

When employees are grouped into teams and given direct responsibility for a product or service, they can more clearly see the link between what they do and the customers' response. With self-management comes a heightened sense of ownership and commitment. When the team has responsibility and authority for its work, each action it takes (or fails to take) reflects on the team members, rather than on their supervisor. With this greater ability to have an impact comes greater commitment to quality, service, and cost reduction.

Reduced Cost

Self-managed work teams reduce the cost of doing business in a number of ways. First, they enable the organization to eliminate expensive management positions and sometimes whole layers of management. Second, when employees are cross-trained, they can easily perform work that is needed at the time without having to wait for specialized input, thus reducing downtime and increasing productivity. Third, teams apply quality improvement tools to the work they do, eliminating unnecessary steps and breaking down barriers to inefficiency. Organizations that have implemented self-managed work teams have reported productivity increases of 30 percent or more.[1]

Design of the Team

The team structure can be incorporated throughout the entire organization or team implementation can be limited to segments of the organization. Although it is difficult to manage both a team and hierarchical organization simultaneously, there are advantages to doing so. The primary advantage is that management's comfort and ability to work with teams can occur gradually, rather than be faced all at once.

Most organizations make the decision to implement teams in stages. They identify which areas will be converted to teams, which ones will not be converted, and where conversion will end. (A complete description of the process is included in chapter 8.)

Self-managed work teams in health care can be categorized into four different types. They are:

- Single-function teams
- Cross-functional teams
- Geographic teams
- Multishift teams

The type of team implemented depends primarily on the type and volume of work needed. It also may depend on how far the organization has advanced in self-management. For instance, housekeeping might be separated into geographic teams if it is one of the first departments to implement teams. However, if nursing has already implemented self-managed work teams, housekeeping employees may become members of cross-functional nursing teams to provide support services to nursing units.

Single-Function Teams

A *single-function team* exists to perform one main work function. The volume of work might be so small and so specialized that it is neither logical nor practical to cross-train employees on several teams to perform the function. Additionally, the work may have little interdependence with other functions in the organization and no specific geographic requirement.

An example of a single-function team may be found in accounts payable in a medium to large hospital. The single function performed by employees in this section is to process payments to vendors. Regardless of how the work is divided—alphabetically by vendor, organizationally by originating department group, or randomly by who has the largest backlog—all the team members basically perform one function: They process vouchers for payment.

The advantage to a team structure in accounts payable is that it enables employees to focus on the quality of the work (correct and timely processed vouchers) and the customer (enhanced satisfaction) rather than on the specific task (their section of the alphabet). To expand the team's job, vendor relations and department relations could be added to its scope of responsibility. If this were to happen, accounts payable team members would develop a commitment to both the originating department and the vendor, as well as a commitment to perform their job function of processing accounts payable transactions.

Cross-Functional Teams

A *cross-functional team* is composed of employees who possess many different skills and who generally are cross-trained to perform a number of different functions. For example, employees on a laboratory cross-functional team can all draw blood, operate various machines, maintain records, complete reports, and communicate directly with customers. These employees have broad job duties and responsibilities, and have been cross-trained to function effectively in their various roles. Thus, each individual laboratory team member understands the entire process and is aware of what is important to patients, nurses, and physicians alike. Likewise, all the team members are aware of team performance data and opportunities for improvement.

When a cross-functional laboratory team is established, it generally exists to serve the needs of a specific patient type and geographic area. Frequently, a satellite laboratory is established, which improves the speed with which samples are obtained and tested and results reported. This means that patients can start treatments earlier and go home sooner.

Laboratory employees on cross-functional teams have variety in their jobs and a commitment to a group of customers. Their work is designed to make team members autonomous, to provide them direct customer feedback, and to enhance their perception that their work is significant.

Within health care, barriers have long existed between nursing and the ancillary and support departments, such as laboratory, pharmacy, business office, radiology, respiratory, food service, laundry, materials management, and housekeeping. One way to overcome these barriers is to develop a cross-functional self-managed work team in which the functions of all or many of the support departments are included. For example, if a patient care unit had incorporated within its personnel the knowledge, skills, and resources to perform all the support functions listed, those employees would be members of the unit and their loyalties and commitments would be to the unit's patients and physicians, rather than to the support departments from which they come.

When hospitals were first created, nursing staff performed all the support functions. However, because of the high cost of nursing services today, that approach is no longer feasible. Cross-training support personnel to perform nursing support functions would go a long way toward diminishing many of the barriers that currently exist between departments.

Geographic Teams

A *geographic team* exists to meet the needs of internal or external customers in a geographic area. It can be a single-function team or a cross-functional team. It is composed of employees who have responsibility for services in either a physical area of the institution or a specific region.

One department that can be divided into geographic teams is housekeeping. Housekeeping employees often are assigned to clean a specific area to which they develop an allegiance. Other employees in housekeeping are specialists who go from area to area to perform "deep" cleaning or special services, such as waxing and buffing. Their allegiance is to their skill.

As often happens, housekeeping's workload in any given nursing unit varies on a daily basis. For example, one day, unit A might be extremely busy with a number of patient discharges in addition to a significant amount of general cleaning. On the other hand, unit B may have very little patient turnover and a normal amount of general cleaning. Thus, the employee in unit A may be exhausted trying to keep up with the workload, whereas the employee in unit B has a very light day.

When housekeeping employees work on geographic teams, they are responsible for cleaning services on a number of nursing units. They can be flexible enough to shift their resources to the unit that has the high workload on their own. Because they are self-managed, they can move resources without calling a supervisor, waiting for the supervisor to assess workloads, waiting for his or her decision, and then having to work with an employee who is angry for being pulled from his or her own area to work in someone else's area. Because they are cross-trained, housekeeping employees typically are not insulted if they have to perform a different role in order to help with a high volume of general work.

The allegiance formed within the geographic housekeeping team is to the customers who occupy that geographic area, the team, and the housekeeping department. In comparison to the traditional organizational structure, the importance of the home department diminishes because of close contact with the customer group.

Some health care organizations are large enough to provide services to patients or physicians in different external geographic regions. For example, a group of employees may do physician office billing. There may be a team that bills for physicians' offices from the north side, a team that bills for physicians' offices from the east side, and so on. These employees have an allegiance to the geographic region they serve, although the employees are centrally located.

Multishift Teams

A *multishift team* is a group of employees who work across shifts. Although rare, multishift teams can help eliminate barriers that often exist between shifts. For example, in a medium hospital in the Southeast, a self-managed team of housekeeping employees is responsible for cleaning the emergency department (ED) on all three shifts. Although the employees on this team work individual shifts (they do not rotate), they feel a commitment to the cleanliness of the ED on a 24-hour basis. Team members communicate with each other through brief meetings and reports, and not all team members attend all meetings.

When the ED housekeeping team members get together, they arrange for training, work out supply and equipment problems, discuss vacation schedules, and assess how well they are meeting customer needs. They have given themselves a team name, "The ED Life-Savers," and have a tremendous amount of team pride. They perceive that they have autonomy and are respected by nursing professionals for the quality of their work and their responsiveness to the needs of the emergency department. Although working on three shifts is a challenge to team cohesiveness, this team has been able to surmount it by assuming responsibility around the clock rather than for the duration of a shift.

Other teams that have tried to overcome the shift barrier have not been as successful. The housekeeping team in the above example had the advantage of being so small that its membership needed to include all shifts in order to have a bona fide team. Allegiance to the shift never became more important than allegiance to the team and the customer.

Size of the Team

Although a number of alternatives for self-managed work teams exist in the health care setting, the key determinant of team size and number is the volume of work to be accomplished. Within the organization, departments with the most customers requiring the most services will have more teams, whereas small departments may themselves become individual teams or be combined to form teams.

Throughout the literature on team effectiveness and group dynamics, there is a general prescription for team size. Teams should have no fewer than 6 members and no more than 18.[2] In addition to the volume of work, team size depends on the variety of functions to be included. Because teams are flexible, they can be assigned more work to accomplish than would ordinarily be assigned to the same number of individuals.

Small Teams

Generally, a team of five to seven members is considered small. An advantage to small teams is that they do not need to perform as much administrative work as larger teams. Team members see each other frequently, get to know each other better, and are better able to establish trust. However, a drawback to small teams is that issues such as performance and personality problems, absenteeism, and scheduled vacations have a greater and more immediate impact on team cohesiveness and productivity.

Medium Teams

A medium team generally is composed of 7 to 12 members. Its size is large enough to be able to introduce significant productivity improvements without being overly burdened by administrative work. In a medium team, cross-training is important, as is skill variety, so that team members can perform a number of different functions. Additionally, this group is still small enough to facilitate effective communication among members.

One disadvantage to medium teams is that their members are less likely to form work groups that are as cohesive as those formed by members of small teams. Additionally, the frequency with which all team members are available to provide input or help with decision making decreases.

Large Teams

When team size exceeds 12 members, it risks breaking apart into two or three smaller teams. A large team of 18 members could easily break into three small teams of six members each. The larger the team gets, the more administrative work it must contend with—for example, completing time sheets, scheduling time off, scheduling training, making copies, distributing mail, and so on.

A larger team size also makes development and maintenance of team spirit more difficult. Because employees on large teams often do not see each other as a body, they tend to break down into small cliques. Communication becomes a real problem. The team has to spend more time ensuring that news and changes are communicated and that problem solving and decision making include the input of all members. It is easier for some team members to avoid participating at all, because the time to get input from everyone is rarely available.

On the other hand, larger teams do not suffer as dramatically as smaller ones when members are either on vacation or out sick. Personality conflicts within larger teams do not create the same level of disruption and distress.

• Structure within the Team

Teams usually are structured as a circle to represent the equality of all members. (See figure 5-6.) They may be homogeneous or single-function, or include people with a variety of skills representing different professions or functions. Within the team, whether on a permanent or rotating basis, one person generally assumes the role of team leader. Other roles within the team can range from safety officer to quality improvement coordinator to record keeper. (The various roles are discussed in detail in chapter 6.)

Team Members

Team membership reflects the variety of work arrangements or schedules that the organization utilizes in its work force. The team may comprise full-time, half-time, weekend-only, one-shift-only, or multishift employees. In some organizations, relief workers, who fill in for absentees, are members of more than one team. However, temporary employees are rarely assigned to a team until they become permanent employees. For the most part,

Organizational Structure

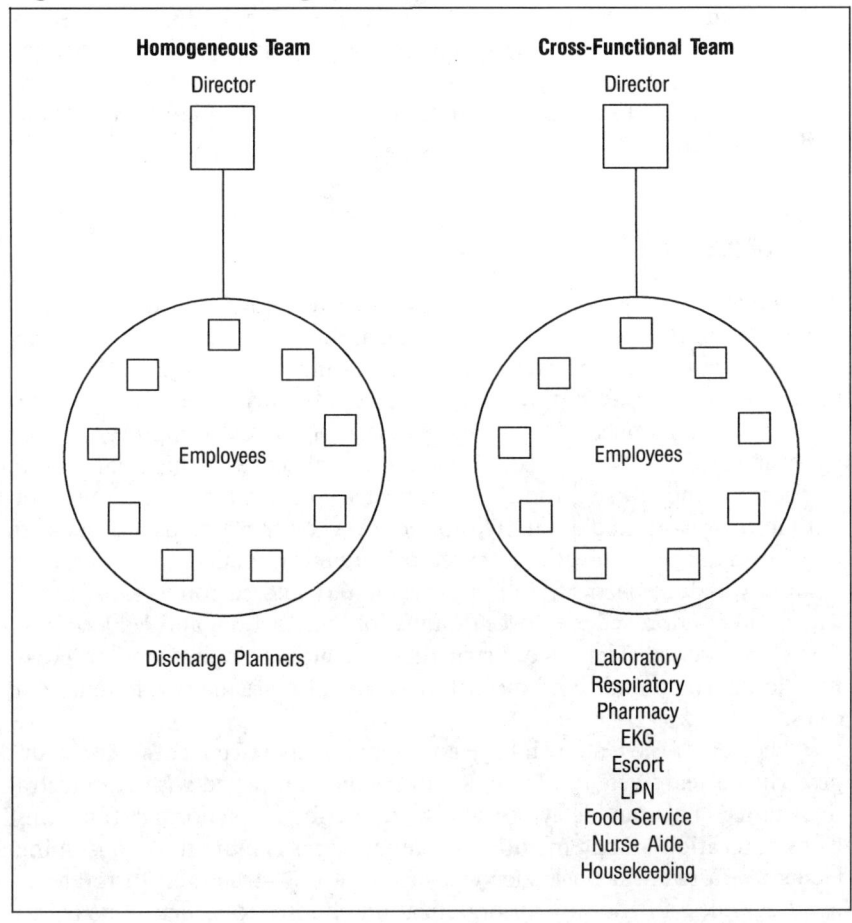

Figure 5-6. Self-Managed Teams

```
         Homogeneous Team                    Cross-Functional Team
              Director                              Director
                □                                      □
                |                                      |

           ( Employees )                         ( Employees )

        Discharge Planners                       Laboratory
                                                 Respiratory
                                                 Pharmacy
                                                 EKG
                                                 Escort
                                                 LPN
                                                 Food Service
                                                 Nurse Aide
                                                 Housekeeping
```

employees belong to one team, which spans one shift only. However, the team may have 12-hour-shift employees, as well as 8- and 4-hour-shift employees.

Team Leader

The team leader position can be permanent or rotating. To a great extent, the decision depends on the team's composition, the team members' previous experience, and the presence or absence of a coach. Most team design models encourage the team leader position to rotate so that one person does not, by default, become a supervisor.

Self-managed work teams espouse the shared leadership concept. Within this concept, each team member has some leadership responsibility and may have a specific leader assignment. For instance, the different administrative functions may each have a leader—a safety officer, a quality improvement leader, a staffing coordinator, a record keeper, a budget officer, and so on. These assignments rotate, giving all team members an opportunity to learn, grow, develop, and display their unique talents. (The role of team leader is described in more detail in chapter 6.)

• Conclusion

The model for employee work groups tends to reflect that of the overall organization. Because health care organizations traditionally are conservative, the pyramidal hierarchy is the most common structure for both the organization and the employee work group. This structure is based on the division-of-labor concept, which assumes that productivity improves as tasks are segregated and simplified.[3] However, social scientists have found that division of labor rarely produces as expected. Rather, employees prefer variety in their work and are more productive when their minds are engaged.

Self-managed work teams flatten the organizational structure, improve flexibility, reduce barriers, and improve quality and customer satisfaction. They lead to improved employee morale, job satisfaction, and reduced cost. There are many different team structures, including single-function, cross-functional, geographic, and multishift. There also are many different team roles.

The size of the team can have an impact on its effectiveness. For example, when a team gets too large, it can become burdened with administrative duties that can delay its ability to perform its normal functions. Communication among members of larger teams is more time-consuming. Generally, a team has a leader whose position is structured to rotate.

Regardless of the way an organization chooses to structure its teams, the team concept offers significant benefits over the traditional alternatives.

References

1. Hoerr, J. The payoff from teamwork. *Business Week* 314:57, July 10, 1989.
2. Orsburn, J. D., Moran, L., Musselwhite, E., and Zenger, J. H. *Self-Directed Work Teams: The New American Challenge.* Homewood, IL: Business One Irwin, 1990, p. 8.
3. Hackman, J. R., and Oldham, G. R. *Work Redesign.* Reading, MA: Addison-Wesley Publishing Company, 1980, p. 47.

Chapter 6

Team Roles, Responsibilities, and Personalities

When self-managed work teams are created and designed, they assume roles and responsibilities both vertically and horizontally within the organization. They begin to perform functions that previously had been performed by supervisors and managers. Additionally, they absorb functions that had been performed by support personnel.

This chapter explores the roles and responsibilities that team members assume as the team structure is implemented and matures. It also outlines the responsibilities of the team coach and briefly reviews team personality and behavior.

• Roles and Responsibilities in Traditional Organizations

In the traditional *command–control* organization, employees perform pieces of work rather than whole jobs. For example, they may draw blood but not test it. They may clean the patient room but not the hallway. They may prepare the salad but not the potatoes. They may bathe the patient but not apply the dressing. This piecemeal approach to work can cause employees to question the value of both their work and their contribution to the organization. In addition, these employees are rarely required to think about or coordinate aspects of their work because their work is supervised by others. As a result, the work does not engage their interest or commitment.

Thus, in an effort to motivate employees, organizations have added recognition and reward programs that focus on pieces of the work. When the work itself is not motivating, it becomes relatively easy for unions and other dissension-provoking groups to enter the management–employee relationship.

Conduction of Traditional Command–Control

The command–control system appears to work best when work is performed principally by low-skilled, low-educated, and low-paid workers (although

TQM has shown that even at this level of the organization, employees who are given permission to think can make substantial improvements to work processes). In fact, the system is most effective when there is little need to integrate work from one area into another and when machinery and equipment are more important to producing a product or service than employees are.

Most command–control organizations operate under the premise that managers are paid to think and employees are paid to do. The roles of manager and employee do not overlap.

The role of the employee is to:

- Do what he or she is told
- Notify the supervisor when a problem occurs
- Wait to be told what to do next

The role of the supervisor is to:

- Decide how to do the work
- Tell the employees what to do
- Obtain and organize resources
- Solve problems and make decisions
- Initiate change
- Watch over employees to make sure they do as they are told
- Keep records and make reports

Drawbacks to Traditional Command–Control

The command–control approach has been successful for a century; however, today it is crumbling. Neither managers nor employees believe that it is the best system. Recognizing its drawbacks, many are seeking new ways of working, including increased employee involvement.

Among the chief disadvantages to command–control is that it does not utilize the full capabilities of the organization's employees and thus, regardless of hourly wage, the organization is not getting its money's worth from its employees. Second, with this approach supervisory productivity is low because supervisors do many tasks employees could do for themselves. Third, the quality of decisions, fixes, and changes that are implemented is lower than necessary because employee involvement is discouraged. Some supervisors are unable to admit they do not have all the answers and may make expensive mistakes. And employees are unable to exercise initiative and implement improvements that are glaringly obvious to them, because (1) they do not have authority and (2) management is not close enough to the work to see the improvements that are needed.

• Roles and Responsibilities in Self-Managed Work Teams

Prior to arranging work, roles, and responsibilities for teams, it is critical that the work be designed, or redesigned, to (1) eliminate unnecessary effort; (2) incorporate support services, administrative tasks, and supervisory work; and (3) become group rather than individual work. (A detailed discussion of work redesign is provided in chapter 8.)

Once the basic work of the group has been designed, responsibilities will have been incorporated, vertically from management and support personnel and horizontally from others who do pieces of the work. The object is to create a whole job, having task and skill variety, in which employees have responsibility for outcomes and through which they have feedback about their success.

Teams can accomplish the work of the organization through their implementation as a basic work unit. Within each team, there are a variety of roles. The most common are:

- Team leader
- Team coach
- Team member

Team Leader

The team leader position can be either permanent or temporary (rotating). Some teams may have no designated leader, in which case leadership is shared among team members. (See figure 6-1.) When the team leader position is permanent, it will incorporate some of the duties formerly performed by supervisors, including:

- Schedule and conduct meetings
- Monitor performance
- Schedule work and make assignments
- Schedule vacations and time off
- Serve as liaison to the rest of the organization
- Maintain team records

However, even though the permanent team leader performs duties that a supervisor might perform, he or she also needs different skills and competencies than a regular supervisor. According to a study by Personnel Decisions, Inc., "the five competencies which were most strongly related to 'head up a self-managed work team'" were:

- Influence others
- Champion change

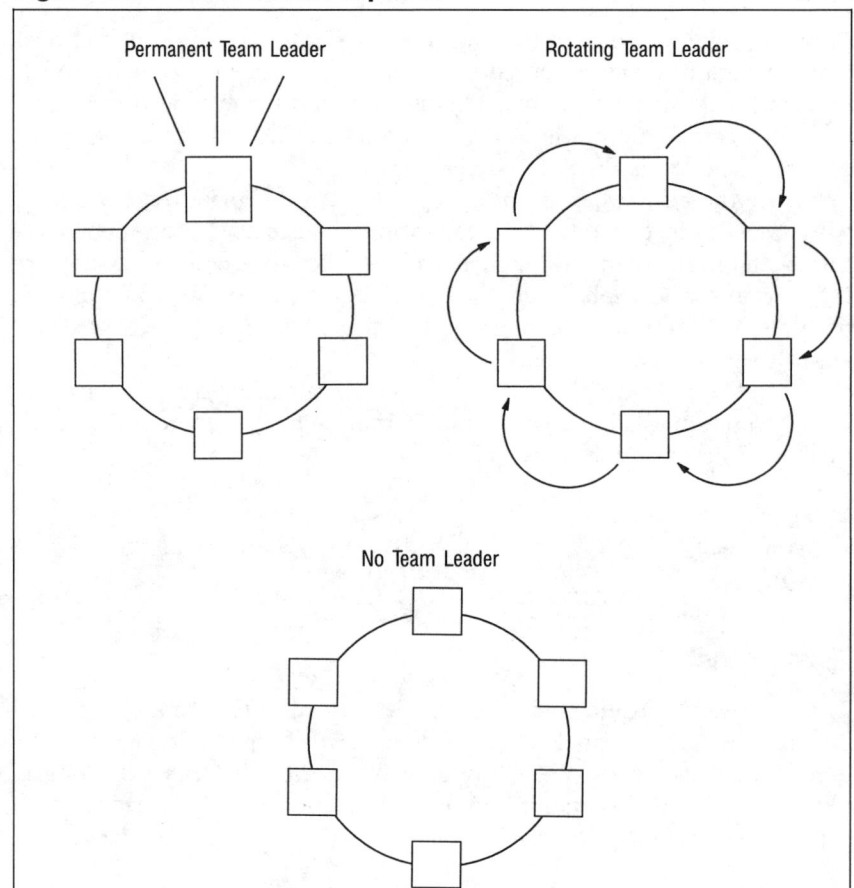

Figure 6-1. Team Leader Options

- Use sound judgment
- Provide direction
- Act with integrity[1]

It is of critical importance that the leader, whether permanent or rotating, be committed to this new organizational structure and method of working. Part of what helps the team survive and succeed is having a leader who is a strong advocate for change and capable of persuading others that change is desirable.

Permanent Team Leadership

When a permanent team leader is assigned, he or she frequently is the team's former supervisor. However, the habits that the supervisor and team members have developed over the years often restrict their ability to function as a self-managed work team, because the supervisor is used to making decisions and the employees are used to deferring problems to the supervisor. Thus, it is extremely difficult to make the transition to a self-managed work team if the supervisor is retained as permanent leader.

Even if the team leader is not the former supervisor, it is difficult for the team to achieve the higher level of commitment to performance and ownership that it can achieve with either a rotating team leader or no team leader. Employees with a permanent team leader see their participation in the work as directed rather than owned. Cost savings that can be generated by reducing the number of supervisors are lost if every team has a permanent team leader who is paid at a level above the team members.

Rotating Team Leadership

The rotating team leader option has advantages over that of the permanent team leader. Generally, leadership rotates from team member to team member on a quarterly basis. Each team member has the opportunity to lead meetings, make work assignments, complete paperwork, and perform other assignments assigned to the team leader position.

One advantage to rotating leadership is that it puts pressure on the current team leader to moderate his or her behavior and *serve* the interests of the other employees on the team. Because the team leader will hold the position for only a few short months, he or she recognizes that the next team leader can retaliate if there has been a perceived injustice.

Another advantage is that each team member will grow and develop knowledge and leadership skills. Throughout the team, there will be a greater understanding of financial matters, organizational constraints, and the complexities involved in leading others.

A disadvantage to rotating leadership is that it tends to load all the administrative work on the leader position. This means that for a period of three months, to a great extent the employee who is team leader will not be performing his or her own work. Thus, every quarter when a new leader is designated, the transitions and shift in assignments can lead to disruption and possibly decreased productivity.

No Team Leadership

Some teams start out with the belief that they can function best without a team leader. Eventually, these teams will either flounder or appoint an informal leader to address the group's need for leadership. Regardless of the group's original intent, all groups want and need leadership. An innovative option to having no leader is for team members to share leadership.

Shared Team Leadership

In the shared leadership approach, administrative and supervisory tasks are distributed throughout the team. Frequently, these tasks are grouped logically into assignments such as quality improvement, scheduling, record keeping, and meeting leadership. Generally, assignments are rotated so that no one person has to do the same things all the time and so that all team members have the opportunity to learn and practice new skills.

Shared Team Leadership in a Council Setting

Sometimes several team members share leadership roles in a structure called a leadership council. Although not all team members participate on the council, the council makes decisions that affect the whole team. For example, in the event a request from another area of the organization is made for increased service from the team, council members meet to discuss the request, review the facts and data, and decide (1) whether to provide the service and (2) which team members will be assigned to provide it. Although the council represents all employees on the team, the employees do not participate in making decisions that affect them intimately.

Leadership roles on the council rotate so that all members of the team eventually have the opportunity to serve. The council has considerable power and team members, when they serve on the council, can implement changes that might not occur if the entire team were involved in the decision.

The leadership council concept works best when the team is large or when team members work many different shifts and schedules. Two advantages to the concept are that it provides an avenue for employee input into decision making and it accomplishes administrative work. However, what it fails to do is to engage each employee in ownership of the team and its decisions. When an employee is not serving on the council, he or she can criticize what "they" are doing to "us." Team spirit can be diminished, and the council can easily turn into a problem-solving, decision-making hierarchy.

Shared Team Leadership outside a Council Setting

One of the most popular methods of providing team leadership is shared leadership without the council concept. Team members are advised of the leadership tasks they must perform during training and team formation. With the help of the team coach, the team itself designates which members will perform different tasks. Every team member is assigned at least one leadership task, rotates through the assignments, and is involved when decisions need to be made. For example, one team member may be assigned to schedule team meetings and put together the agenda, another to complete monthly activity reports, and still another to take charge of inventory control and purchasing.

Because all employees have leadership assignments, when the leadership team meets, the whole team meets. The leadership tasks identify management-level work that the team must do, rather than management-level positions that the team must have. Team members participate equally in decision making and share responsibility for managing the team.

Team Coach

Generally, the team coach, or team facilitator, performs his or her role outside the team. (See figure 6-2.) In some organizations, the position of team coach has replaced that of supervisor. A coach may work with five or six teams, whereas previously a supervisor may have worked with only one group of employees.

Figure 6-2. Team Coach

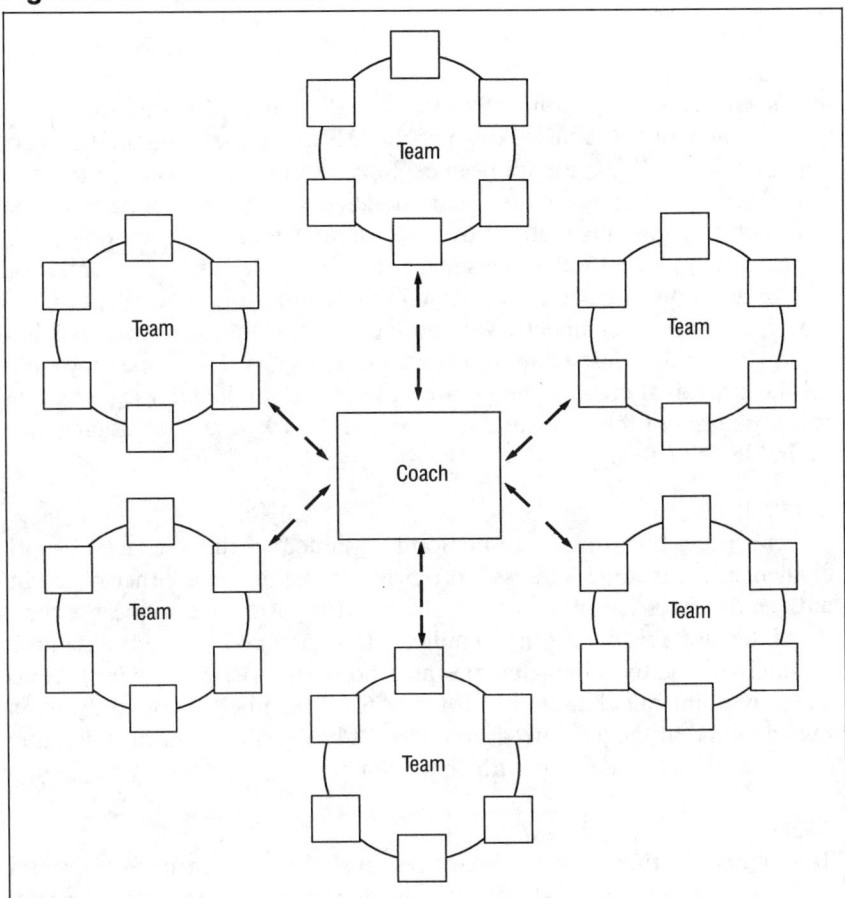

The team coach's primary purpose is to guide and support the team as a whole, as well as its individual members, as skills are developed in teamwork. To a great extent, the ease with which a team moves from individual to group work and assumes new management and support roles and skills depends on the capabilities of the team coach.

Functions of the Team Coach

The individual who serves as team coach must assume a number of different roles. His or her responsibilities can be grouped into five specific functions:

- To counsel
- To confront
- To train
- To coach
- To support

Counseling

In the counseling function, the coach actually guides the team through its thinking and/or decision-making process. He or she may ask questions and suggest avenues that have not been explored but have a bearing on the decision. He or she may encourage team members to gather more data, further consider the long-range impact of a decision, or look at a decision's political ramifications and seek out a sponsor at a higher level in the organization.

In addition, the counseling function may take a more personal focus. The coach may work directly with an individual team member who is having difficulty demonstrating positive team behaviors. He or she may counsel the individual one-on-one in order to describe and clarify expectations, identify causes of the behavioral problems, and work toward developing more desirable behaviors.

Confrontation

Generally, the confrontation function is assumed when the coach abruptly challenges the team to address a problem that he or she is either observing at the moment or has observed repeatedly in the past. For example, the coach may interrupt a team meeting to indicate that members are exhibiting limiting and/or negative characteristics as a body (that is, *groupthink*). He or she may point out that respect for one team member is not being maintained, and that the team needs to revisit its basic values and consider alternative methods of dealing with that member.

Training

Training is not the coach's primary responsibility; rather, team training is performed by the organization's training department or an external consultant. However, because the coach knows what to do on a team, how to do it, and how to communicate, he or she is in a position to reinforce training, help improve skills through guided practice, and correct or expand the learning level that a team member has achieved.

In this function, the coach may review meeting leadership skills with the team member who has just rotated to the leadership position, review chart and graph development with the employee who has just been assigned the quality improvement role, and teach team skills to new members or new skills to experienced members. Additionally, if there is a point in time when a trained coach has no teams to coach, he or she would make a good team trainer organizationwide.

Coaching

Coaching involves observing team behavior, assessing where the team is in relation to its goals, identifying roadblocks or opportunities for improvement, and then working with the team or individual members to improve performance. For example, the coach offers suggestions before, during, and after team meetings to help improve their effectiveness.

Generally speaking, the coach tries to bring problems to the team's attention and then help team members address and solve them. To this end, the coach may have to assume one of his or her other roles—for example, counseling. Sometimes the coach tries to prepare team members to deal with a problem that he or she anticipates. For example, if the coach is aware that team members are harboring strong feelings about a particular issue, he or she may meet with the team leader before the meeting to discuss this issue in order to coach the leader through possible scenarios and responses.

Finally, the coach serves as the team's cheerleader, recognizing improvements both large and small that the team is making and encouraging the team after a disappointment, such as the rejection of a proposal. Additionally, the coach may give individual team members immediate positive feedback when they perform a new skill, take a risk, or help out a colleague.

Supporting

The coach also functions in a supporting role. For example, he or she may accompany the team as a silent participant when it is making a presentation to management. He or she may act as a behind-the-scenes advocate for the team, helping the organization to more clearly understand the team's needs and perspective.

Although the coach does not have a voice in decision making, he or she may confront the team when it appears to be taking a direction that may be detrimental to performance. The coach serves the team as both a resource and a support by listening, observing, questioning, and reinforcing, rather than by directing and controlling.

Qualifications of the Coach

The team coach position may be filled from within any level of the organization. The individual in this position needs to be a strong communicator who is able to listen, observe, and assimilate impressions. He or she also must demonstrate sensitivity and persuasiveness. Ideally, the coach is the type of person who can readily fade into the background and yet be formidable enough to inspire team members to do their absolute best.

If the candidate for the position is either experienced with teams or knowledgeable about what makes teams effective, has organizational savvy, and demonstrates basic communication skills, he or she can easily be trained to serve as a team coach. In terms of attitude, the coach must be able to see the potential that different people possess regardless of background or experience and must be able to recognize the value of drawing on employee differences to make better decisions and formulate better solutions.

Often supervisors displaced by the implementation of self-managed work teams make excellent coaches. However, these individuals need special training to prepare for the role shift. They, themselves, also need coaching to help them maintain role integrity in order to avoid reverting to their former "boss" role.

Training of the Team Coach

The team coach should receive the same training that managers and team members receive. However, they should receive their training in advance of the team. That way, the coach can help guide, support, reinforce, or correct team behavior. (The training program is discussed in greater detail in chapter 11.)

Team coaches need to learn all about self-managed work teams—why teams are being implemented and what the organization's expectations are. The team coaches need to be well versed in small-group dynamics concepts and the methods that teams and groups have for working together. Coaches need skills in communications. They will be helping teams work out problems by asking the right questions, clarifying and confirming meaning, and summarizing agreement and progress.

Team coaches need to know the policies of the organization and how to get things done. Additionally, they will help the team get resources and information from the organization. Therefore, as resources to the teams, they should have the training, skills, and information needed to help the teams be effective.

Team Members

To envision the role of self-managed work team members, it is helpful to think of the teams as freestanding companies that contract their services to the hospital. Within these companies and without outside supervision, employees work together to perform a number of functions that enable the organization's work to get done.

Functions of the Team Members

Team members perform a number of different functions. The self-managed work team is designed to absorb work both vertically and horizontally, and may incorporate all supervisory roles in addition to all support roles. Generally, team members have responsibility for the following six functions:

- Planning
- Performing the work
- Measuring and improving performance
- Solving problems and making decisions
- Conducting meetings
- Training other team members

A self-managed work team may perform all of these functions or only a few of them, depending on the degree to which it has been empowered to do so by the organization. The degree of empowerment depends on the nature of the work, the preparation of the employees to do the work, and the organization's culture and values.

Planning
A critical element in team effectiveness is establishment of the basic framework from which the team will function. This basic framework includes the team's mission or purpose, its values and vision for the future, its primary and secondary customers, and its short- and long-term goals.

Team members need to know from the outset what the team is, whom it interacts with, and what it is trying to accomplish. The team needs to operate from a plan that considers what the needs are, what must be accomplished, and the time frame that is available to achieve its goals. Teams need a goal and a plan structure in the same way that departments do in order to help the organization accomplish its long- and short-term objectives.

Performing Work
Teams exist to do work. Often new team members are hesitant to help each other, even though they have been given permission to do so. They find the transition from individual work to teamwork difficult and sometimes need time and coaching to make it.

In addition to doing the work and helping their teammates, team members also must plan, structure, and assign the work. In some hospitals, a daily beginning-of-the-shift conference has been initiated to assess what needs to be done and to decide who will do it.

Another important part of this function is follow-up. It is as critical to teamwork as it is to individual work. The team needs a system to help it remember who said they would do what and by when. If this system is coordinated with the daily work assignment system, most teams will find that work will go smoothly.

Measuring and Improving Performance

Self-managed work teams shine in the area of work improvement. In large part, their success may be due to the release of ideas and feelings held by employees who for years had said to themselves: "If they'd ever ask me, I could tell them a better way" or "If I was in charge, things would be different." Whatever the reason, the results can be impressive. For example, at its very first meeting at Memorial Mission Hospital in Asheville, North Carolina, the self-managed housekeeping team identified 27 opportunities for improvement. Most of their ideas were eventually implemented and resulted in measurable improvements in productivity, quality, and customer satisfaction.[2]

Teams often are eager to begin to measure their work performance. They want to be able to show immediate improvements in productivity and customer satisfaction. As in other areas of life, teams can become discouraged if they do not see continuous improvement. Sometimes a team will outperform itself for several consecutive weeks or months and then experience a downswing. Although downswings may have many causes, they all have the same effect on the team: They lower morale.

Downswings can be caused by interpersonal problems on the team that lead to two team members arguing and thereby causing tension on the team. Communication patterns that worked well before are disrupted and team members start to take sides or withdraw from team interaction.

A change in expectations from a department that the team serves can cause a downswing. The methods and procedures the team was using have to be modified and changed to meet new expectations. The team may see these changes as a drain on their energy and time and become frustrated.

A downswing also may occur when a team loses a member who has had a strong personality and been involved in keeping team morale high. The loss of this individual may cause the team to go through a grieving cycle before the members are able to work again with the same energy and enthusiasm.

As a final example, some high-performing teams will plateau for weeks or months before they are able to achieve new breakthroughs in performance. These plateau periods can cause a downswing in team energy and performance.

Solving Problems and Making Decisions

Teams take their management roles seriously. Many team members have never been given authority or responsibility for actually solving a problem or making a decision, even though their input may have been solicited.

A major component of self-management lies in the performance of this function. For example, if team members are having problems with supplies, they investigate, contact the department or vendor involved, and work to solve the problem. If the team needs to select a replacement product, members must go through the investigative and decision-making process. If they do not perform these problem-solving and decision-making functions, they will have very little self-management.

Conducting Meetings

A meeting is a basic component of the teamwork system; without it, teams have no way to reinforce the team concept and members cannot function as a group, rather than as individuals. Meetings allow members to communicate: Team members can share ideas, express opinions, reach consensus, solve problems, and make decisions. Thus, time and space must be provided for teams to get together to conduct business.

Training Other Team Members

Team members are expected to train each other. If the team is cross-functional, some team members may possess knowledge and skills that others do not. Thus, they will be asked to train their teammates so that all team members can fill in for each other, enhancing the team's flexibility. In the case of new employees being introduced to the team, experienced team members will be expected to orient and train them to do the work. In the event that team members have developed unique ways of doing their work that have improved overall performance, they may be asked to train their colleagues to use the same methods.

Other Responsibilities of the Team Members

It is empowering to add new roles and responsibilities to individual workers' jobs. Employees can perceive the addition of responsibilities and the expansion of roles as signs that they are respected for their competence. They see new job duties as an opportunity to demonstrate skills they have not been able to use in their previous work environment, and the challenge gives them a new sense of purpose. However, the addition of work must be accompanied by the delegation of authority to make and implement decisions and to initiate change. Otherwise, employees will feel that they have merely been "dumped on." Empowerment gives employees the opportunity to add value and make a meaningful contribution to the work of the organization.

Among the additional responsibilities that members of self-managed work teams may be asked to perform are a number of management functions, including the following:

- Managing people resources
  - Interview and select prospective team members

- Orient new team members
- Train team members
- Keep time and attendance records
- Schedule vacations and days off
- Provide relief coverage for absences, vacations, and days off
- Maintain safety records and teach safety
- Schedule overtime
- Set standards for work performance
- Evaluate team and individual performance
- Administer discipline
- Terminate employment of team members
* Managing financial resources
  - Develop and maintain the budget
  - Purchase supplies and materials
  - Recommend pay increases
* Managing equipment resources
  - Evaluate equipment
  - Propose capital equipment purchases
* Performing administrative and liaison functions
  - Complete reports and daily paperwork
  - Provide input to higher-level management decisions
  - Take action on problems
  - Contact support departments directly

Employees also may be asked to carry out the following maintenance and housekeeping functions:

* Maintaining and repairing equipment and facility when minor problems occur
* Maintaining the work environment

Some team members will be asked to assist with the following quality improvement functions:

* Analyzing and improving work processes
* Maintaining quality control data
* Communicating with suppliers
* Working directly with customers (patients, families, physicians, payers)

Finally, most if not all team members will play a role in maintaining the team. Functions involved in this role include the following:

* Designating/selecting team leader
* Sharing management responsibilities

Team Roles, Responsibilities, and Personalities 75

- Conducting team meetings
- Resolving interpersonal conflicts on team
- Being accountable for mistakes and successes
- Celebrating and recognizing each other's accomplishments and team performance
- Conducting peer reviews
- Working without supervision
- Learning the jobs of other team members

• Star System for Shared Leadership

One of the basic tenets of self-managed work teams is that team members share management and leadership roles and responsibilities. One method for clarifying the shared leadership functions is the star system. (See figure 6-3.)

Each point of the star represents a leadership role. Team members are able to anticipate their transition from one responsibility to another because responsibilities are clearly depicted on the star. A team can plan rotation from one function on the star to the next for the entire year. For example,

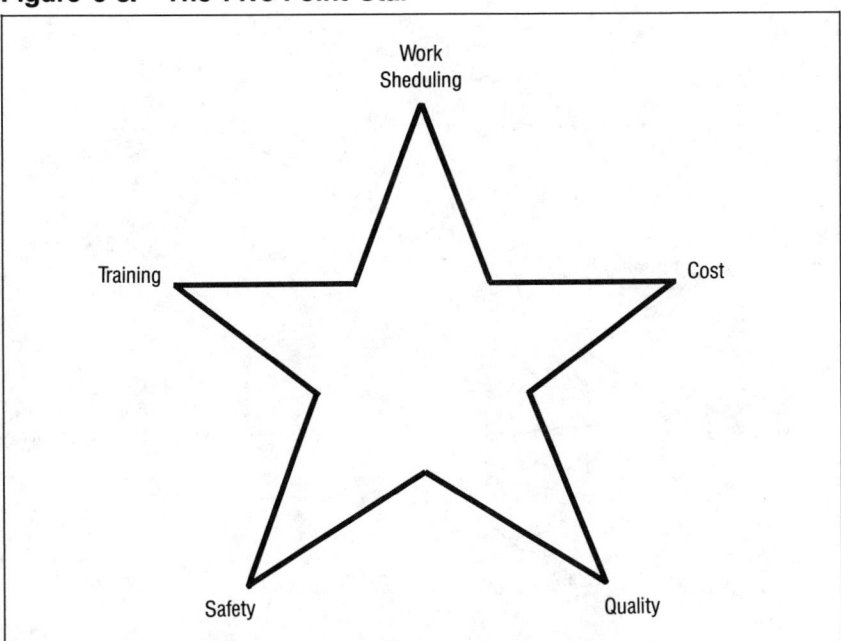

Figure 6-3. The Five-Point Star

```
         Work
       Sheduling


Training                    Cost




      Safety        Quality
```

Source: This five-point star was adapted from the Hannaford Brothers Star.

the team can decide who will be in charge of safety in the first quarter, second quarter, and so on. To help the organization know who the point of contact is for each responsibility, the star points can contain the employee's name as well as the function he or she performs. The star can then be updated quarterly to reflect team member rotation.

Five-Point and Ten-Point Stars

The five-point star was developed by the Hannaford Brothers.[3] This star depicts five leadership roles that are rotated quarterly so that everyone has an opportunity to learn how to manage each responsibility (point of the star). As figure 6-3 shows, the points of this star represent five responsibilities: work scheduling, cost, quality, safety, and training.

The Alliant Hospital System in Louisville, Kentucky, also uses a star method, but its star has 10 points representing high- and low-task responsibilities.[4] (See figure 6-4.) When an employee rotates off a high-task assignment, he or she is given a low-task responsibility. Some of the responsibilities that may show up on the star are: inventory control, staffing, equipment maintenance, recognition, housekeeping, cost control, customer relations, record keeping, and training.

Figure 6-4. The Ten-Point Star

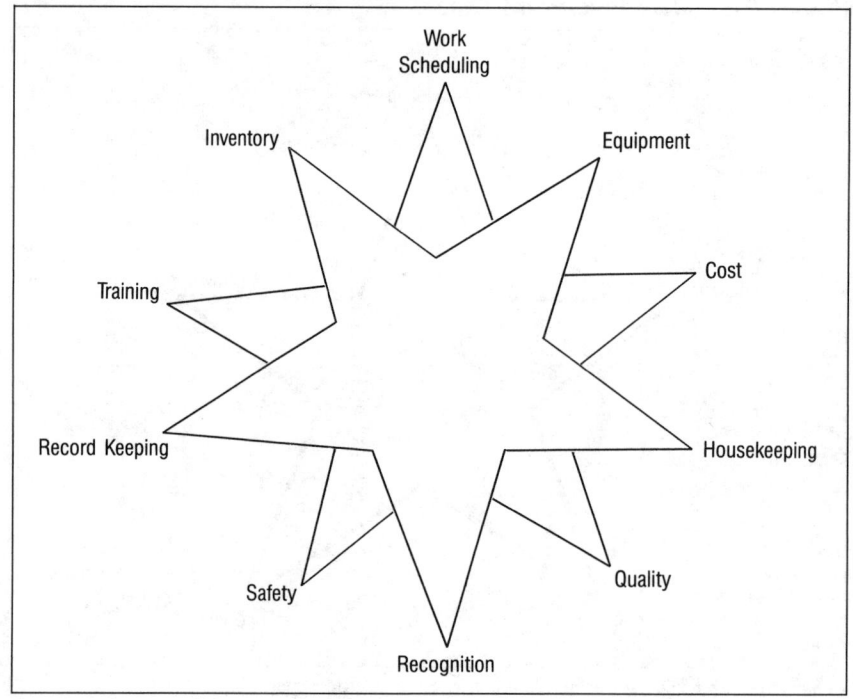

Support Groups

Other organizations have taken the five-star system a step further. They have organized "same point teams" as support groups composed of employees from teams throughout the organization who are assigned the same responsibility represented by each point of the star.

For instance, each team in the organization may have an employee assigned the role of team trainer. On a monthly basis, all the team trainers meet in their support group to learn more about training, share training problems and concerns, and offer each other support for the duration of their assignment as team trainer. (See figure 6-5.)

Each of the other points on the star also would have a support group—for example, a record-keeping group, a cost group, a quality group, and a safety group. The support groups provide training to team members, ensure

Figure 6-5. Same Point Teams

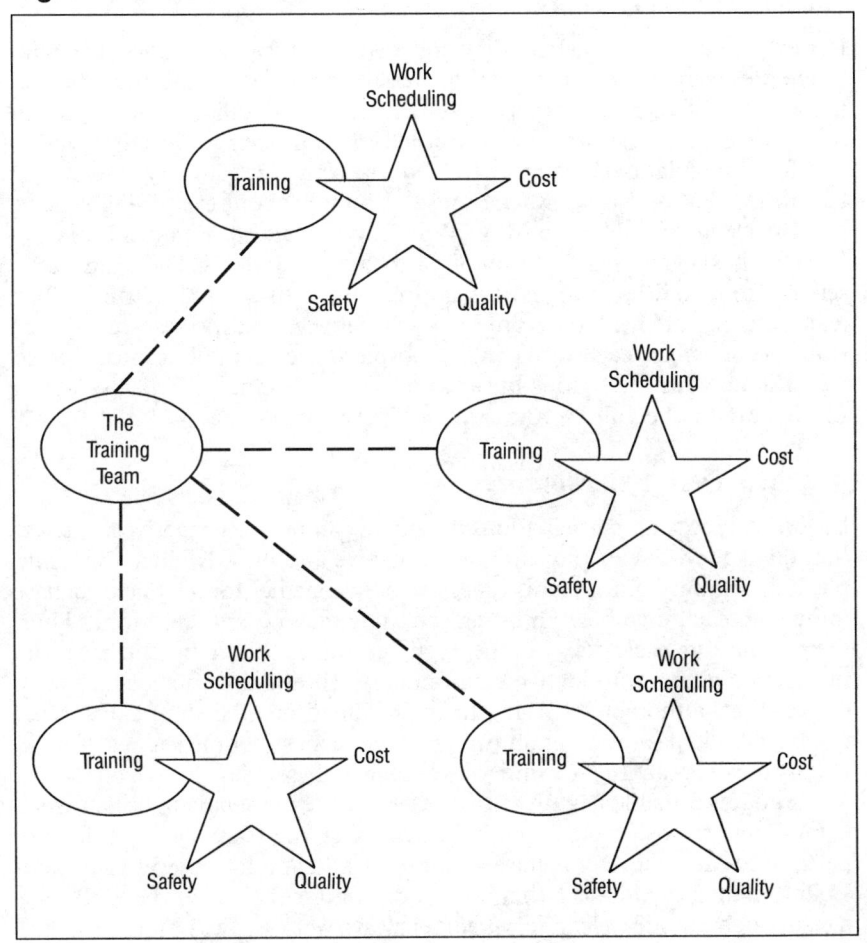

continuity as team members move in and out of those responsibilities, and provide resources to deal with questions and problems.

The support groups may have permanent leaders consisting of supervisors or managers who have been displaced due to the implementation of self-managed work teams. Former supervisors may have a special interest or expertise in an area represented by one of the star points.

• Team Personality

Generally, all self-managed work teams are similar in a number of ways. They all hold meetings, set goals, and have someone in a leadership role. However, no two teams are exactly alike. Teams reflect the personality of their members and their leaders just as departments in the organization do.

Positive Team Behaviors

Regardless of how and where they are created, all teams are very different. Some are energetic, creative, and aggressive about achieving their performance goals. Others are structured, methodical, and diligent in the pursuit of their work. Still others are concerned more about form than function and focus on relationships more than work. And, occasionally, a team will be formed that displays a wacky sense of humor about everything it does.

For example the "Have Mop, Will Travel" team at Memorial Mission Hospital has a great sense of humor, as their name reflects. The team leader sets the tone and has imbued the entire team with a sense of fun. When team meetings are held, the team jokes while it accomplishes its work. When team members see each other in the hospital, they share humorous greetings. Along with the serious business of accomplishing their tasks, having fun is part of the culture and spirit of the team.

Negative Team Behaviors

Unfortunately, team participation sometimes can provoke negative behaviors that make the work of the team unproductive and unsatisfying. For example, it is not unusual for teams that have been together for a while to behave in unison, each member exhibiting the same feelings and emotions. Thus, the purposeful exclusion of one member of the team by the majority produces a counterproductive environment. Additionally, teams can form cliques that, although satisfying to their limited membership, can subvert team goals and destroy team unity. Sometimes teams become jealous of other teams and take actions to undermine their cohesiveness.

Another possible negative consequence of team behavior occurs when team members lose their individual identity to the team. When this happens, team members can behave irrationally and at a lower level of responsibility than they would if they were working on their own. For instance, a team might decide to let a few members leave work early. Eventually, everyone on the team is leaving early. In order to avoid losing pay, team members might collude to falsify their time records. The result is that everyone ends up taking advantage of self-management by behaving irresponsibly and immorally because, as members of a team, they may feel that they no longer are individually responsible for their behavior.

A further example of negative team behavior can be found in the concept of *groupthink*.[5] In this phenomenon, individuals tend to support a team decision even though they have strong reservations about it. Team training needs to focus as much attention on managing agreement as it does on managing conflict. When team cohesiveness is a strong force, members often do not want to upset the team by disagreeing. When this happens, the quality of the team's decisions is diminished.

Groupthink manifests itself in a number of ways, including:

- Risk-taking behavior that indicates the group believes it can behave outside established norms
- Group efforts to silence dissent
- Immoral or unethical behavior
- Failure to reveal adverse information to the group

Negative behaviors require attention from the start. During the training process, trainers need to express the likelihood that negative behaviors will arise and to alert team members to watch for problem behaviors emerging in the group. Because the team's social interactions have as much impact on team performance as its task-related behaviors, team coaches need to be as adept at identifying and correcting team behavior problems as they are at identifying and correcting work performance problems.

Additionally, it is important that teams be allowed to work out their own problems. This encourages team maturity and team effectiveness. The opportunity to manage themselves is one that teams truly value. Because team member behavior and interaction are so important to team effectiveness, member satisfaction needs to be one of the team's goals.

When management evaluates team performance, it needs to look at team member satisfaction as well as productivity and customer satisfaction. A high-performance team will be successful in task-related goals as well as in social interactions. When a team's performance falters, its likely cause can be traced to internal interpersonal problems.

• Team Performance Assessment

When an organization establishes a self-managed work team, it also identifies performance expectations. The team routinely assesses its performance against those expectations. Additionally, management also wants reports on how well teams are performing.

Team coaches and team leaders get together monthly to look at team performance from the perspective of all teams in the organization or department. Organizational barriers to team effectiveness, team leader training needs, team system needs, and team member training needs are identified. Goals are established for addressing problems, and ways of recognizing and communicating successes are identified.

• Conclusion

A team-structured organization offers many improvements over the traditional alignment of roles and responsibilities. Although all the work still has to be done, teams provide energy, enthusiasm, and commitment that are not always present in the functional organization structure.

A team framework encompasses three primary roles: team leader, team coach, and team member. Team leadership may be permanent, rotating, or shared. The shared leadership concept has proven effective in many organizations, as illustrated by the star system.

The team coach is a valuable resource. He or she serves in a number of functions that help the team achieve superior performance. These functions include counseling, confronting, training, and supporting. The coach does not participate in decision making. Often the team coach position is assumed by a supervisor displaced by implementation of a self-managed work team, although a supervisor should not coach his or her own former employees if it can be avoided. This is because it is too difficult for the coach and the team members to stay within their new roles.

Team members assume many roles and responsibilities, depending on the degree to which the organization is willing to empower them. Although the majority of these new roles are management-related, others involve maintenance of equipment and the environment, quality improvement, and team maintenance.

Teams develop personalities that reflect their membership. They may be creative, highly structured, or playful. Teams also can exhibit negative behaviors that are detrimental to performance.

If they are to succeed, teams must be allowed to grow, develop, and mature. Management can aid their progress by helping teams focus on performance and to monitor team member satisfaction as well as productivity and quality improvements.

References

1. Hazucha, J. F. Leading self-managed work teams: what are the key competencies? Paper presented at the 1992 International Conference on Self-Managed Work

Teams, Sept. 1992. Also published in *1992 Conference Proceedings,* University of North Texas, Denton, p. 132.
2. Team notes from the first team meeting of the "6th Floor Sharpies," Memorial Mission Hospital, Asheville, NC, Aug. 1992.
3. Wellins, R. S., Byham, W. C., and Wilson, J. M. *Empowered Teams: Creating Self-Directed Work Groups That Improve Quality, Productivity, and Participation.* San Francisco: Jossey-Bass, 1991, p. 114.
4. Telephone interview with William B. Newkirk, coordinator of education and development, Alliant Health System, Louisville, KY, Aug. 13, 1993.
5. Glaser, R. Avoiding groupthink in self-managing teams. Paper presented at the 1992 International Conference on Self-Managed Work Teams, Sept. 1992. Also published in: *1992 Conference Proceedings,* University of North Texas, Denton, p. 194.

Chapter 7

The Role of Supervisor

When hospitals implement self-managed work teams, they take one of two approaches: They either implement a team in an area that has lost a manager or allow a maverick manager to implement a team within his or her department. In either approach, the direct impact on supervisors is minimal. In some hospitals, supervisors remain in their current role as the team develops. The transition to "no supervisor" takes a long time, involves the supervisor, and does not result in the loss of the supervisor's job.

In industry, however, the transition to self-managed work teams generally occurs more rapidly and on a larger scale. According to Carr in an article titled *Managing Self-Managed Workers,* "When an organization chooses to empower employees to manage themselves, the supervisory role (as an independent position) largely vanishes."[1] However, if the supervisor's role vanishes, what happens to the supervisor? This question must be given serious thought before an organization implements self-managed work teams.

This chapter describes supervisor reaction to implementation of self-managed work teams in health care and presents some of the options that are available to supervisors during the transition. It also takes a look at the manager's role and how it changes as the organization moves toward self-management.

• Supervisor Reaction to Self-Managed Work Teams

At Memorial Mission Hospital in Asheville, North Carolina, the supervisors in housekeeping helped conceive, plan, and guide the process of implementing self-managed work teams in their department. Their reaction could not have been more positive: "We were delighted. We believed the employees could do it and that the whole department would benefit. We weren't worried about our jobs. I guess we had blind faith."[2]

On the other hand, William Newkirk reports that supervisors at the Alliant Health System in Louisville, Kentucky, were pretty scared. "At the management level, it was a goal, tied to incentives, to implement self-managed teams. The managers were committed and the employees generally thought it was a good idea. The supervisors were the resistors."[3]

Generally, the latter scenario is the more frequent one. With rare exceptions, supervisors fear the transition to self-managed work teams. They see their job security threatened, regardless of management promises to the contrary. They fear loss of prestige, power, and self-esteem, as well as reduction in pay. Often they are unsure about their ability to function in a newly designed job or one that has recently been vacated elsewhere in the organization. And perhaps most important, they want to know what they should tell their families. At this point, they need validation of their worth to the organization, not platitudes or false promises.

This presents a situation in which management honesty is critically important. Employees can tell when they are not being told the truth. They will appreciate a clear explanation of both the business reasons for the change and the expected outcomes, particularly with respect to their future in the organization.

When self-managed work teams are implemented in industry, the number of supervisors is reduced dramatically. In some cases, team implementation eliminates entire layers of management. The same could be true in health care. Hospitals are facing tremendous pressure to cut costs and increase productivity and if self-managed work teams were implemented in large areas of their operations, supervisor positions would be eliminated. However, in the initial stages, only a very few supervisor positions would be affected and attrition could easily open other employment opportunities within the organization.

The transition to self-managed work teams takes time. On average, team implementation takes 18 months to two years, from conception to self-sufficient operation. During this time, displaced supervisors have the opportunity to take other positions within the organization that have been created because of team implementation—for example, team coach or technical advisor.

Generally, such roles are filled with employees from within the organization, including displaced supervisors. Those supervisors selected are trained, prior to team formation, to assist and facilitate the implementation process. The training department or the self-managed work team consultant provides the training to help displaced supervisors develop the skills and knowledge they need to succeed in their new roles.

• Role Options for Displaced Supervisors

Depending on background, experience, and skills, supervisors can make a smooth transition to new roles within the self-managed organization. Following are several employment options.

Transition Planner

As the transition from the supervisor-managed structure to the self-managed structure takes place, the supervisor has the option of staying in his or her position in order to facilitate the transfer of duties and responsibilities. As mentioned earlier, some supervisors will welcome the opportunity to participate in the empowerment of their employees. However, others will find the task overwhelming, not because they lack the ability to do it but because to do so is counter to everything they have been taught.

If the supervisor stays in the position to help his or her work group through the transition, he or she needs to be involved, along with the team, in planning the transition. The supervisor may identify the range of tasks or duties that need to be passed on to the employees and, in collaboration with the team, may set priorities and time lines.

This option of leaving the supervisor with his or her employees as both parties attempt to make the change does not always happen smoothly. Both team members and supervisor need coaching to make the transition work, primarily to prevent them from reverting to old, familiar roles.

Team Coach

The supervisor may transfer into a team coach or facilitator position. When this option is exercised, the transition to self-management can occur more rapidly and with fewer problems than it does when the supervisor remains with the team. Supervisors should complete their training before the teams do in order that they will be able to facilitate as soon as the teams are ready to start. While the supervisors are learning how to coach, the employees will be learning how to function as teams. (See chapters 6 and 11 for more information on subjects that supervisors will need to learn to become team coaches.)

Although the transfer of duties and responsibilities is a collaborative effort, senior management and team members may press for faster implementation than the supervisor believes possible. Sometimes supervisors erroneously believe that no one on the team is capable of learning supervisory duties. Consequently, they may be reluctant to help facilitate the transfer of these duties, which can slow down the process. In other instances, the organization may not really recognize the monumental shift that employees are making and is not allowing employees the time they need. Collaboration among all parties is essential to ensure that the timing of the transfer of duties is effective.

Many supervisors who step into the team coach role characterize it as highly rewarding and satisfying. They enjoy seeing their employees demonstrate new skills and competencies, and like to see the change in commitment that employees feel as they move toward self-management.

Technical Advisor

In health care, employees frequently are promoted to supervisory positions because they are technical experts. Before becoming supervisors, they may have been the best technologists in the chemistry lab or the most knowledgeable critical care nurses. As supervisors, they also may have developed areas of expertise, for example, in budgeting or in leading quality improvement teams.

Whatever their expertise, supervisors may be asked to take the role of technical advisor to help others develop skills, knowledge, and performance ability in that area. Being asked to take such an assignment is perceived as positive. However, technical advisor positions do not last forever. They are extremely important at the beginning of team implementation and when team members are learning new skills and knowledge; but teams eventually achieve the level of knowledge they need, at which point the technical advisor's services may no longer be needed. Thus, supervisors who accept this role will want to know the duration of the assignment so that they can assess their job security.

The team implementation plan is a good guide to follow in deciding how long the technical advisor role will be needed. Generally, the role will be phased out approximately one year after the last team is started.

Trainer

It is obvious that a great deal of training will have to occur to enable groups of employees to function as self-managed work teams. If the move to self-management takes place one department at a time, more than likely the existing training staff, with the supervisor's help, can implement team training. However, if training staff is limited and several teams are being started simultaneously, additional trainer positions will be needed.

If a supervisor has the opportunity to become a trainer, the move can be seen as positive depending on the reputation of the training function within the organization. Once again, the supervisor will question the duration of the assignment, looking for reassurance about job security. Like technical advisors, additional trainers will be needed only as long as there are teams to be trained.

Support Team Leader

If the hospital implements the star system of shared management (discussed in detail in chapter 6), support teams will likely be established to support team members who rotate into the star point roles. If the organization implements a number of teams, several supervisors will find opportunities as support team leaders. Generally, these positions have an unlimited duration.

Multiteam Manager

Some supervisors may have the opportunity to become the manager of several self-managed work teams. (They function like a department director.) In this position, the supervisors provide leadership to the teams, rather than function as a supervisor or team facilitator. An opportunity such as this could mean a pay increase and enhanced prestige within the organization.

As multiteam managers, they will keep their teams informed about changes in technology, market presence, and community needs. Multiteam managers will communicate boundaries to the teams so that teams will understand their financial, quality, and legal parameters. They assess and work to improve team performance and strive to remove organizational barriers to team effectiveness. They perform in the role of leader and at the director level in the organization.

Unfortunately, very few of these positions will exist. If the current ratio is one manager to 15 employees and the goal of self-management is to increase the span of control to 30 or 50 employees, reductions in management positions will be the rule (see table 7-1).

Team Member

In health care, many supervisors elect to join self-managed work teams as members. Having functioned as working supervisors, they see in this transition little loss in prestige and an opportunity for increased job security. In many health care organizations, employees, particularly in nursing, transfer in and out of management positions with little disruption.

Because, historically, there has been a shortage of health care professionals, internal opportunities for supervisors who will accept a demotion generally are available. Management can smooth the transition back to a staff position by permitting the supervisor to keep his or her existing salary level.

Table 7-1. Example of Number of Management Positions Needed as Self-Managed Teams Are Implemented

Hospital Size (Number of Employees)	Number of Managers (per 15 Employees)	Number of Managers (per 30 Employees)	Number of Managers (per 50 Employees)
1,000	66	33	20
2,000	133	66	40
3,000	200	100	60
4,000	266	133	80
5,000	333	166	100

- ## Guidelines for the Transition

To ensure that most supervisors support and advocate the change to self-managed work teams, four guidelines should be followed. Management should:

- Provide supervisors with real jobs
- Involve supervisors in the transition
- Model appropriate behaviors
- Train and coach supervisors

Provide Supervisors with Real Jobs

As much as possible, roles and responsibilities for supervisors should be developed and communicated as the team concept is introduced into the organization. Supervisors can be involved in learning and changing along with the employees they used to supervise. Often the challenge and excitement that come with learning something new can energize supervisors and lessen the impact of losing their old positions.

Nothing is sadder than to watch supervisors experience the decline of their role when the organization has provided no other opportunity. Normally, supervisors are an extremely valuable asset to the organization, ostensibly having been drawn from the best and brightest of the employee group. An organization that makes no effort to retain its supervisors in its new structure risks losing a tremendous amount of knowledge, skill, and performance capacity.

If the organization is expanding when the move to self-management is made, opportunities will exist for supervisors to assist with the growth, establish work teams in the new areas, and maintain a high level of activity and involvement. On the other hand, if the organization is not expanding, it may be possible to reduce staffing levels through attrition and move supervisors into staff level jobs. Although this is not the most desirable alternative for supervisors, it often is preferable to having no job at all.

Involve Supervisors in the Transition

Management should involve supervisors in designing team implementation. Supervisors are closer to both the work and the employees than high-level management is, and can help identify (1) ways to group employees on teams, (2) tasks that may need to be eliminated, and (3) potential resistors to, as well as potential leaders of, change.

Ways to include supervisors from the outset include providing education, arranging site visits, sharing reading materials, and soliciting their participation in identifying barriers, needed systems changes, and employee strengths and development needs. Supervisors will have knowledge and opinions on every aspect of the transition, and can be a tremendous asset to the organization during this process.

Model Appropriate Behaviors

Management has long known that it must model the behaviors that it expects to see in its employees. For self-managed work teams to be successful, management will need to model at least three basic traits. The first of these is honesty. Supervisors will want answers to tough questions, such as: "Are some supervisors going to lose their jobs?" If the answer is yes, they should be told. Managers should describe the situations that would cause a supervisor to lose his or her job, and discuss what the organization is prepared to do to help in those situations. Supervisors need to know when they will learn about their job security and how much time they will have to find another position.

If supervisors will be given the opportunity to take other assignments or will be demoted to staff jobs, they will want to know the financial impact of those decisions. Management should be prepared to clearly describe the alternatives and the financial impact of each. If possible, supervisors should be in contact with representatives in human resources who can discuss their individual situations.

Another trait that management should model is the willingness to make tough business decisions and carry them through. For example, if management knows that a staff reduction is needed and knows the number of positions that must be reduced, they need to decide who and when. They then must communicate and implement this decisions. It is demoralizing to lose one's job. It is more demoralizing to hear conflicting rumors and to continually wonder "who's next," "how many need to go," and "when will it happen for me?"

Finally, management needs to demonstrate respect for its employees. The supervisors should be treated as adults who can understand the importance and value of the business decisions behind the organization's decision to implement self-managed work teams. Management should give supervisors time, be empathetic when they express their personal concerns, and show compassion by having *real* jobs for them as an alternative to layoffs.

Train and Coach Supervisors

The employees who are embarking on teams and self-management are not the only ones who need support during the transition. Supervisors also will need training and coaching to succeed in their new roles. They will need to hear praise and receive positive feedback as they risk their security to try to take on a role they have never had before. Additionally, they will need leeway to make mistakes as they try out their new skills.

If possible, supervisors should be given a copy of their new job descriptions and performance expectations early in the process. Having the actual paper to study and reflect on provides a sense of security and is a step toward accepting the reality of the change. Regardless of age or experience, supervisors are no better able to deal with dramatic change in their work environment than any other employee.

• The Role of the Manager

If implementation of self-managed work teams is going to cause the number of supervisory jobs to diminish and the remaining jobs to change, it will have an immediate impact on managers' jobs. Prior to team implementation, a manager might have had as many as 10 supervisors reporting to his or her position. However, with the changes that self-management brings, there might no longer be a layer between manager and teams. Although team coaches and facilitators will exist, they have no position in the direct chain of command. An example of the division of management roles in the self-managed environment is shown in figure 7-1. The following subsections describe the level of participation that middle managers will have in each of these roles.

Strategic Planning

Middle managers will continue to play a major role in the area of strategic planning. In addition to participating in decision making with senior

Figure 7-1. Management Roles in the Self-Managed Environment

Management Roles	Senior Managers	Middle Managers	Self-Managed Teams
Strategic Planning			
Operations Management			
Communications and Integration			
Employee Development			
Change and Innovation			
External Relations			

management, middle managers will have to ensure that the organization's direction is clearly communicated to teams. In conjunction with team coaches, managers will need to ensure that teams develop goals that will move the organization in the direction defined by the strategic plan.

Operations Management

After the implementation of self-managed work teams, middle managers will be less involved in operations management. Teams will manage the daily work and, in some organizations, also will manage budgets. However, in some departments it is more common for the manager to continue responsibility for the budget. Nonetheless, team members will make decisions that affect it and will need to be provided with productivity and budget guidelines.

Communications and Integration

Whereas the team concept focuses on horizontal integration within the organization, managers will be working to ensure vertical integration. The alignment of goals and direction will be critical. Part of the manager's role will be to disseminate information to teams from within the larger organization as well as information on issues that affect the organization from outside.

Additionally, managers will be responsible for providing feedback to teams. Feedback will be extremely important as teams take on new responsibilities and try new ways of doing things. Although team coaches will be in a position to provide recognition, coaching, and individual feedback, feedback from managers will continue to be critically important to teams as self-managed bodies. Managers may want to establish routine meetings in which they can bring teams up-to-date on accomplishments and involve them in management-level decisions.

If an aspect of the team structure is not working well, managers need to know and be involved in trying to fix it. Sometimes managers may need to address organizational roadblocks that are affecting several or all of the self-managed teams.

Employee Development

A major focus at the middle management level will be to ensure that continued emphasis is placed on developing employees at all levels. Because people are the only organizational asset that can appreciate in value, and because the organization will be relying on fewer people, the continued growth and development of the organization's employees will be critical to success. For example, technology and consumer expectations will continue to change. To provide the information needed by physicians, patients, and families alike, more and more employees will need to be computer-literate and higher levels of empowerment will continue to occur. Consequently, management must anticipate the need for new skills, ensure that training resources are available, and make provisions in budgeting and productivity forecasting for employee time away from work to continue the learning process.

Additionally, the performance review system may need to be modified to become a performance development tool that will outline the development needs of the team and its individual members. This tool can help determine the quantity of education needed and the subjects that need to be taught.

Change and Innovation

Another role that will become middle management's responsibility is that of change agent. Middle managers will be asked to help the organization adapt to its rapidly changing environment. The ability of managers to obtain buy-in and commitment to change will be an important skill in shaping the organization's future.

External Relations

Although senior management will continue to play the largest role in external relations, middle management responsibilities are likely to increase in this area. For example, if a middle manager has responsibility for a specific service or product, he or she will be expected to maintain external contacts with customers and suppliers to assess the continued effectiveness of the service and to anticipate needed changes.

• Conclusion

Supervisors can play an integral part in the organization's successful transition to self-managed work teams because they have served as management's link to employees in the past and can bring their former influence to bear on the transition process. Because of their value in the process, management needs to involve them in the transition from the outset. A number of guidelines are available to assist management in acquiring the participation of the organization's supervisors.

When self-managed work teams are implemented by an organization, many supervisory duties are absorbed within the team and some organizations find that they can reduce the number of supervisor positions. However, this does not necessarily mean that the employees in those positions must be eliminated. Former supervisors can assume a number of roles in organizations that have moved to self-management. In addition to continuing to serve as supervisors, they can become transition planners, team coaches, technical advisors, trainers, support team leaders, multiteam managers, or team members.

When the supervisor's role changes in a self-managed team organization, so will the manager's role. Managers will be less involved in managing operations and more involved in developing people and ensuring that change occurs. Both supervisors and managers can play key roles in the transition to self-managed work teams and should be given the opportunity to participate in the organization's new venture.

References

1. Carr, C. Managing self-managed workers. *Training & Development* 45(9):38, Sept. 1991.
2. Personal interview with Ruth Owenby and Decie Sherlin, housekeeping supervisors at Memorial Mission Hospital, Asheville, NC, July 17, 1993.
3. Telephone interview with William B. Newkirk, coordinator of education and development, Alliant Health System, Louisville, KY, Aug. 13, 1993.

Chapter 8
Work Redesign

When self-managed teams are implemented and work content, flows, and systems are redesigned, employees will have greater responsibility for the quality and efficiency of the service they provide, as well as increased commitment to the work. They are responsible not only for performing the work but also for managing it and ensuring that it meets the needs of the organization's customers.

The redesign of work can be approached in four ways. It can be done organizationwide, all at once. It can be phased in. It can be done department by department using a pilot or model approach. Or the redesign can be done by department as supervisor positions are vacated.

This chapter discusses the benefits of work redesign to the organization and its employees and customers. Additionally, it describes the effects of work redesign on the organization's structure and systems, and explains the implementation options just mentioned.

• Benefits of Work Redesign

The benefits of work redesign are shared by three groups: the organization, the employees, and the customers (patients, physicians, and payers). Following are descriptions of the benefits each group enjoys.

Benefits to the Organization

From the perspective of the organization as a whole, redesigning work so that it can be performed by teams instead of individuals reduces the cost of doing business. For example, it reduces the number of high-paid positions needed because many of those responsibilities can be assigned to lower-paid employees. Thus, the cost of providing services is less and charges to customers can be reduced, which also may lead to improvement of the organization's market presence.

Additionally, work redesign improves flexibility: Employees can perform more than one function and move to the work, rather than be restricted by assignment to a single function. Improved flexibility leads to improved productivity. For example, it can reduce the time it takes one department to respond to the needs of another or one employee to respond to the needs of a customer. As flexibility increases, employees can absorb a larger amount of work, which also helps reduce cost.

Another benefit is that employee innovation and creativity are stimulated when work is designed for self-managed teams. Instead of restricting problem solving and planning to the management or supervisory level, all employees participate in these functions, bringing with them a wider range of experience and ideas. This expanded scope of ideas can enhance the quality of the resulting plan or decision, as well as ensure its appropriateness.

Yet another benefit of work redesign is that it strengthens employee commitment to the work. In recent years, health care organizations have been concerned that new hires often seem to lack the work ethic or values that older or more experienced employees have. Work redesign provides a link between employees and work that increases their commitment. When employees are able to see the impact of their work on their customers and know that they are directly responsible for their success, their commitment grows stronger.

Finally, work redesign leads to improved quality. Often unnecessary steps are eliminated and delays in service are reduced. Patients, families, and physicians alike receive a higher level of care and service than they have in the past.

Benefits to the Employees

Employees who are highly involved in their work environment experience greater job satisfaction. In large part, their satisfaction comes from having control over their work. They have a say in what is done, when it is done, and how it is done.

Their satisfaction also comes from an increased level of feedback. Work is designed so that employees have more direct contact with their customers. With the supervisor no longer there to filter customer response, employees can see for themselves that patient satisfaction is the direct result of a service or group of services they provide.

Another benefit is that employees have the opportunity to develop and use a wider range of skills, as well as to see real meaning in what they do. They can put more of themselves into their work and better appreciate the value of their contribution.

With increased commitment to the work comes increased self-esteem. Employees are in a position to take credit for an end result and to receive the credit their work merits. Because they are more aware that it was their decision making that achieved the end result, they find their work more meaningful, which enriches their self-worth.

Benefits to the Customers

The principal benefits of work redesign to customers, whether they be patients, family members, physicians, or payers, are improved service and quality. For example, waiting times are reduced and employee responsiveness is increased. Health care staff have greater and broader knowledge and possess a wider range of skills. And of growing importance to both patient and payer, the cost of service can be reduced.

• Cost of Work Redesign

Even though redesigning work so that it can be performed by self-managed teams provides many benefits, it does not happen without generating a number of costs. The major cost of implementing work redesign is in the *time* that it consumes. Whether the whole organization or a section of the organization moves to self-managed work teams, senior and middle management will need to devote time to learning, discussing, and developing implementation plans. Site visits to service organizations or industries that have implemented teams are a valuable way to see firsthand their impact on the organization and its employees. Following are the major factors in the process that will incur costs and time:

- Employees will need to be trained and involved in design and implementation planning.
- Once teams have been implemented, employees will need ongoing training and meeting time. Although team implementation eliminates the expense of supervisors, teams will still need the services of team coaches, whose training will be yet another expense for the organization.
- Managers also must learn new skills and new ways of doing their work. Like the employees, they need to learn team skills, problem-solving skills, and improved interpersonal skills. The investment in training is spread over the implementation of teams and also is incorporated as an ongoing expense.
- Policies, procedures, systems, and work methods will need to be changed. These changes will involve principally paper consumption, meeting time, and communication time, and generally are not exorbitant.
- As employees learn new skills and new ways of doing things, they will make mistakes. For the most part, these mistakes will not be costly, but they can result in increased rework costs during the transition and learning phase.

• Structural Redesign

If the organization decides to redesign its entire structure to implement the self-managed team concept, the redesign will require moving the organization to a product or service structure. This new structure could revolve around groups of either related diagnoses, such as cardiac and oncological, and/or related patients, such as women and children. Patient care teams and patient support teams would need to be formed, and within these teams, the work would have to be restructured.

According to Hackman and Oldham, there are five critical components of work design for groups:[1]

1. The work has variety and requires many different skills.
2. It is a whole job, not a piece of a job.
3. The work is significant.
4. The work allows the team to make and implement decisions.
5. The team receives direct feedback and has greater accountability for the work.

Generally, a work design team is assigned the task of developing the actual structure of the work, which relates directly to the flow of work processes. As work is redesigned, inefficiencies frequently are identified and removed. (The methods that work design teams can use are described later in this chapter.)

• Organizational Systems Redesign

Along with arranging for the redesign of the work, senior management also must assess and redesign the organizational systems that support the work. Every organization has several such systems. In addition to the work of the organization, they are designed to reinforce the power, authority, and role of management. If these systems are not adjusted or redesigned to support team implementation, they may become impediments, barriers, and roadblocks to effective team functioning. Following are descriptions of the major systems and discussion of how they must be redesigned when the organization chooses to implement the team concept.

Communication

The communication system is the method that management uses to pass information up and down the organizational hierarchy. It reinforces the organization's chain of command and power structure. Information that is categorized as highly important and highly confidential is not passed beyond the senior management level. Information that is categorized as important and confidential generally goes to middle managers and sometimes supervisors. Information that is neither important nor confidential is available to all employees. Thus, employees have access to information about the time and place of the employee picnic but not about the organization's loss of a managed care contract.

Even in organizations that are not team based, employees need information in order to do their jobs. Access to job-related information can be provided through meetings, electronic media, or print media. In many health care organizations, employees have limited access to all of these communication methods. They request information from their supervisors who in turn must go through the chain of command to get it. If the information is held in another department, it often is obtained by playing the time-consuming and inefficient "communication game" (see figure 8-1).

The communication redesign needed to provide employee/team direct access to information and information sources must be current and timely. Employees should be able to read financial reports and talk directly to accounting or engineering personnel to get needed information. They also should be able to participate in meetings in which decisions are made that affect them. Additionally, they should have computer passwords so they can monitor information that is generated by the work they do.

Customer Relations

In many health care organizations, the senior manager, the department director, or occasionally the supervisor is empowered to work directly with customers when problems occur. Employees are empowered to express empathy but must refer problems to management to solve. Thus, customer contact, other than service provision, is reserved for management; and managers interpret, codify, and occasionally relay customer feedback to employees.

In the self-managed work team environment, the team has to become the customer contact point. The redesign that is needed is to allow team members to communicate directly with customers so that they can know firsthand what is satisfactory or unsatisfactory about their work and so that they have the opportunity to problem-solve in order to improve customer relations and better meet customer needs.

Problem Solving

In health care organizations that have implemented TQM, employees serving on temporary teams increasingly are involved in problem-solving efforts. However, assignment to a problem-solving team is a special event, not a routine part of the employee's everyday job.

With self-managed work teams, problem identification and problem solving are integral parts of the team's role. When problems arise, the team is notified and calls on organizational support for assistance in solving the problem, as needed. The team investigates the problem, gathers data, considers alternatives, makes the decision, develops the change plan, and implements the solution.

Figure 8-1. The Communication Game

Financial Management

In most organizations, budgeting is the responsibility of management. Managers prepare and justify the budget, analyze discrepancies, assess problems, adjust expenditures, and work to comply with the budget. Regardless of whether they are on teams, employees do what they are told when it comes to a budget. Some have never even seen one.

When work is redesigned for teams, access to budget information and the ability to make decisions regarding expenditures is important. If teams are expected to function within financial limitations and to perform in a cost-effective manner, they need to have some financial control. However, health care organizations vary considerably in the degree to which they are willing to delegate budgeting responsibilities to teams.

If the team is a department or a major section of a department, it may be given budgeting responsibility equal to that at the director level. However, if the team is a small unit of a department, it may be given limited or no financial information. The decision regarding the extent of team involvement in financial management depends on the degree to which the team's behavior can affect the budget, the degree to which cost reduction is an important team goal, the time the team has to prepare and monitor the budget, and the educational level of the team members.

Personnel Selection

One responsibility that team members truly enjoy is that of selecting replacement personnel for team vacancies. Although some organizations do not give teams this responsibility until they are mature, most teams believe they can and should perform this function early in their development. The selection process that gives team members responsibility for choosing their coworkers is different from the selection process in which department directors choose their subordinates.

Ordinarily, department directors work with human resources to screen, interview, and select replacement personnel. The director (and occasionally the supervisor) will conduct interviews, but the director makes the final decision on which applicant will work in the department. In most organizations, employees do not even meet their new coworkers until they show up for their first day at work.

When teams choose their own replacement employees, the whole team is involved in the selection process. Teams conduct group interviews. Following the interviews, the team discusses the candidates' strengths and weaknesses and selects the individual they believe will fit the best with their team. The team members are likely to select the candidate who possesses a skill the team needs, as well as a personality the members felt most comfortable with in the interview process. Because the team is involved in the selection process, the members are committed to the success of their new team member from the start.

The traditional selection process only gives attention to work experience, educational level, and references. When selecting applicants for teams, attention is also given to whether the applicant has previously worked in a team environment and the degree to which he or she will respond to growth, development, participation, and self-management.

In *Work Redesign,* Hackman and Oldham include an uncopyrighted job diagnostic survey.[2] Section seven of this tool, or some modification of it, can be used in the screening process to help select personnel who would function well in a self-managed work team environment.

On a Likert scale or range, the survey asks what type of job the respondent likes most. The comparisons show whether a job that allows for creativity, a job with responsibility, and a job with challenging work are preferred. See figure 8-2 for a sample comparison question.

Training

In most health care organizations, training is a centralized function that focuses on safety, clinical skill development, and management development. In recent years, organizations have placed added emphasis on customer relations and quality improvement.

In the self-managed work team environment, team members need training in technical and supervisory skills to be able to function in an expanded role. They also need to acquire team skills and improved interpersonal skills. Training to support team functioning needs to be developed and implemented. And finally, team members need to learn to train each other so that they can become cross-functional in their approach to work. The addition of any or all of these skills will then need to be reflected in team member job descriptions.

Figure 8-2. Sample Comparison Question

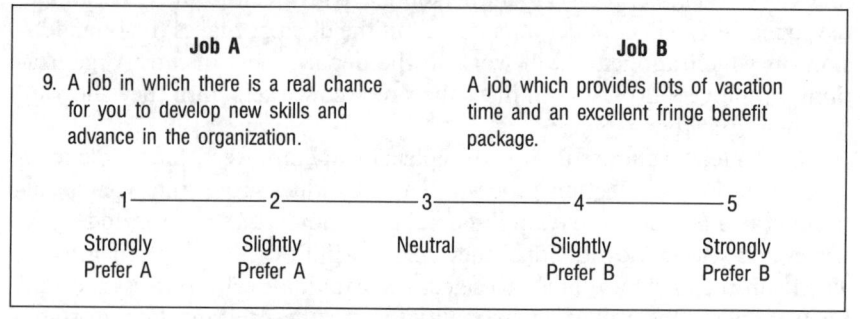

Job A	Job B
9. A job in which there is a real chance for you to develop new skills and advance in the organization.	A job which provides lots of vacation time and an excellent fringe benefit package.

1	2	3	4	5
Strongly Prefer A	Slightly Prefer A	Neutral	Slightly Prefer B	Strongly Prefer B

Source: Hackman, J. R., and Oldham, G. R. *Work Redesign.* Reading, MA: Addison-Wesley, 1980, p. 292.

Performance Appraisal

When a bona fide supervisor is not part of the organizational structure, the supervisor-administered appraisal no longer is effective. Several methods for evaluating performance can be used with self-managed work teams.

Some teams implement a self-evaluation instrument that focuses on the results of teamwork and on team effectiveness, in which team members receive feedback on their individual contributions. Other teams use a peer evaluation system, in which members receive feedback from teammates on individual performance and skills. Still other teams use a method called the 360-degree appraisal, in which team members receive feedback from teammates, the director, the coach, and customers.

Whatever performance appraisal system is used, it will need to be modified to focus on team member behaviors, growth and development, new skill acquisition, and the degree to which team performance achieves the goals established for it. If pay is tied to performance, revision of the performance appraisal and compensation system is critical to the effectiveness of the team approach.

Compensation

Historically, hospitals have had conservative compensation systems. They tend to use longevity step-pay and/or pay-for-performance compensation systems. Longevity step-pay provides employees with a small pay increase for each additional year they work for the organization up to a maximum number of years. The pay-for-performance system is a merit pay approach in which individuals who perform the best receive the highest pay increase. Health care organizations that have implemented self-managed work teams have modified their pay practices. Generally, these modifications are in the form of team performance bonuses, rather than adjustments to the basic compensation system. Other organizations have implemented skill-based pay systems and gainsharing systems to tie pay to performance.

To send a clear message on the value of teamwork and the self-managed work team system, some method of recognizing and compensating high-performance teams is essential. If individuals can receive "bonuses" or base pay adjustments for outstanding performance but teams cannot, the compensation system will likely create competition among individuals, reinforce individual performance, and deter employees from developing strong team performance.

However, team-based rewards also can have disadvantages. One disadvantage is that teams may strive for high team performance to the detriment of overall organizational performance. (Team compensation is discussed in greater depth in chapter 13.)

Planning

In most health care organizations, planning is a top-down process in which senior managers determine broad goals for the year(s) and directors use these broad goals to develop more specific ones for their departments. In many organizations, employees see neither the organization's goals nor their own department's goals. With self-managed work teams, broad goals are still set at the top of the organization, but teams develop annual goals and plans based on the goals of both the organization and their division or department.

Delegation of planning responsibility to teams requires communicating the organization's direction to the team. It also requires a system that will "close the loop," so that team goal accomplishment is directly related to and supports organizational goal accomplishment.

Record Keeping

Both the organization and the team need to decide what information the team needs and how it should be kept. For example, the team may need to keep training records, attendance records, performance records, quality records, and so on.

It is important that the team not be burdened with too much administrative detail. Part of the design process is to determine whether required records help improve patient or customer outcome. If they do not, the rationale for keeping them should be evaluated and extraneous records should be eliminated.

Support Services

Each line function in the organization requires a number of support services. Most hospitals have large housekeeping, engineering, laboratory, pharmacy, and respiratory departments that are designed to provide support services to patient care units.

Support departments can be organized to support teams in several ways. First, the support department can remain a separate functional department organized into self-managed work teams. Maintaining functional separateness when implementing teams is less jarring to the traditional health care organization, but doing so does not always produce the greatest flexibility and economies.

Second, service departments can be disbanded completely, with their functions absorbed by the self-managed work team in the patient care unit. And third, they can disperse all but a core group that remains in a matrix relationship to the dispersed employees.

For example, at Memorial Mission Hospital in Asheville, North Carolina, housekeeping was reorganized into self-managed work teams, with each team taking responsibility for the cleanliness of a geographical area.[3] The housekeeping teams are not cross-functional and thus do not perform other support services for units in their geographical location. On the other hand, at Sutter General Hospital in Sacramento, California, personnel from a number of support departments have been assigned and cross-trained to provide a patient care unit with support functions.[4]

Hospitals experiment with decentralized services from support departments when they implement satellite labs and pharmacies. This arrangement maintains the centralized control and support of the satellites, while improving service and response to patient care units. The satellite groups provide their employees with expanded autonomy and work variety. Although the satellites are rarely self-managed, they do present an acceptable intermediate step from the hierarchical structure to the matrix structure.

• Design Implementation Options

As management moves toward the decision to implement self-managed work teams, it also must choose an implementation approach. Basically, health care organizations can effect implementation in four ways: They can (l) implement teams all at once throughout the organization, (2) phase in teams in stages, (3) introduce a team as a pilot in one department or section, or (4) convert a section or department that has lost its supervisor. Each of these options has advantages and disadvantages.

Organizationwide Implementation

The health care organization that decides to implement teams throughout in one fell swoop sends a clear signal of its commitment to the team concept. This approach enables the organization to flatten and restructure all at once, rather than segment by segment. All departments change at one time, as do all their support systems. In a segmented implementation, parallel systems may need to be put into place in order to support individual work and teamwork simultaneously.

Advantages to Organizationwide Implementation

The all-at-once, organizationwide approach offers a number of advantages. Following are two of them.

People Costs Can Be Reduced
In health care organizations, people costs are the major variable expense. Moving from individual work to teamwork enables the organization to become lean and reduce salaries and benefits. When the entire organization is transformed at once, these cost savings can be realized in a relatively short time frame.

Staff Work Can Be Reduced

Team implementation organizationwide allows management to evaluate, adjust, and reduce staff (versus line) roles. Staff work can be a burden to the organization unless it adds true value to the services the organization provides. Staff people in all organizations tend to increase the work of line people. It is particularly important to assess and evaluate staff positions when looking at opportunities for job expansion on teams.

Disadvantages to Organizationwide Implementation

There are several drawbacks to an all-at-once approach. First, the scope of implementation makes the change difficult to organize and coordinate. Second, a tremendous amount of training needs to take place all at once, and more training resources are needed for the implementation phase. Finally, the daily work of the organization can slow down and be disrupted.

When one area is changed to teams, only 20 to 100 employees are involved, who need to be scheduled for training and receive new job descriptions and roles. If the entire organization is involved at once, 500, 1,000, or 2,000 employees will be attending training and trying to perform in new job roles. The number of training staff, classrooms, and overtime hours (or replacement staff needed) is overwhelming to consider.

Phased-in Implementation

A better alternative to the all-at-once approach is phased-in implementation. With a step-by-step process, all the planning and organizing are done just as they are in organizationwide implementation, except that the impact on the organization and support resources is greatly minimized.

Although the phased-in approach takes longer, it enables managers and employees to work out problems and improve systems more quickly because they have learned from their experiences elsewhere in the organization. Additionally, support resources do not have to be expanded and staff reductions can occur over time rather than all at once. This approach enables the organization to let turnover and retraining replace layoffs as the method of staff reduction.

Pilot/Model Department Approach

Health care organizations most commonly use the pilot or model department approach to team implementation. In this approach, self-management is implemented in one department or section of the organization, and is assessed and evaluated before being expanded into other areas of the organization. From the organization's standpoint, this approach is less risky than the other implementation options. It is easier to organize and implement, and if it does not work, few resources have been expended.

However, the pilot approach can lead employees to believe that the organization's support for self-managed teams is limited. It emphasizes the uncertainty that management feels about dramatically changing the organization culture and structure. It also produces an ambivalent response among the employees who participate and who are in the role of supporting the pilot. They may question the need to exert themselves for a new management idea that has limited organizational commitment. If a pilot is not successful, the whole project can be cancelled.

The model approach is similar to the pilot approach in that it implements teams in one area or department at a time. However, when management states that the department was chosen as a model for all other departments who may want to implement self-managed teams, it engenders a higher degree of commitment and buy-in. The model approach offers the first department to serve as an example that other departments can copy. Its results will be a standard for the form, structure, and systems that other departments can use.

The primary problem with the model or pilot approach is that none of the organization's systems are aligned with it. Thus, the systems can block the team's ability to function.

Team Implementation by Default

A number of self-managed work teams have been started in health care organizations when a department or section has lost its supervisor. Management takes advantage of the opportunity to experiment with the team concept. This approach to implementing self-managed work teams has worked in some instances, but generally is considered to be the least effective of the possible options.

The drawbacks to this approach are similar to those discussed in the section on pilot or model implementation. The organization's systems have not been aligned to support the self-managed work team, and the organization may be little prepared to exert itself to make the team effective. The decision to make the group of employees a self-managed work team is an expedient one, without regard for the impact on the employees or the organization. Knowledge of teams, awareness and training programs for teams, rarely exist when a team is implemented in response to a supervisor vacancy.

However if the supervisor vacancy is difficult to fill, and the employees are functioning well without a supervisor, the decision to make the employees a self-managed work team can appear logical and justified. The primary benefit of this approach is that there is no current supervisor to ease into a new role.

• Design Methodology

The first step in designing self-managed work teams is to determine the organization's goal for team implementation. For example, some organizations choose to implement teams because they see them as a way to improve employee morale and job satisfaction. However, although employee satisfaction can be a result of team implementation, as a goal it limits the potential benefits to the organization of the team concept.

A more desirable goal would be one that is more specific in terms of what the organization hopes to achieve, for example, to "improve service and quality for customers, while reducing cost by 20 percent." Not only is this goal one that self-managed work teams can accomplish, but it also is a goal the organization is willing to invest in.

It is the organization's goal that guides the implementation strategy. Once the goal has been established, the design team should follow three basic rules and consider three environmental factors.

Basic Rules

There are three basic rules in designing self-managed work teams. These are:

1. Keep the process simple.
2. Use work design principles.
3. Involve those who will be affected.

Although the move to self-management is complex and can involve and change the entire organization, it can be implemented carefully and in steps.

Design

Three primary environmental factors need to be considered in the design phase. These are:

- Technical or physical
- Social
- Boundaries

Each factor has its own components and requires making a number of decisions.

Technical or Physical

This refers to the physical environment in which the team is located and the work methods, equipment, and materials needed by the team to provide its service. A self-managed team consultant or a group of employees who work in the department can construct a flow diagram of the work, overlaid on a floor plan. The floor plan also will note the location and movement of equipment, supplies, and people.

By looking at the flow diagram, the design team can begin to identify areas of concern or areas where restructuring would be logical. The team then may be able to relocate equipment or supplies, remove doors or walls, and improve the speed of the process and access to support personnel. Just by making physical changes in the work environment, the design team may be able to reduce the cost or time necessary for the work team to provide its product or service.

Social

This refers to the organizational structure of the team and the department, as well as to the design of the jobs that the team members perform. It also includes policies, procedures, work and communication systems, organizational culture and values, and relationships with customers. This part of the design affects what work people do and how they do it. During this phase of work redesign, work found to be unnecessary can be eliminated. At the completion of social redesign, job descriptions can be developed, needed new skills can be identified, and training can be planned and implemented.

Boundaries

The third factor that the design team considers is the boundaries senior management has established for the team. These define the areas that the team can and cannot change and those that are open for discussion.

Armed with the boundaries and information on the technical and social aspects of the work, the design team can prepare a new environment for a self-managed work team, rather than a group of individuals.

• Conclusion

There are many advantages to work redesign that can benefit the organization, the employees, and the customers alike. Chief among them are that cost can be reduced, service improved, and employee satisfaction increased. However, in the initial stages, the process of work redesign takes time, costs money, and consumes many resources.

As health care organizations explore implementation of self-managed work teams, they may decide to transform the entire organization all at once or one department or section at a time. Other design options include starting with a model or pilot, or converting a department to a self-managed work team when a qualified supervisor cannot be recruited.

Regardless of the method chosen, work redesign must occur for the greatest benefit. Additionally, changes must occur in the systems that support the work. These systems include communications, customer relations, problem solving, budget/financial, employee selection, training, performance appraisal, compensation, planning, record keeping, and support services. Despite the complexity of the process, it must be kept simple, incorporate design principles, and involve the employees who will be affected by the change.

Three other factors must be considered in the decision to redesign work: the technical (or physical) environment, the social environment, and the boundaries established by senior management. When these are all incorporated, the end result is work that is enriching, efficient, effective, and supportive of self-managed teams.

References

1. Hackman, J. R., and Oldham, G. R. *Work Redesign.* Reading, MA: Addison-Wesley, 1980, pp. 171–72.
2. Hackman and Oldham, pp. 275–306.
3. A proposal for self-managed work teams and incentive pay in the housekeeping department, prepared by the housekeeping department, Memorial Mission Hospital, Asheville, NC, Aug. 26, 1992.
4. Telephone interview with Sylvia Swarner, nursing education, Sutter General Hospital, Sacramento, CA, Aug. 5, 1993.

Part Three
Team Development

Chapter 9

Introduction of the Team Concept to the Organization

Whether the impetus for self-managed work teams comes from an employee, a middle manager, or a senior manager, the approach used to introduce the concept to the rest of the organization will be basically the same. However, how well the concept is received will depend in large part on how well it is presented by the individual introducing it—*the team advocate*. And the effectiveness of the team advocate's presentation relies heavily on the strength of his or her personal vision and the extent of his or her personal knowledge of the organization.

This chapter identifies key factors within the organization and the community that the team advocate must assess in order to determine the viability of introducing the self-managed work team concept. It also presents a plan for introducing the team concept to members of each of the organization's levels—senior managers, middle managers, supervisors, and employees and their unions. The chapter closes with an illustration of a six-phase communication plan.

• Personal Knowledge of the Concept and the Organization

To begin, the team advocate must have a personal vision of what the organization will be like once it has implemented self-managed work teams. In all likelihood, his or her vision will be based on knowledge of the team concept gleaned from books, articles, and conversations with those who have had experience with self-managed teams. This vision may take several forms. It may be a picture of committed employees working together on teams, a flattened organizational structure devoid of bureaucratic layers, or an enhanced bottom line.

In addition, the team advocate must thoroughly understand the organization and its operations in order to know how successfully the team concept will fit the organization's needs. For instance, he or she should know what programs and/or work arrangements the organization has already implemented that increase employee involvement and support the concept of teamwork. Following is a list of work arrangements that may already be in place:

- Committees
- Task forces
- Shared governance groups
- Problem-solving teams
- Employee input groups
- Employee focus groups
- Project teams
- Partnerships
- Cross-functional patient care consultation teams

The organization also may be supporting and reinforcing those work arrangements through policies and behaviors such as the following:

- Team recognition
- Team-building activities
- Adoption of team-related terminology
- Team training
- Incentives or compensation linked to teamwork

Additionally, the team advocate should be familiar with other elements that can have an impact on the organization's decision to proceed with team implementation. These factors include the concept's fit with the organization's strategic plan, organizational values that would support the team concept, the opinions of key leaders within the organization, any perceived barriers to implementation of the concept, and environmental factors, as well as examples of successful team implementation within the community in which the hospital is located. These factors are discussed in greater detail in the following subsections.

The Strategic Plan

The self-managed team advocate should be able to identify how team implementation will accomplish the goals set forth in the organization's strategic plan. (If self-managed work teams seem to be directly counter to the goals of the strategic plan, that information also is important to know.) For example, the strategic plan might contain a goal of reducing the cost of key marketable services so that the organization is in a low-cost leadership position. An organization has to change substantially to significantly reduce cost. The implementation of self-managed teams is one way that an organization can greatly reduce cost, and, therefore, the goal would be compatible with the strategic plan.

If it was a strategic goal of the organization to improve employee productivity by providing bonuses for individual employees who excel, then the implementation of self-managed work teams would not be an effective way to achieve that strategic goal.

Organizational Values

The organization may already be committed to values that are complementary to those that exist in a team-based organization. Examples of such congruent values include commitments to:

- Quality
- Employee involvement
- Continuous improvement
- Customer satisfaction
- Employee growth and development
- Innovation
- Trust and respect for others
- Encouragement of decision making at the lowest possible level
- Employee empowerment
- Cost reduction
- Teamwork

If the organization has made a commitment in writing and/or practice to all or some of the values in the preceding list, implementation of the team concept will be relatively smooth. The team advocate can point to the organization's commitment to those values as a step toward supporting the team concept. However, if the organization's values differ considerably from those listed, team implementation will be very difficult. For example, an organization that is committed to individuality and freedom to act independently would not embrace the value of teamwork.

Leaders' Opinions

Every organization has a number of formal and informal leaders whose opinions help shape its direction. The support of these leaders for self-managed teams would facilitate the introductory phase considerably. By the same token, however, their opposition to the concept would make its introduction so difficult that it might best be postponed until a more opportune time.

Development of a chart listing supporters and those opposed would provide a useful tool to help determine the level of consensus that exists among the organization's current opinion leaders (see figure 9-1). Incorporated in this

Figure 9-1. Opinion Leader Assessment

Opinion Leaders	Assessment of Opinion	In Favor	On the Fence	Opposed
President	Has initiated and supported major change in past. Is in favor of team concept.		X	
Vice President, Finance	Resists change. Can be influenced by financial benefits.			X
Vice President, Operations	Believes in planned change. Is not a risk taker. Is supportive of concept.	X		
Vice President, Nursing	Has implemented shared governance in several units. Willing to try innovation.	X		
Vice President, Human Resources	Is concerned about impact on the policies. Has initiated much change in past, but slowly. Believes in team concept.		X	

chart should be information that is known about the opinion leaders such as change initiatives they have supported in the past, values they endorse, their willingness to take risks, their own teamlike behavior, and their existing knowledge of self-managed teams. In addition to learning who among the opinion leaders support or oppose the team concept, the chart should help team advocates gain some understanding of why teams might be opposed and how to persuade those opinion leaders who oppose them to reevaluate their attitudes about self-managed teams before they are formally asked to express their opinions by the organization.

Perceived Barriers

Any individual, process, event, or physical aspect of the environment can either work to support self-managed work teams or become a barrier to their implementation. Once barriers are identified, advocates of self-managed teams can use a force-field analysis to help identify actions that can be taken to eliminate or reduce the effect of those barriers. A force-field analysis is a graphic display of the barriers to change and the driving forces to overcome the barriers. The barriers are identified first by brainstorming. Then, the group that is developing the force-field analysis identifies remedies or driving forces that can be used to overcome the barriers. A force-field analysis is displayed in figure 9-2.

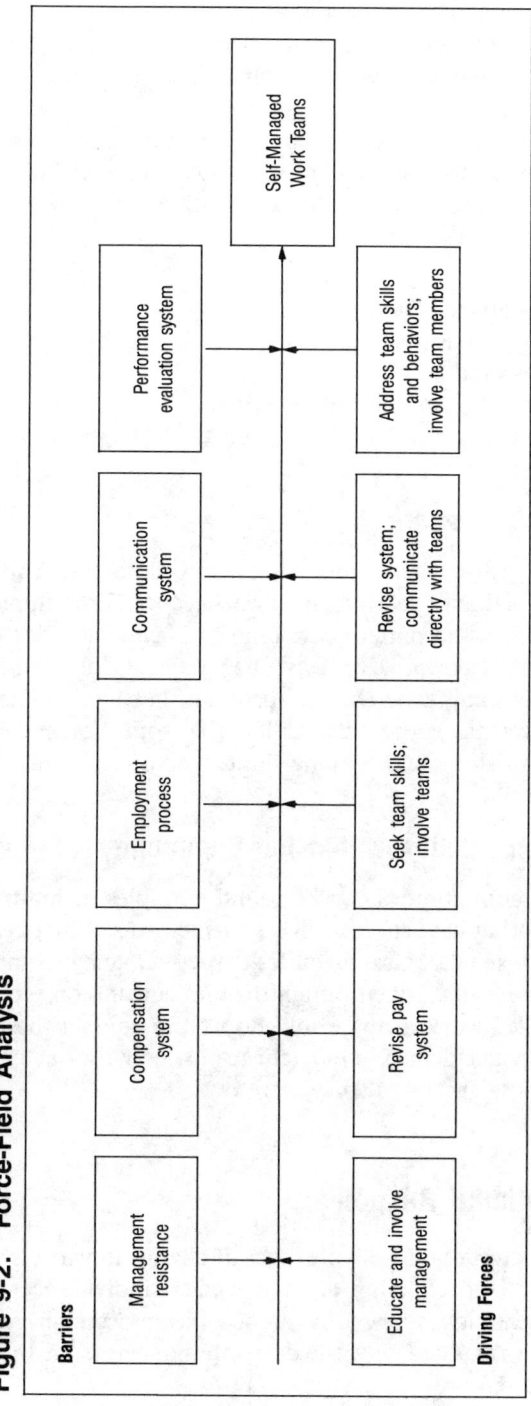

Figure 9-2. Force-Field Analysis

Barriers

| Management resistance | Compensation system | Employment process | Communication system | Performance evaluation system |

Self-Managed Work Teams

| Educate and involve management | Revise pay system | Seek team skills; involve teams | Revise system; communicate directly with teams | Address team skills and behaviors; involve team members |

Driving Forces

Opinion leaders who resist change or who are opposed in principle to team organization will present strong barriers to team implementation, as will entrenched managers who see self-management as a step toward chaos and confusion.

Systems and processes that reinforce organizational hierarchy and focus on individual performance will impede successful team implementation during both the conceptualization and transitional phases. Examples of such systems and processes are:

- The management system
- The communication system
- The employment process
- The performance evaluation system
- The compensation, rewards, and recognition system

Environmental Factors

Other factors within the organization also will have an impact on the successful introduction of self-managed work teams. For example, if the organization is in crisis and patient care units are being closed, the organization may be extremely receptive to trying new ways of doing business. However, if the organization is experiencing success or has just initiated a major program that affects the entire organization, the motivation and energy to implement a new work system may be limited or nonexistent.

Team Implementation within the Community

Within most communities can be found examples of industries and other organizations that have successfully implemented self-managed work teams. Some of the hospital's board members may even manage companies or plants that have successfully gone through the implementation process. Advocates of self-managed work teams would do well to contact these companies to learn why they decided to implement teams, how they achieved implementation, and how successful they were.

• Organizational Response

Organizations respond to the prospect of change in various ways; typically, their response is a reflection of their leaders' individual personalities and risk-taking mentality. A new idea can become an overnight reality or quickly fade into oblivion. Generally, the determining factors are the organization's structure and culture.

Organizational Structure

Within a health care organization, there is the opportunity for some departments to implement the change to self-managed work teams and for others to take a "wait-and-see" attitude. Thus, because it is composed of different physical units that are geographically separate, the hospital may be an ideal setting for team implementation. One part of the organization can be "doing," while the other parts are watching and learning.

This opportunity exists particularly in organizations that have a matrix or product line structure. When faced with change, matrix or product-structured organizations tend to be more flexible than functional organizations. One reason is that in a functional organization, teams are more difficult to form. When one department or division does make the transition to team-based work, if often does so amidst a good deal of skepticism from other departments. The barrier to structural change in a functional organization is formidable.

Organizational Culture

If the organization's culture is conservative and traditional, and in many health care organizations it is, management will tend to perceive the team concept as a fad. However, if the organization is open to innovation and has been a leader in implementing change, management will likely be more receptive to the idea.

There are many examples in the service industries, including health care, that indicate that self-managed work teams can help the organization improve both productivity and quality. It is a concept that is difficult to reject when studying actual experience within the service and health care industry. Justification for the resistance that exists is in the thoughts and opinions of managers. It is not found in the experience of organizations that have successfully implemented teams.

- ## Introduction of the Team Concept to the Different Levels of the Organization

As with all change efforts, the vision for the change must be carried by an individual who has influence within the organization, usually someone in senior management who either has the idea or is willing to be its advocate. As mentioned previously, the team advocate will need to:

- Research the concept, gathering information from articles, books, and local organizations that have implemented self-managed teams
- Know how the organization's strategic plan and values support the concept

- Understand the systems and other barriers that may block team implementation
- Have a clear personal vision and compelling reason for advocating self-managed teams

This individual also will need to be aware of what the different groups within the organization will want and/or need to know in order to make a decision about implementation. These groups are at all levels of the organization and include senior managers, department directors, supervisors, employees, and the unions. The wants and needs required of these particular groups to make a decision about implementation are discussed in the following subsections.

Senior Managers

Senior managers will want the type of information they generally need to make any major decision. They will want to know the benefits and risks, and the financial implications. Following are the key questions to which management will need answers:

- How long will it take to implement teams?
- What are the benefits?
- When will the benefits be seen?
- What resources will be needed?
- How much will implementation cost?
- What proof is there that the benefits and costs are accurately projected?
- Who else endorses or has implemented self-managed work teams?

Questions such as these should be anticipated and researched in preparation for introducing the concept to senior management.

Department Directors

Department directors and head nurses are the middle management core of the organization. They are close to employees and also close enough to senior managers to have a top-level perspective. Generally, there are more risk-takers at the middle management level than there are at the senior level. Thus, the members of this group are more likely to be willing to support the team concept and to try it out.

However, this does not mean that they are willing to support the concept without reservation. Department directors will want to know whether there is senior management support for self-managed teams. This group will be more likely to follow if the concept is introduced by a high-level manager, preferably the chief executive officer (CEO). Department directors also will want to know the benefits to the organization, the time frame, and their role during and after implementation. Generally, they will be looking for practical and detailed information, rather than philosophy. Many of them will be ready to roll up their sleeves and get started, and some will be pleased to serve on a steering committee or design team.

Supervisors

Supervisors are the group most likely to resist the concept of self-managed work teams. Because key to productivity improvement in the team concept is a reduction in the number of supervisors, this group will bear the negative aspects of team implementation.

At this level, it is critical to the concept's success that it be introduced by the CEO or another highly trusted and visible member of senior management. The more supervisors can be told about how they will be involved and affected, the better. The more they can be assured that they will continue to have a valuable job in the organization, the better. They must be told what the business reasons are for making the change, and they must understand the concept's benefits to patients, other customers, and employees alike.

The supervisors' response to self-management will be the one most likely to influence the employees' reaction. Thus, if supervisors perceive only negative outcomes to the implementation process, employees also will perceive the process negatively.

It is important to remember that supervisors must learn about self-managed teams before their employees do. If possible, they should be involved on the design team for their department or division from the outset. Ideally, supervisors will have the opportunity to read articles and books and participate in site visits. They will be involved in discussions of whether teams will work on the organization and then participate in helping to make decisions about how teams in their areas will be structured. With this information and involvement, supervisors can be a knowledgeable resource for their employees.

Employees

It is best that employees be told about the team concept by their department director or other person in the organization who understands the functions and operations of their department. Like the other groups, they will want to know how self-managed work teams will benefit the organization, patients, and themselves. They will be interested specifically in when the change will occur and what will happen. Additionally, they will want to know about organizations in the area that have implemented self-management.

More than likely, employees will respond very positively to the team concept. However, they are likely to be cynical and question senior management commitment. They will look for guarantees that the move to self-management will be a lasting change. They also will want to know whether their department is the only one that has to implement self-managed teams.

Unions

If the organization already has a good relationship with its union leadership, the introduction of self-managed work teams should be relatively easy. Union leaders should be involved and educated along with senior management. They should be consulted and included in structuring the approach within the organization. However, if the union–management relationship is strictly adversarial, unions can seriously retard the implementation process.

If several unions are representing different categories of employees, they should be approached separately and involved as "partners" in the transition to teams as it affects the employees they represent. However, regardless of when self-management is implemented in their area of the organization, they should learn about the concept at the same time that the rest of the organization does.

Additionally, employees who serve as union stewards need to be treated as respected members of the organization. They should be included in the information and education plan, and should receive information from the organization, not just the union. Specifically, they will want to know how the change to self-managed work teams will affect their role.

It may be helpful to have information on departments within the organization where self-managed teams and unions are peacefully coexisting. This information should be shared with union leaders when they are introduced to the concept.

• The Communication Plan

Successful introduction of the team concept depends in large part on the team advocate's communication plan. This is the strategy that he or she will use to promote self-managed work teams throughout the organization.

The communication plan has six phases. These phases are:

- Phase 1. Research
- Phase 2. Precommunication
- Phase 3. Introduction to senior management
- Phase 4. Introduction to middle management

- Phase 5. Introduction to supervisors
- Phase 6. Introduction to employees

Each phase involves specific strategies and participants. (For overview, see table 9-1.) It is possible to shortcut any phase of the strategy, depending on the success of the preceding phase. However, there needs to be a planned approach for communicating with each of the key participants or groups listed.

Phase 1. Research

During this phase, the participants are the initial core group of advocates for self-managed work teams. Their overriding strategy is to *obtain the information that will sell teams to the organization.*

They explore the organization's strategic plan, values, and existing degrees of teamwork, as well as seek out examples of successful team implementation in the surrounding community. At this stage, the team advocate also attempts to identify any potential barriers to and supports for the team concept.

Phase 2. Precommunication

In this phase, the participants are expanded to include those opinion leaders who are "definitely in favor" and those who are "on the fence." Opinion leaders perceived to be "definitely opposed" are not included. The strategy of those in favor is to *persuade all opinion leaders that the organization should implement self-managed work teams.* One means of doing this is to provide the opinion leaders with all the information gathered during the research phase.

Phase 3. Introduction to Senior Management

The participants in this phase are all senior managers, even those opposed to implementation. The strategy now is to *introduce senior management to the benefits of self-managed teams through articles, community and health care examples, and site visits.* The influencing of others is now in the hands of senior managers who are for and those who are against team implementation. It is at the end of this phase that the decision whether to implement teams is made.

If the decision is to implement teams, senior management then needs to decide where and when. This decision will determine the content and audiences of phases 4 through 6. It is during phase 3 that the board of directors and union leadership are brought into the process, once approval is obtained from senior management.

Table 9-1. The Communication Plan

Phases	Participants	Objectives	Methods
1. Research	Initial core of group advocates	To identify information that will help support team implementation; to identify barriers; to assess position of opinion leaders	Research strategic plan, values, existing team structures, barriers, position of opinion leaders, examples of teams in the community
2. Precommunication	Initial core group and opinion leaders who favor teams	To provide this group with supporting arguments from the research so they can be effective advocates	Share and discuss research; develop strategies for overcoming barriers
3. Introduction to Senior Management	All senior managers Board of directors Union leaders Medical staff leaders	To educate senior management about self-managed work teams and to obtain their approval to proceed If senior management approves, this phase expands to include obtaining endorsement from the board, union leaders, medical staff leaders	Share articles, books, testimonials; take site visits; overcome barriers through discussion and reference to examples Repeat above as needed with board directors, union leaders, medical staff leaders
4. Introduction to Middle Management	All middle managers	To obtain interest, awareness, and enthusiasm for self-managed work teams; to get volunteers for a model department; to overcome barriers	Senior management to introduce idea in large and small group meetings; conduct one-on-one discussions between vice presidents and middle managers; distribute articles; take site visits
5. Introduction to Supervisors	All supervisors	To obtain interest, awareness, and enthusiasm for concept; to calm fears; to overcome barriers	Chief executive officer or vice president to introduce idea in large and small group meetings; conduct one-on-one discussions between director and supervisor; distribute articles
6. Introduction to Employees	Small groups of employees in departments that will implement first	To obtain knowledge of teams, their role in coming months; to obtain buy-in, commitment, and enthusiasm	Meet with director and supervisor; receive articles; receive outline of plan for implementation; discuss when and how employees will be involved

Phase 4. Introduction to Middle Management

In this phase, middle managers are added to the participants. The strategy is to *generate enthusiasm and commitment, while educating this group about self-managed teams.* Communication with middle managers can be done one-on-one with the vice president, by division, or organizationwide. At this stage, senior management also may look for volunteers to participate in a self-managed team model or may announce the rollout plan, which eventually will affect all middle managers.

Phase 5. Introduction to Supervisors

Supervisors make up the next group of participants. They learn of self-managed work teams after management has made the decision to implement them. At this stage, the strategy is to *introduce the concept of self-managed work teams and reassure supervisors that there is a valuable place for them in the organization.* Both supervisors and department directors will look at teams from an extremely practical viewpoint and will want as many specifics as the organization can provide.

Phase 6. Introduction to Employees

Depending on the scope of implementation, only a small number of employees may become participants in this phase of the initial communication plan. The strategy here is to *introduce the concept of self-managed teams, reassure employees about the permanence of the change, and generate enthusiasm for the concept and a willingness to participate.*

• Conclusion

The individual within the organization who is the initial advocate for self-managed work teams must begin with a clear vision of how the organization will be once the concept has been implemented and then communicate that vision to management. To support the vision, he or she needs to conduct research and canvas the organization's opinion leaders for their perspectives on teamwork. In addition, he or she must identify the barriers and driving forces that can prevent team implementation.

Introduction of the team concept into a complex organization such as a hospital requires that the key questions and concerns of employees in the different levels of the organization be identified and later addressed in the communication process. This is accomplished through development of a communication plan.

The communication plan is carried out in six phases and incorporates communication strategies that bring relevant information to the identified participants at each phase. The success of the communication plan can significantly affect the overall organization's reception of the self-managed team concept.

Chapter 10

Skills Acquisition

As the health care organization prepares to establish its first self-managed work team, consideration must be given to the skills that team members are expected to possess or acquire. Employees who will work on new self-managed work teams may need few new skills if they already have been working in a participative environment and if the team is going to be single-functional. However, if the team is going to be cross-functional, employees may need to develop a whole range of new skills just to do the work of the team.

Regardless of the type of team or previous experience, employees who participate on teams will need to possess skills from four different skill categories—technical, interpersonal, teamwork, and supervisory. This chapter examines these four categories and describes the skills that each comprises.

• Technical Skills

Technical skills are the specialized skills that employees need to help their team produce the product or service that it is designed to produce. For example, a housekeeping team is single-functional, which is to say that its members perform basically one service—cleaning. They may already possess the basic technical skills to clean different types of surfaces and different areas of the organization, and may only need to learn new cleaning routes. However, if the team is going to use special types of cleaning equipment, it is likely that team members will need to acquire new skills to operate and maintain the equipment.

On the other hand, the nursing unit support services team is cross-functional, meaning that its members will perform a number of different functions. Thus, members of this team must possess a variety of technical skills, such as EKG administration, phlebotomy skills, basic respiratory care skills, and nurse aide skills.

• Interpersonal Skills

Interpersonal skills are those skills that enable people to talk to each other in an open and honest manner; in other words, these skills facilitate communication. Although some people may disregard the importance of interpersonal skills for team members, experienced team facilitators agree that lack of interpersonal skills is the single most disruptive problem a team faces. Poor communication can quickly diminish team productivity, create disharmony, and lead to disbandment.

Following is a list of interpersonal skills that each team member needs to possess:

- Asking for help
- Clarifying and confirming
- Confronting
- Enhancing customer relations
- Giving feedback
- Giving praise
- Receiving praise
- Listening with empathy

Asking for Help

Before team implementation, employees operated independently in the performance of their daily assignments. Often they were discouraged by co-workers and supervisors from approaching others for help with their individual assignments. In a team environment, although there are still individual assignments, the work is seen as belonging to the team. Team members can and should help each other. It improves productivity and enhances the sense of team. Employees begin to feel like "this is our work" rather than "this is my work." Asking for help is a new job requirement and a new skill. If it is not handled effectively, it can lead to disharmony on the team and reduced productivity.

However, the team concept creates an environment in which employees are free to ask each other for help and in which working together presents the opportunity to improve productivity. Because of old barriers such as pride, habit, past experience, and attitude, many team members will find it difficult to ask for help; however, they must realize that the team cannot help them unless it is aware that they need help.

Clarifying and Confirming

These are two of the most important communication skills that team members can possess. They can be used to transform potentially explosive situations into situations of mutual understanding. As a result, productivity is increased and lost time and waste are reduced because employees have been able to clarify direction and assignment, rather than proceed on false perception and misunderstanding.

Further, clarifying and confirming skills can help team members reinforce the trust they must feel with one another. For example, if one team member says something that offends another, the offended employee has three options. He or she can: (1) take the hurt and anger, and swallow it; (2) retaliate; (3) use clarifying and confirming to identify what was intended by the hurtful comment. Obviously, the third option is the most effective and the one employees on the team should be encouraged to use.

Confronting

Confronting is the process by which team members speak up, and speak out, to ensure that their ideas and talents are appropriately considered, understood, and utilized by the team. This skill also is helpful in the same situations that clarifying and confirming skills are. Confronting helps to clear up misunderstandings before they lead to broken friendships and permanent alienation.

Enhancing Customer Relations

A number of interpersonal skills are important to team members as they learn to work directly with their customers, rather than through a supervisor or other intermediary. These skills are called customer relations skills and include negotiating, listening, responding to concerns and complaints, providing good first impressions, and so on.

In health care organizations, employees may have worked directly with internal and external customers in the past. However, they rarely were given responsibility for ensuring customer satisfaction. Generally, that responsibility has been reserved for managers and other personnel within the organization. Because in a self-managed environment responsibility for customer relations frequently is assigned to the team, all team members need to possess these skills.

Giving Feedback

It is a primary responsibility of team members to give each other feedback regularly, whether it is asked for or not. If used effectively, feedback is one communication skill that will enhance individual learning rate and improve team productivity.

By providing feedback to each other, team members can help correct problems in performance, improve team morale, draw out shy or hesitant team members, and enhance the self-esteem of those with whom they work. Team members also can use this skill to help clarify roles and responsibilities among themselves, as well as with the team supervisor or coach.

Giving Praise

Responsibility for giving praise is shared equally by team members. When employees begin to praise each other spontaneously, it is a clear sign that they are beginning to work together as a team. Employees who have worked in an individual-oriented environment throughout their careers are used to competing with each other for praise from the supervisor. And certainly they are not accustomed to giving praise to their coworkers.

When recognition is freely given by one team member to another, team spirit improves. The team environment lightens and team synergy begins to occur more often.

Receiving Praise

Although the skill of receiving praise effectively is not difficult to learn, its importance cannot be overemphasized. Some employees, when receiving praise, will gloss over their accomplishment saying, "It was nothing." In the process, they may offend the person giving the praise. Employees should respond to praise with a simple "thank you" or better yet, "I really worked hard on that, thanks for noticing." When a team member responds appropriately to praise, it reinforces the praise-giving behavior and encourages it to happen again.

Listening with Empathy

Effective listening is a skill that team members need to utilize in their communication with each other and their customers. It is a key element of the interpersonal skills category. Listening with empathy involves taking in the emotions as well as the words of the speaker. It also can involve the added skill of being able to interpret body language. How the speaker relates physically to those around him or her can speak volumes.

Employees who are skilled at listening with empathy respond to their coworkers with a greater depth of understanding. For example, a coworker says, "I just have to take tomorrow off to go to my daughter's school." The untrained response might be, "well go check with the team leader." The empathetic response, however, addresses feelings. "You are worried that the team leader will say 'no' and you don't want to let your daughter down."

• Teamwork Skills

Teamwork skills are those skills that enable employees to function effectively as a group. Employees are able to merge their individual behaviors in order to focus on producing group outcomes. Without these skills, employees brought together to work as a team will continue to function as individuals. Teamwork skills reinforce team member equality and enable members to participate equally in the decision-making tasks and management of the team.

Following are many of the teamwork skills that employees will need to learn as they participate on teams:

- Brainstorming
- Celebrating
- Conflict resolution
- Evaluating team performance
- Group decision making
- Influencing others
- Meeting participation
- Multivoting
- Nominal group technique
- Participation
- Peer appraisal
- Problem solving
- Quality improvement

Brainstorming

Brainstorming is a group activity in which a large number of ideas are generated spontaneously. It is one of the most frequently used teamwork skills and needs to be learned early in the team development process. Brainstorming exercises can help employees become comfortable with working in groups and can help them build trust as team members.

Celebrating

Employees are not accustomed to taking time from their work to celebrate their accomplishments. However, celebrating is an important team ritual. It emphasizes that the accomplishment was the result of efforts made by the entire team and that the entire team, rather than just one individual, deserves the credit. Guidelines for celebrations, as well as for permission to celebrate, are developed in the team training sessions. Following are some sample celebration guidelines:

- We will celebrate the week following completion of our project.
- We will involve our director, team coach, and others who helped us achieve our goal.

- We will spend no more that $5.00 per person for our celebrations.
- Everyone on the team participates in celebrations.

Conflict Resolution

Conflict may arise between as few as two team members or as many as all the team members. Thus, team members need to develop skills to deal with conflict one-on-one as well as within a group. Generally, teams establish guidelines for dealing with conflict before it happens, so that team members know the expected behaviors in advance.

Team members also will need to learn how to resolve conflicts that arise with members of other departments. Self-managed work teams are expected to deal with such conflicts themselves rather than turn them over to a supervisor to handle, which was the course of conflict resolution in the past. If employees, even after they have been members of teams for a period of time, try to revert to their formerly dependent behavior, supervisors and team coaches should be prepared to redirect responsibility for conflict resolution back to the team.

Evaluating Team Performance

In the course of their development, teams need to stop to reflect on how they are doing. Early in the process of training team members, a form, format, and system should be developed for evaluating team performance. High-performance teams establish specific measures and focus on successes and opportunities for improvement at least monthly. The team evaluation process involves brainstorming and/or other idea-generating methods for identifying causes of, and possible solutions to, poor performance.

Group Decision Making

Group decision making is another area in which team members need to break old habits. Traditionally, if asked for a decision, employees either referred it to a manager or made it themselves. Within the self-managed work team environment, most decisions are team decisions. Team members need to learn to consult with each other, develop criteria for decision making, explore alternatives, and determine when decisions can be made by either majority or consensus, or by individual members.

Influencing Others

Because no one team member has authority to make decisions by himself or herself, all team members need to learn how to influence others. They need to be able to present information, opinions, and ideas in ways that will make them acceptable to people who are involved in the decision-making process.

Meeting Participation

Very few employees have had to either lead meetings or participate in them prior to becoming team members. Because most communication occurs in formal and informal meetings, acquisition of a wide range of meeting skills is particularly important. A lack of these skills ultimately can lead to a decrease in productivity. Team members need to learn how to determine meeting objectives, prepare agendas, keep track of time, and keep the team focused on the agenda and the topic under consideration. Team members must also learn to summarize progress and agreement, control disruptive behaviors, and obtain participation of all team members in discussion and decision making.

Multivoting

Multivoting is a group decision-making or prioritizing method. It involves several stages of voting to reduce options (produced by brainstorming, for example) to those most preferred by the group. This simple technique is easily learned and helps speed the decision-making process.

Nominal Group Technique

The nominal group technique is another method for generating and prioritizing a large number of ideas. It is similar to "silent" brainstorming in that group members do not talk to one another while they are generating ideas. However, they all participate in selecting the best idea.

In the nominal group technique, team members, using sticky notes or 3 × 5 cards, generate ideas, one per card or note page. All these cards and note pages are given to one specified individual who groups or sorts them into similar categories. Each idea grouping is discussed, both its positive and negative aspects. The group then votes to implement the idea or ideas that have the most merit.

This technique is useful when trust is still tenuous and team members do not feel comfortable exposing their ideas to group ridicule. It also is an effective tool if one team member tends to dominate the brainstorming process.

A limitation of this technique is that it requires all members of the team to be literate. Thus, this technique will not be useful for teams whose members do not possess basic reading and writing skills.

Participation

Participation is the skill of offering suggestions, ideas, input, and feedback. To some team members participation will come naturally. Others may need to be coaxed by direct questions such as, "What do you think of this idea?"

Effective participation requires skill in the phrasing of the input or feedback. To maintain harmony and the team members' self-esteem, it is not acceptable for someone to say, "That is a terrible idea." Instead, the participating team member might say, "What would happen if . . .," or "Let's take a few minutes to look at it this way."

In addition to being a skill, participation is an expectation that needs to be made clear to new team members. Some team members believe it is acceptable to assume the role of "the quiet one." They do not recognize that they are depriving their team of the value of their thoughts, ideas, and experiences. The team's potential performance level is diminished when one or more members decide to limit their participation to just doing the work.

Peer Appraisal

The organization may adopt a form of peer appraisal for team members to replace or supplement the individual performance appraisal that is common in nonteamwork environments. Peer appraisal is an advanced team skill and not one of the first skills taught to team members.

In a peer appraisal, team members are asked to assess strengths and opportunities for improvement. They may give their feedback either verbally or in writing. Team members need to focus on specifics, including any actual examples that they have observed. They must avoid generalizations such as "You always do this" or "You never do that."

Peer appraisal is an important tool for improving the performance of the team when used correctly. If not used with correct training, however, it can lead to bruised egos and broken friendships.

Problem Solving

In some hospitals, problem solving is no more than simply defining the problem, investigating possible causes, proposing alternative solutions, and selecting the best one. In others, problem solving is described and defined by the quality improvement process. In this case, facts and data, the work process, and customers also are included in the problem-solving effort.

Self-managed work teams are expected to solve their own problems, and this empowerment is a gift that teams particularly covet. In order to be effective at problem solving, team members will need to develop or refine skills they have not had to use frequently in a supervisor-led work group.

Quality Improvement

Many health care organizations have implemented and are committed to a quality improvement process. If self-managed work teams are formed in those organizations, quality improvement will be a major component of their role. To the degree that quality improvement is a team performance expectation, it is a skill that team members will need to learn.

Quality improvement is a problem-solving or work improvement process. One of its foundations is the definition of quality. In health care organizations, quality is frequently defined as "meeting or exceeding the needs and expectations of those we serve." The quality improvement process is a formal method that involves several steps, including: defining customer needs, measuring the performance of the work process that is intended to meet the customer need, identifying improvement opportunities, identifying the root cause of the current performance deficiency, and selecting and implementing a solution. Quality improvement involves skills in gathering and displaying data, establishing priorities, using charts and graphs, interviewing customers, brainstorming, and analysis, among others.

• Supervisory Skills

Supervisory skills, also referred to as *administrative skills,* are the skills needed for planning, organizing, staffing, directing, and controlling the work of the team. Any skill that enables the team to take on the role or responsibility of a supervisor is a supervisory skill. All the team members must learn supervisory skills because they all share team leadership responsibility. Some organizations limit the supervisory duties and responsibilities that are transferred to teams; others transfer them gradually so that teams have time to prepare to take them on, but transfer all supervisory responsibilities.

If the team is truly self-managed, the supervisory skills team members acquire will have a great impact on the way the team functions and performs. Following are examples of supervisory skills that all or most team members will be expected to learn:

- Budgeting
- Business writing
- Coaching
- Disciplining
- Goal and priority setting
- Hiring
- Ordering, purchasing, and scheduling supplies
- Orienting new team members
- Performance reviews
- Planning

- Record keeping
- Safety assessment, monitoring, and improvement
- Scheduling personnel
- Time management
- Training others

Budgeting

Budgeting is the skill of determining the resources that will be needed to meet the team's annual plan in advance of its implementation. It involves the ability to project into the future, and to monitor and control expenditures.

Very few team members have been exposed to a budget or cost information before being assigned to a self-managed work team. However, most team members are familiar with budgeting their personal resources and generally can assume budgeting responsibilities successfully.

Business Writing

Business writing includes the preparation and issuance of memos, reports, letters, and so on. The form and format of business communication within the organization and outside usually are not of concern to employees below the supervisory level. When written communication leaves the department, it generally is either prepared by management or prepared by secretarial support and signed by management.

Business writing may not be a skill that the whole team needs to learn; however, at least two team members should be proficient at it. This way, one team member can perform the function in the other's absence.

Coaching

Coaching is a training technique that helps others grow and develop without being *told* what to do. It is a method of sharing knowledge and information, and mutually exploring alternatives to help others attain skill mastery. The degree to which team members are expected to acquire many skills determines the degree to which coaching skills will need to be taught to team members.

Disciplining

In most hospitals, the disciplinary process is administered at the supervisory or management level in conjunction with the department of human resources. When self-managed work teams are implemented, they may be given authority to administer formal disciplinary counseling, although this responsibility is one of the last to be transferred from management to the team. Disciplinary counseling involves the team members or the team leader documenting a personnel policy violation by completing the required form and communicating the violation to the team member.

Before responsibility is transferred, team members and human resources will need to work together to establish a system for discipline and to develop team member skills in completing the paperwork, documenting the reasons for disciplinary action, conducting the disciplinary interview, and following up to either reinforce improved behavior or take additional corrective action.

Goal and Priority Setting

From the outset, goal and priority setting will be two skills that team members need to develop or refine. Goals are the building blocks of all self-managed teams; they guide team actions and help determine team performance.

Writing a goal involves having clear written communication skills and knowing the components of and the requirements for a goal. Goals should be specific, measurable, important to the organization, and achievable. A goal should state what is to be accomplished and include a time frame or deadline in which to do so.

Setting priorities requires the ability to assess the relative importance or value of several goal options. A goal that provides the greatest benefit should have priority over the others.

Hiring

Whenever possible, teams need to be involved in hiring replacements to fill vacancies. The skills of interviewing and selecting from among a group of candidates can be taught "just-in-time," right before the team has to interview candidates for its first vacancy. In addition to interviewing and employee selection skills, team members will need to learn the legalities involved in the hiring process, as well as the processes and forms required by human resources.

Ordering, Purchasing, and Scheduling Supplies

Most organizations have dollar control limits and organization position controls concerning the initiation of purchase orders. If this system is not changed to permit team purchasing power, team members need only acquire general knowledge of the purchasing process in order to work with the supervisor or director who will do the purchasing for the team.

If the team receives purchasing authority, policies and procedures will need to change to reflect that authority. In addition, team members will need to learn skills such as how to purchase, inventory, and determine reorder levels.

Orienting New Team Members

Team members should participate as a group in a facilitated process to design new member orientation. In addition, they should receive training on how to orient and coach new employees as they learn the organization, the job, and the role of being a team member.

Performance Review

Initially, responsibility for conducting performance reviews will remain with management. However, as the team matures, it may provide input into an individual appraisal conducted by a supervisor or director, or it may be responsible for completing the annual individual performance review. Ideally, individuals will be evaluated differently under the self-managed team structure. Their performance review needs to include feedback from the team, as well as the coach and the customer.

Performance review skills can be taught just-in-time, that is, immediately prior to their use. They are not skills that team members need early in the maturation process. Ordinarily, performance review training will include information on the purpose and benefits of the performance reviews; skill development in assessing and documenting performance; information on the legalities; practice in planning and conducting performance reviews; and training on the internal policy, forms, and procedures.

Planning

All teams need to learn how to plan and set goals. If the team works in a quality improvement environment, planning will need to include customer and supplier participation. The organization's planning process will need revision to ensure that team input and participation are part of it. Training in planning skills can occur as the team develops its first plans.

Record Keeping

Record keeping is a skill that teams need to develop from the very beginning. They will need to become familiar with existing record-keeping forms and systems, and may want to develop new ones that will complement the goals and procedures the team sets. Among the records that teams need to keep are time and attendance, budget and supplies, customer feedback, and performance.

Safety Assessment, Monitoring, and Improvement

Every team in the organization needs to know how to report and respond to fires and what its role will be in case of an internal or external disaster. Teams need to know about the hazardous chemicals they work with and how to lift and move objects or people without injuring themselves. Health care workers also need to know about infection control and universal precautions techniques. Along with this knowledge, teams also need to exhibit safe behaviors. The work team needs to schedule and document its safety training, monitor the team's safety performance, and initiate improvement actions in areas where safety incidents have occurred.

Scheduling Personnel

In some organizations, scheduling personnel is not complex because every employee works the same shift, the same number of hours, and the same days in a week. When health care teams begin scheduling, they may have a simple task, or they may be trying to provide coverage with employees who rotate shifts, work two or three days a week, work four, eight, or twelve hours a day, and are needed in quantities determined by a computerized patient acuity staffing program. The complexity of the scheduling process will determine the amount and type of training that team members will need.

Time Management

When a team is self-managed, it no longer has a supervisor who tells team members what to do and when to do it. Team members need to review the work of the day, the week, and the month to ensure that they have scheduled time to accomplish it all. Teams will need planning calendars to help them manage their work and their time. They will need training on how to use the calendars and on how to incorporate time for performance reviews, budgeting, and planning, into time that had previously been devoted to working.

Training Others

Team performance depends on a continuous emphasis on growth, development, and learning. Team members possess skills and knowledge that will benefit their coworkers. Training coworkers is a skill that all team members need. They will need to learn basic adult education principles as well as how to develop and conduct minitraining sessions.

• Conclusion

Employees who become members of self-managed work teams need to develop a large number of skills. Generally, these skills fall into four categories: technical, interpersonal, teamwork, and supervisory.

Most of these skills can be taught in a phased learning plan. Skills and knowledge that are needed initially relate to these questions:

- What is a self-managed work team?
- What is expected of us as team members?
- How do we work together?

Initial training focuses on group process skills such as meeting participation, brainstorming, and multivoting. Teams begin to establish guidelines for how they will work as a group, laying out training plans and initiating self-scheduling. They move into refining their interpersonal skills midway through their development and learn supervisory skills as they mature.

The training process for a newly formed team may take six months to a year, depending on how many responsibilities management transfers to the team. It is important to time and phase the training carefully. Otherwise, team members will be overloaded and productivity will decline.

Team members are not the only ones who will need training as self-managed work teams form. Supervisors, facilitators, coaches, and employees throughout the organization need to learn about the teams and how to relate to them as organizational entities.

Chapter 11
Team Training

According to Peter Drucker in his book *The Post Capitalist Society*, "Achievement is addictive."[1] Employees who are given the opportunity to grow, develop, and achieve at new levels are exhilarated by the experience and want more. Training for self-management provides a learning environment and promises a work environment in which employees will flourish. If health care management is ready to adjust the work environment to support the concepts learned in training, the results will justify the time and expense involved in the process. However, if management is not willing to adjust the work environment, the investment in planning and training will be wasted.

This chapter describes the training program used to help employees make the transition to self-managed work teams. It also discusses the adjustments the organization will need to make in order to ensure the training program's success.

• Developing the Training Program

The purpose of the training program is to help self-managed work teams acquire the knowledge and skills they need to meet the team's goals and satisfy the organization's expectations. Ideally, it will encourage team members to bring forth and use skills and knowledge they use in the world outside work, thus enabling the team as a whole to excel by capitalizing on the strengths of each of its members.

The training's immediate objective is to help employees learn to function effectively in their new team environment. Its ultimate objective is to encourage employees to grow, strive, and achieve in an environment that continues to change and requires new skills at a remarkable rate. The role of team trainer, whether a trainer, coach, or supervisor, is to motivate team members to work toward that objective.

The training program is a five-phased plan that is applicable to all self-managed work teams, regardless of function. These phases are:

- Phase 1. Preparation
- Phase 2. Assessment
- Phase 3. Selection
- Phase 4. Connection
- Phase 5. Education

(See also figure 11-1.) The following subsections describe the elements of each phase.

Phase 1. Preparation

In this phase, managers and team members work together to define the team's objectives and the organization's expectations. The one certain quality of high-performance teams is that they know what is expected of them. It is not enough for management to say, "Now that you are a self-managed team, we expect to see productivity improve." Rather, management needs to say, "Now that you are a self-managed team, we expect productivity to improve by at least 20 percent."

Phase 1 involves three tasks. Team objectives must be defined, the knowledge and skills that teams need to achieve those objectives must be identified, and knowledgeable staff must be involved in the process.

Define Team Objectives

Defining team objectives should be a process of negotiation. The process can involve the manager, the facilitator, and all the team members. Regardless of who is included in the process, its success depends on the degree to which team members are committed to the objectives defined by the participants. Team members need to believe that (1) the objectives and expectations are achievable and (2) they have the support they need to implement the changes necessary to achieve those objectives and expectations.

Identify the Knowledge and Skills That Teams Need

In addition to defining objectives, the preparation phase involves identifying skills and knowledge that are necessary to achieve those objectives. The skills and knowledge needed generally are divided into four categories: technical, teamwork, interpersonal, and supervisory. (See chapter 10 for discussion of these skill categories.) Most self-managed work teams need training in all of these areas, and certain teams may need additional knowledge and skills to help them achieve their specific objectives.

Team Training

Figure 11-1. The Five Phases of Team Education

Phase 1. Preparation
- Define the team's objectives
- Identify the knowledge and skills needed to achieve those objectives
- Involve knowledgeable staff

Phase 2. Assessment
- Decide whom to assess for which skills
- Identify team members' strengths

Phase 3. Selection
- Identify the knowledge and skills team members need to acquire
- Research and locate training materials

Phase 4. Connection
- Select the training methodology
- Share strengths among team members
- Develop training plans for individual team members and for the team as a whole
- Purchase or develop appropriate training materials

Phase 5. Education
- Implement the training plans
- Generate enthusiasm for and commitment to learning and achieving

Involve Knowledgeable Staff

The organization should involve its trainers and personnel job analysts in determining the skills and knowledge that teams will need to achieve high performance. They can work with team members, facilitators, and managers to translate productivity expectations into job tasks and responsibilities, and can help identify related knowledge and skills the team will need to achieve its goals.

Phase 2. Assessment

This phase involves the design and administration of a team skill and knowledge assessment. Once again, training and/or employment screening personnel should be involved in this phase of the training program. They will know the appropriate mode of assessment for each skill—for example, interview, paper-and-pencil test, individual or group activity, or demonstration. In this phase whom to assess for which skills will be decided and team member strengths identified.

Decide Whom to Assess for Which Skills

It may be neither necessary nor desirable to assess all team members for all skills and knowledge. Some skills will be needed by only one or two team members, whereas other skills will be needed by the entire team.

It is important that the assessment process be as nonthreatening as possible. Although some employees will volunteer their participation, others will be terrified and determined to refuse. Thus, the assessment should be conducted by someone all the employees trust. A useful way to communicate the process is to characterize it as an "assessment for development in a changing role."

Identify Team Member Strengths

A major benefit of the assessment process is that it helps identify team member strengths and hidden talents. For example, the process may reveal a mathematician, a writer, or a consensus-builder on the team. If these employees have never been called on to demonstrate their skills in the workplace, in all likelihood, no one has ever known they existed. Once skills such as these are identified, they need to be celebrated and utilized to help the team. Each employee who participates in the assessment process can be designated the team resource for her or his strength in a specific skill.

Phase 3. Selection

In this phase, a comparison is drawn between the knowledge and skills the team possesses and those it needs. Any identified gaps should be addressed through a learning activity, although not all of them at once. Training materials should be researched and located. And training subjects should be prioritized so that they can occur throughout the year as the team moves further along the continuum toward self-management.

Identify the Skills and Knowledge Needed

After assessment is completed, existing skills are compared systematically to needed skills. Some team members will have several skill gaps; others will have only a few. Training plans should be prepared for the team as a whole, as well as for each individual on the team.

Research and Locate Training Materials

Much of the material the organization has used to train employees and facilitators on TQM is directly applicable to training employees on how to function on teams. For example, the organization's customer relations training programs can be adapted to help teams increase their awareness of customer needs and how to respond to customer complaints and concerns. Additionally, management development programs on coaching, counseling, feedback, effective communication, planning, budgeting, financial reports, time management, meeting management, and so on can all be adapted for team member training.

A number of outside companies and organizations are possible resources for training materials and consultant services. Major training companies such as Development Dimensions International and Zenger-Miller have packaged team training programs. Training materials catalogs contain page after page of prepackaged materials that can be purchased and adapted to meet the specific needs of self-managed work teams. Additionally, the American Society for Training and Development can be contacted to secure the services of consultants and trainers who specialize in self-managed work teams. The Association for Quality and Productivity offers seminars and other resources to help organizations interested in exploring team implementation. The University of North Texas, in Dallas, has established an Interdisciplinary Center for the Study of Work Teams and is an excellent resource and referral source for information.

Phase 4. Connection

Because each team is composed of employees with many different strengths and abilities, team members can become significant training and development resources for each other. Whereas the assessment phase helps identify team member strengths, this phase identifies ways that members can share their strengths with each other. It also connects the appropriate training methodology with the specific training need. Training plans for individual team members or for the team as a whole are formulated, using employee resources as well as the appropriate training materials.

Select the Training Methodology

Whether a team member will provide the training or whether it is developed or purchased by the training department, the basic rule is that *knowledge* can be learned from books, self-study materials, and attendance at professional meetings and seminars but that *skills* are best learned through practice or by working with a buddy, either on the job or in a workshop.

Share Strengths with Team Members

One way that employees can share their knowledge with each other is to conduct in-services or demonstrations. Another way that employees can work with others to share skills is to set up a buddy system. In this system, a team member who has a specific skill is paired with a team member who needs to learn that skill. This pairing may take place on the job or after the team member who needs the skill has just completed a seminar or workshop.

Develop Training Plans for Individual Team Members or for the Team as a Whole

The training plan, whether for an individual or the entire team, is the road map for self-management. It outlines the skills that will be needed for success.

Individuals may want to develop their own training plans. Following the assessment phase, each team member receives information on his or her current skills, knowledge, and developmental needs. Armed with this information, and with the help of the team facilitator, each employee can map out his or her direction within the new system.

Skill development needs that are common to the entire team are best taught to the team as a whole. This allows team members to practice with each other, as well as coach and reinforce each other. Providing situations in which team members can learn together gives additional opportunities for team building to take place.

Training should occur immediately prior to the transferal of new levels of responsibility. The most efficient training occurs immediately before the employee or team is placed in a situation requiring the application of a new skill or knowledge. For example, when an employee knows that he or she will be leading the team meeting within a few days, his or her interest and readiness to learn are at their peak. When team members know they will be interviewing applicants for the first team vacancy within a week, their readiness to learn interviewing and selecting skills is at its peak. Knowledge and skill are more easily retained when they can be put to immediate use.

Purchase or Develop Appropriate Training Materials

When training plans are complete, the training department must decide whether it already has the necessary training resources or whether additional materials should be purchased or developed. The type of materials needed will depend on the subject matter and the learning methodology selected.

When a team member is going to teach a skill to others, he or she will know the subject matter well enough that training materials will not need to be purchased. However, this individual may need to be trained in adult learning principles—for example, in how to structure the training experience.

Phase 5. Education

It is in this phase that individual and team training plans are implemented. The implementation process should incorporate an effort to encourage enthusiasm for and commitment to learning.

Implement the Training Plans

The timing, phasing, and sequencing of training are critical. No team will thrive and achieve if it is constantly in training. Teams need the opportunity to implement what they have learned and to attain proficiency. They need to see how the training experience helps them achieve results at new and improved levels.

For its part, the organization cannot afford to have groups of employees in constant training. Work must be done; patients must be cared for. Training needs should not be allowed to overshadow work needs. By the same token, work needs should not be allowed to create continuing delays in training.

Generate Enthusiasm for and Commitment to Learning

There are several ways that organizations can create enthusiasm for learning. The organization can make questioning and reflecting a part of its culture; it can use adult learning techniques in the departments as well as the classroom; and it can recognize learning with the same level of support that it gives to quality improvement and cost-reduction activities.

In the future, the greatest benefit of the training process to the organization and the team will be the commitment to and enthusiasm for learning that team members have developed. Technology will continue to increase at a rapid pace, and health care as it is practiced today will change. Knowledge and skills that employees learn in the 1990s will have to be replaced with new knowledge and skills in the next century. Thus, the need to learn is ongoing. The team and its individual members will find future growth and development easier and less daunting if they come away from this process with a healthy respect for learning.

• Adjusting the Work Environment

If employees are trained to develop new skills but return to a work environment that does not allow them to apply what they have learned, the training time and experience are wasted. In order for team members and the organization to benefit from the training process, the work environment also needs to change. Change needs to manifest itself in the organization in two areas: the work systems and management behavior.

The Work Systems

If teams are taught decision-making skills but the supervisor or coach continues to make team decisions, not only will the team forget its new skill but it will perceive self-management as no more than a fad that the organization does not intend to support. If skills continue to be stifled because the organization's work systems do not allow them to be used, the entire program will be jeopardized. Employees will stop participating, performance will decline, and self-management will fail.

For this reason, the work systems within which teams will be functioning need to be reassessed to see whether they support teamwork or whether they will reinforce the current practice of individual performance and managerial direction and control. Not all of the organization's work systems will need to change, nor will they all need to change at once. Changes can be phased in as teams develop and learn how to operate in new arenas.

The importance of changing work systems cannot be overemphasized. The culture and work systems that exist in organizations today were not designed to support teamwork or self-management. Additionally, the organization should act expeditiously when the need for change is apparent. A delay in changing a work system that has blocked team performance for an unwarranted amount of time will create a situation in which employees will already have experienced the negative consequences of trying to swim against the current. The next time, these employees will not be as enthusiastic or as willing to continue trying.

In most organizations before the implementation of teams, supervisors give direction and make work assignments. Once teams are formed and trained, the employees on the team expect to make their own assignments.

The work system of supervisors directing employees should no longer exist after the first few hours of team training. If employees return to work having made their own assignments and the supervisor immediately changes or challenges the assignments, the employees will become disenchanted and disoriented. They will question the supervisor's involvement and wonder what went wrong between the training and the workplace reality. The employees will not be able to go against old behavior patterns indefinitely and will revert to the "the supervisor manages–the employee works" system.

Managerial Behavior

Managers will need an overview of their new role, including what behaviors are and are not expected or wanted. They should participate in an assessment of their attitudes and skills to identify changes or improvements that will be needed to help them succeed in a self-managed team environment.

Another reason that managers will need to behave in ways that are congruent with the new system is that they will be expected to perform the roles of coaches and facilitators. If they are unable or refuse to change, the organization will need to take action to either help improve their motivation or remove them from their positions so that they can neither harm nor impede the transition.

When team implementation is still in the planning stage, the organization and its management staff would benefit from attending workshops on self-management and teamwork. Following are some of the topics that might be addressed:

- Self-managed work teams and their benefits
- Work design concepts
- Organizational systems
- Team methods
- Team development stages
- Barriers to team effectiveness
- Employee involvement and the manager's job

If teams learn how to function before managers do, the lack of supporting management behaviors could slow or stop the transition to self-managed work teams.

Among the skills that managers will need to learn in their new role are change management, teamwork techniques, team system management, and interpersonal and coaching skills. The following subsections examine these areas.

Change Management

Managers will be expected to lead the change and transition to self-managed work teams. If they do not understand the change process or have skills in facilitating change, they will need to participate in a change management workshop to prepare themselves for employee reaction to the new way of doing business.

Teamwork Techniques

Teams use a number of techniques to make decisions and move the team forward that are not common in an individual-oriented environment. Managers need to know these techniques so that they can use them, model them, and coach teams in their application. Following are some examples of team techniques:

- Brainstorming
- Multivoting
- Nominal group technique
- Team decision-making options
- Team problem solving
- Conflict resolution
- Team performance measurement
- Team celebrations
- Peer appraisal

Team System Management

Managers also will need to learn how systems will change to support teams. Ideally, they will be involved in changing these systems. Examples of systems that may change are:

- Planning and goal setting
- Budgeting
- Purchasing
- Reporting
  - Time and attendance
  - Productivity
  - Budgets
  - Quality control
  - Safety
- Performance review
- Discipline
- Compensation
- Employment

Interpersonal and Coaching Skills

Managers at all levels have received communication and interpersonal skills training at some point in their careers. However, they may need a renewed vision of the appropriate communication style to use when dealing with a team. The first thing they need to understand is that team communication occurs with a group, not an individual. The manager needs to think: "I will ask the team," not "I will ask Joe." (Interpersonal skills are discussed in chapter 10.)

Managers also will need to modify their communication style from telling, directing, and controlling to coaching, guiding, and influencing. Skills that managers will want to brush up on include:

- Clarifying and confirming
- Coaching
- Influencing
- Questioning
- Giving feedback
- Praising
- Listening with empathy

• Conclusion

The purpose of team training is to provide team members with the knowledge and skills they need to accomplish their goals and to meet the organization's expectations. In addition, team training should motivate them to want to continue to learn, long after teams have been implemented. The work environment will continue to change and a work force that is committed to learning will be a distinguishing asset in the future.

The team training program comprises five phases: preparation, assessment, selection, connection, and education. The phases are designed to build on each other so that employee strengths are emphasized and that the whole process is efficient, effective, and motivational.

In addition to training team members, the organization needs to change the systems and environment in which teams will work. Failure to change these areas will cause the training to fail and ultimately will lead to the destruction of the entire team concept.

In some cases, managers also must be retrained. They are a critical ingredient in the transition to teams. They must learn about self-managed work teams before employee training occurs and will be expected to model teamwork skills and to support teams as they develop.

Reference

1. Drucker, P. *The Post Capitalist Society.* New York City: HarperCollins Publishers, Inc., 1993, p. 202.

Chapter 12

Team Development

Employees on self-managed work teams develop in two ways: They develop the ability to perform assigned tasks in an environment of self-management, and they develop the ability to function socially as a team. Although in both instances they experiment, learn, and grow, the developmental stages they go through are different for each.

As team members learn their tasks and become increasingly self-managed, the team grows in a linear way, with each new skill building on the last one until the team achieves competence. However, as employees develop social interaction, the team's development can go in all directions. Just when members appear to be attaining a high level of efficiency and effectiveness resulting from good communication and interpersonal relations, they can suddenly revert to behaviors demonstrating low levels of trust, discord, and disharmony. Tuckman calls this fluctuating behavior "forming, storming, norming, and performing."[1] Although its pattern is normal, this behavior can be frustrating to team members and team facilitators alike.

In order to manage team implementation within the organization, it is important to understand both the task-related and social aspects of team development. Team members, team leaders, team facilitators, and managers all need to know what to expect as they strive to create and maintain teams. Otherwise, the frustration of watching a high-performance team revert to the storming stage may cause supporters of the team concept to falter. However, if they understand that teams do not stay in any of the social development stages indefinitely, they will be better able to practice patience and continue their support through to the final stage—performing.

This chapter describes the stages of team development and discusses the behaviors that can be expected in both its task-related and social aspects. It also offers strategies for making the performing stage of the process endure.

• Team-Related Development Stages

Self-managed work teams make the transition to autonomy from almost total dependence on supervisors for direction. Although the stages of the transition are not clearly delineated, they can be discerned by the degree to which team members manage themselves and the degree to which they depend on their supervisor for direction. Following are the general stages of this process:

- Stage 1.   Preteam
- Stage 2.   Early team
- Stage 3.   Learning team
- Stage 4.   Mature team
- Stage 5.   Fully autonomous team

(See also figure 12-1.)

Stage 1. Preteam

At this stage, the supervisor controls and assigns work, develops the work schedule, maintains work records, obtains resources for the team, relates to other departments in the organization, solves problems, initiates change, and deals directly with customers and suppliers to resolve disputes. This stage is characterized by a high degree of authoritarian behavior on the part of the supervisor and a low degree of participation on the part of the employees.

In the preteam stage, employees function as individuals and rarely collaborate or cooperate with others in the performance of their work assignments. Often they try to outperform each other and compete for recognition from the supervisor and the organization.

Communication in this stage moves in one direction—from supervisor to employee. It also tends to take place one-on-one more often than it does in a group setting. When employees attend a staff meeting, they perceive themselves as individuals having the same supervisor, rather than as a team.

Stage 2. Early Team

By this stage, some of the responsibilities previously held by the supervisor have been transferred to the employees, and the employees are beginning to recognize their existence as a team. They have had their first meeting to (1) learn what self-management is, (2) clarify assignments, and (3) begin to learn about the new skills they will need to acquire in order to perform their new tasks. However, actual skill training has not yet begun. The concepts of cooperation and collaboration are still being thought about and tentatively approached.

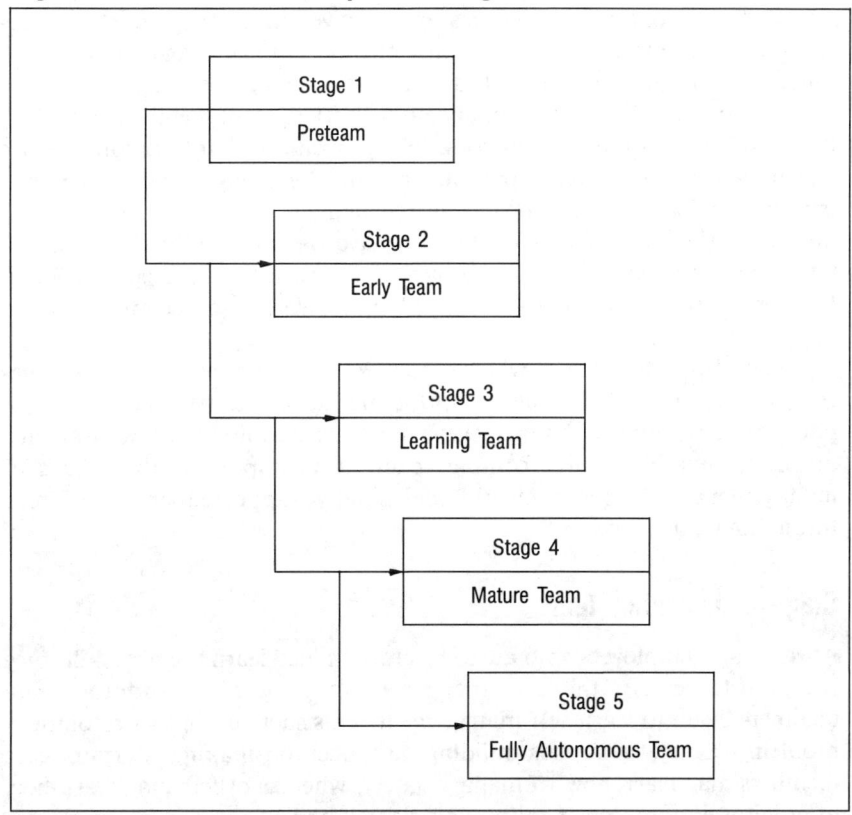

Figure 12-1. Team Development Stages

- Stage 1: Preteam
- Stage 2: Early Team
- Stage 3: Learning Team
- Stage 4: Mature Team
- Stage 5: Fully Autonomous Team

Typically, the first task that is transferred from supervisor to employees is management of the daily work assignments. This responsibility is particularly important to employees because, although they may not make many changes, the sense of freedom to arrange work as they think best lifts their spirits and generates their initial enthusiasm for the team concept.

Prior to making changes in work assignments, it is not unusual for team members to get together without either the team facilitator, team leader, or supervisor so that they can begin to discuss options and reach agreements on their own. Informal leaders tend to take charge of the process, and the changes that employees have wanted to try are tentatively approached.

In addition to managing daily work assignments, the team may take responsibility for some of its record-keeping or paperwork tasks. As team members strive to initiate actions to try to solve some of the problems they face in their daily work, they learn to hold meetings and practice group communication skills.

The amount of change that occurs in this phase depends in large part on the degree to which employees were allowed to participate in management decisions prior to their becoming members of teams and on how committed they think management is to the self-management concept. In an environment that has been strongly authoritarian, team members will likely be slower to take on responsibilities. In organizations that traditionally have encouraged employee participation, team members may already be empowered to problem-solve on their own and manage their daily work assignments. In the case of employees who have been empowered to manage task-related responsibilities in the past, the growth that is needed tends to be more in the social area—learning how to work and accomplish goals as a team.

This also is the stage at which employees often perceive mixed messages from management. If management does not appear to be cohesive in support of teams, employees may believe they have permission to work against or sabotage their newly forming team. It is important that the self-management concept be clearly and solidly supported and reinforced throughout this stage.

Stage 3. Learning Team

At this stage, employees who are to be cross-trained learn the new skills they will need to perform the tasks they have been assigned. In addition, team members begin to learn self-management skills such as conflict resolution, problem solving, consensus building, and decision making. Certain team members may learn how to manage safety, whereas others may learn how to monitor and improve quality. This stage is an exciting one for employees because they are being given the opportunity to learn and grow and to experience limited self-management.

By this point, the team has had many meetings and members are problem-solving together, taking risks, and testing boundaries. Although there may be some dissension among members, basically the team is in a strong growth mode. In addition to improving its meeting and participation skills, the team has started to relate to other departments, has initiated change in how work is done, and is beginning to perform management work and job tasks with greater skill.

Stage 4. Mature Team

By this stage, the self-managed work team has learned many new skills and is performing its assigned tasks competently. Additionally, it has learned and is performing many management skills. Although some team members may be coaching problem team members, the team has yet to take on responsibility for administering discipline when dealing with personnel problems such as absenteeism, tardiness, unsatisfactory work performance, and poor interpersonal communication.

However, at this stage team identity is solid and members have developed a sense of loyalty to the team. The team routinely spends time evaluating its progress and is comfortable giving members praise and constructive feedback. Although some team members may still be hesitant about confronting issues, working through conflicts, and dealing with differences, the team as a whole is managing its diversity effectively.

Also at this stage, the team is providing input into budget development and capital equipment decisions. It is maintaining and reordering inventory, monitoring performance against the budget, and has had experience with goals and quarterly plans.

Stage 5. Fully Autonomous Team

At this stage, the team starts to perform the supervisory roles of hiring, firing, and administering discipline. Some teams also are determining compensation for their members. They are developing budgets and providing input into higher-level management decisions. They also are participating in long range-planning efforts. This final stage is the one in which the team begins to evaluate its own performance, initiates change for improvement in work processes, and basically is performing at the highest level.

Team members know what their relationships are to each other and to the organization. They have weathered some interpersonal storms and have survived. They have dealt with each of the social development stages at least once and feel capable of surviving them if they reoccur. And finally, they are participating freely and fully in the work and management of the team. The team is now structured, focused, and fully capable of sustaining high-quality performance.

• Social Development Stages

During the lifetime of a self-managed work team, it moves through four stages of social development. These stages are:

- Stage 1.   Forming
- Stage 2.   Storming
- Stage 3.   Norming
- Stage 4.   Performing

Each stage has unique characteristics that are observable to both team members and those outside the team. Contrary to Tuckman's theory that these stages build on each other, most other work with groups indicates that teams move through these stages randomly in response to changes in their external work environment and to changes within the team.

Whatever stage the team is in reflects the collective behavior of the majority of its members. Not all members of the team move from one stage to the next at the same time. Whereas some team members may still be trying to adjust to the new work environment, others have fully accepted the change and are in the norming stage.

Because team members can observe their group's behavior individually, they are able to identify the stage the group is in. This ability to stand back and assess where the team is helps the team make the necessary adjustments to prolong the more desirable stages and reduce time spent in the most disruptive ones.

Stage 1. Forming

Forming is characterized by the opening of the mind to new possibilities and the willingness to take risks. At this stage, there will be changes in the way the group and individuals perform.

In the beginning, when employees are first brought together to form the team, they have a number of basic questions. Questioning and exploring new options are part of the forming process. The questions that group members will ask, either silently or aloud, are:

- Why are we to be a team?
- Why am I on this team, instead of another one?
- Is this team worthy of me? Am I worthy of it?
- What is the purpose of this team?
- What is my new role?

If answered to the employees' satisfaction, these fundamental questions can help clarify their identity and start their development as team members. Team members are thus able to achieve a degree of comfort with their new situation. If the questions are not answered to the employees' satisfaction, the storming stage may begin before the employees have the opportunity to bond as a team.

Assuming that the employees are willing to open their minds and try this new way of organizing work, they will begin to learn about the team's purpose, customers, and relationship to the organization. They may select a name for their team, develop a vision, and begin to try out their new roles and responsibilities. Those team members who have learned new skills will be performing them for the first time. Even though this is all still new, team members will begin to develop a sense of security, feeling that "We are in this together."

Stage 2. Storming

Storming can occur at any time in the life of the team. As the name implies, this is the stage during which team members often display tumultuous behavior. They may decide they no longer trust or respect each other and no longer want to be on a team together; in short, they begin to behave as individuals. They challenge the team leader, the facilitator, and any other authority figure who works with the team.

The storming stage can be caused by a change either in the environment outside the team or within the team itself. For example, a change brought about by external forces might be that the team is required to change its physical location. Or management might relegate the team to obscurity because of changing priorities in the organization. Within the team, the change may be brought about by a disagreement between two members in the course of a decision-making task, resulting in a division of the team into opposing factions. Team members may already be feeling edgy because of overwork or learning overload. Whatever the cause, unrest, disarray, and dysfunction are the outcomes.

Certainly one of the most common causes of a team entering this stage is when one team member believes that he or she has been betrayed by another team member. The betrayal may be in the form of gossip, failure to support, failure to endorse ideas, or failure to show respect. The result is that the team member who feels betrayed no longer trusts his or her co-worker. This lack of trust can lead to team dysfunction.

Fortunately, the team does not stay at this stage forever. At those times when the team seems to be tearing itself apart, team members, the team leader, and the team coach can all work to pull the team back together. Eventually, members will regain their team identity and can refocus on the positive aspects of being on the team. By working actively to rebuild the team, they often find they can put bad experiences behind them.

Stage 3. Norming

Frequently, the *norming* stage follows the storming stage. At this stage, exhausted from all the interpersonal conflicts and disruptions, team members have been able to establish truces. Because team members are walking on eggshells to avoid further conflict, behavior settles down to team norms and members make a special effort not to step outside them.

It is during this stage that the phenomenon of groupthink is most likely to occur. In order to maintain team stability so soon after the storming stage, members tend to agree to be agreeable — even when they disagree. Now the need is to manage group agreement rather than group conflict, which had been the focus during the preceding stage.

This norming stage can be likened to middle age. The team has settled into a way of behaving, has achieved a high level of comfort, and is looking forward to a smooth, quiet, blissful retirement.

What, then, happens to cause the team to move on to the next stage? Most frequently, it is that team members begin to experience boredom. The excitement of the forming stage, when everything was new and every team member was learning to function at a different level, has passed. The tumult and excitement of the storming stage has subsided. And now the comfort of the norming stage has become unsatisfying. Team members need to look for new challenges and increase the team's level of performance.

Stage 4. Performing

At the *performing* stage, the team is functioning as a finely tuned machine. Each team member understands his or her role and is adept at performing it. Systems for decision making, problem solving, and conflict resolution are in place and working. The team members understand their relationship to the organization and are comfortable with it. The new ways of working as a team are now familiar and second nature.

The team has excelled and is recognized by the organization for its achievement. Members feel tremendous pride in and loyalty to the team. The energy and enthusiasm they felt in the forming stage is once again present at this stage. The difference is that the earlier excitement of the challenge has now been replaced by the excitement that comes with success.

However, no team can perpetuate these feelings of euphoria indefinitely. Team members need to be faced with additional challenges and opportunities for growth. If they are not, they may become bored or restless and eventually revert to either the storming or norming stage. The task of keeping the team on track so that it will continue to perform at the highest level is an extremely difficult one that requires the attention of the team coach as well as all the team members. Otherwise, the performing stage may last no longer than a month or two.

• Strategies to Make the Performing Stage Endure

Several strategies may be implemented to try to keep a team at the performing stage, although none of them offer guarantees. As the team reaches the pinnacle of its success, anything within the internal or external environment can be disruptive. The highest levels of performance are vulnerable not only to attack from others but also to self-destruction. Following are three specific strategies that can be used to help the high-performance team stay on top:

- *Raise the level of the challenge.* For instance, if the team has met or is meeting its goals for quality, customer satisfaction, and financial performance, it should be asked to:
  - Think about what it can do even better
  - Set goals that stretch the team's talent and ingenuity
  - Set its efforts as a model for the organization on cost reduction
  - Document the steps it takes to cut deeper inroads into the cost of the procedure it performs, while maintaining a high level of quality and customer satisfaction
  - Report regularly to senior management on team progress. This strategy causes the team to focus on the future and to concentrate its efforts on the new challenge. It introduces change, challenge, and excitement into the work environment, and also provides regular feedback and recognition from senior management.
- *Have the high-performance team adopt a team in the forming stage and help it achieve success.* The high-performance team can help the newer team clarify roles and expectations and establish goals and feedback. For its efforts, the high-performance team should share in the recognition given the new team for its success.
- *Change the team's work assignment.* This will create a situation in which team members will have to learn new skills, establish new organizational relationships, and basically re-form. When the high-performance team goes through a rebirth cycle, it becomes so involved in learning and restructuring that it does not have time to become bored or complacent, or frustrated and irritable.

Each of the preceding strategies introduces change to the high-performance team's status quo and is designed to take the team to a new level of performance. Additionally, each strategy gives the team the freedom to design its own approach to implementing the strategy and incorporates feedback and recognition for the team's efforts.

• Conclusion

In the team development process, employees learn to (1) perform work-related tasks in a self-managed environment and (2) acquire the social skills needed to work together as a team. Work-related skill development progresses linearly, with each new skill built on skills that have been previously acquired. However, social development progresses randomly, passing through four stages identified by Tuckman as forming, storming, norming, and performing. It is important that team coaches, team facilitators, and team members alike understand the team development process so that they can help facilitate the team's progression, particularly through the difficult stages.

Not all teams develop at the same rate. One team may quickly progress to the performing stage, whereas another may become hopelessly embroiled in the constant upheaval of the storming stage. Further, not all teams are equally interested in acquiring new skills. Some teams are eager to become self-managed, whereas others tend to cling to leadership from outside the team. However, whatever their individual personality and developmental patterns, all teams will develop with the support and coaching provided by the organization, other teams, and their own team members.

It also is important to remember that the work of team development is ongoing. Once the team has reached the final stage and has achieved a high-performance level, it must continue to be challenged and its efforts must continue to be recognized if it is to maintain its enthusiasm and productivity.

Reference

1. Tuckman, B. W. Developmental sequence in small groups. *Psychological Bulletin* 63(6):384–99, 1965.

Part Four

Compensation and Rewards

Chapter 13
Pay Systems

When an organization implements a major change such as the transition to self-managed work teams, it must alter many of its systems to support that change. Of all the system changes that an organization can make, a change in the pay system is the one most likely to capture employee attention.

If the pay system is aligned with the new organizational structure, the alignment reinforces the structure and confirms to employees that management is serious enough about the change to invest in it. When pay is aligned with new performance expectations, it quickly focuses attention on the new expectations and starts employees on a course of behavior modification. When pay systems are not aligned, employee behavior modification still may occur but generally not as quickly.

Because the employee compensation system comprises approximately 50 percent of the health care organization's expense budget, it should not be adjusted without extensive study and deliberation. Perhaps for that reason, and because they are innately conservative, health care organizations have been slow to change their pay systems.

This chapter explores three pay systems that support implementation of self-managed work teams. It also examines one traditional system—merit pay—that presents roadblocks to the self-managed team strategy.

- ## Pay Systems That Support Team Implementation

The organization can implement a number of pay program changes to support self-management, teamwork, and employee growth and development. Three of these are: gainsharing, skill-based pay, and broadbanding.

Gainsharing

Gainsharing is a compensation system that pays employees a bonus based on the organization's overall performance. Several health care organizations have tried gainsharing, and others are looking at it as a potential compensation system for the future. Gainsharing is a logical approach for nonprofit organizations because unlike profit sharing, its prototype, it is not necessarily based on profits.

Historically, gainsharing systems have been used effectively in the United States by both manufacturing and service industries. Among the many U.S. companies that have implemented gainsharing programs are Lincoln Electric, Herman Miller, Nucor Steel, Holiday Inn, and Taco Bell.[1]

Advantages of Gainsharing

Gainsharing is particularly effective in organizations whose products and services are produced interdependently, that is, resulting from the efforts of many employees working together. The system generally is implemented when employees have control over their work and the ability to make decisions that can influence the outcome of their work. Thus, for these reasons, gainsharing supports self-managed work team implementation.

In health care, employee behavior, input, and decision making can help reduce the cost of services in a number of ways. For example, they can:

- Reduce overtime and other special pays
- Decrease the number of man-hours required to provide services
- Reduce the use of high-cost products (for example, by changing to less expensive types or brands of medicines or supplies)
- Reduce the frequency with which specialty services are required

In addition to cost reduction, gainsharing can be used to encourage employees to improve quality and customer satisfaction, as well as to accomplish other measurable goals.

To establish a gainsharing program, the organization has to have a period of stability defined as the *base year*. Subsequent-year cost reductions, customer satisfaction improvements, and quality improvements are then compared to performance in the base year and employees receive a quarterly, semiannual, or annual bonus as a percentage of the dollar improvement. (See table 13-1.) Although gainsharing is not difficult to implement, most organizations use the services of a consultant during at least the first year of the program.

Disadvantages of Gainsharing

There is a downside to gainsharing, however. If the organizational environment is unstable and many changes are affecting the organization at once, it is difficult to tell what the causes of improvements are. Also, over a period of time the leadership of the organization may lose enthusiasm for the pro-

Table 13-1. Gainsharing

	Base Year	Gainsharing Year
Payroll costs		
Overtime	$ 900,000	$600,000
Call pay	25,000	8,000
Other costs		
Supplies	90,000	75,000
Total cost	1,015,000	683,000
Cost reduction		332,000
Employee share	50%	166,000

gram or decide to modify the base year. Once gainsharing has been implemented, employee reaction to either eliminating the program or tampering with it will not be positive.

Skill-Based Pay

Skill-based pay is a compensation system that pays employees additional increments when they learn to perform new skills. This concept can be used to support organizations that wish to encourage multiskilling among employees in order to increase worker flexibility. There are both advantages and disadvantages to skill-based pay.

Advantages of Skill-Based Pay

This pay practice has been used effectively in manufacturing and textile industries to compensate assembly line workers for learning a group of skills related to building a product. According to Lawler, skill-based pay has been used since the 1960s at General Electric and is growing in popularity. In a 1992 report of *Fortune 1000* company pay practices, 51 percent were using a skill-based pay system in some part of their organization.[2]

The skill-based pay concept fits well with self-managed work teams, particularly when they are cross-functional. When employees are assigned to teams, they are expected to learn new skills in four areas: technical, interpersonal, teamwork, and supervisory. (See chapter 10 for further discussion of these skills.) Although some employees will be excited about learning new skills, others will likely resent having to put forth the effort. Organizations that implement cross-functional self-managed work teams use skill-based pay to reward and encourage employees to step out of their traditional roles, to take risks associated with performing different and new skills, and to commit the time and effort needed to develop and maintain new skill proficiency. Thus, skill-based pay is a way of providing a "carrot" to encourage employees to learn the new skills.

When a team of employees possesses many common skills, it is more flexible and better able to adjust to rapidly changing work loads or other business requirements. According to a Tower-Perrins report of 80 skill-based pay programs, the advantages to skill-based pay are improved productivity and quality, lower operating costs, and lower turnover.[3]

Examples of skill-based pay programs abound in health care organizations. They take the form of certification pay, career ladders, and team competency bonuses. *Certification pay* frequently is given to registered nurses for achieving a specialty certification such as CCRN (Critical Care Registered Nurse). When the nurse passes the certification exam, he or she may receive a bonus, an additional increment in base pay, or both. Organizations that have implemented certification pay systems have found that many nurses willingly exert the effort to achieve this reward. Benefits to the health care organization are distribution of advanced skills throughout the work force and improved quality of patient care; benefits to the employees include increased compensation, higher skill levels, and enhanced value in the marketplace.

Health care organizations that have implemented *career ladders* in the past had a system that resembled skill-based pay. Generally, the clinical ladder had three steps, each of which had certain knowledge and skill requirements and provided an additional increment of pay. For example, within this system a critical care nurse who had achieved advanced clinical knowledge or certification and thus could perform a higher-level skill such as intubation would be paid at a higher rate than nurses who had not.

Within the Alliant Health System in Louisville, Kentucky, a type of skill-based pay system is used for self-managed work teams. At Alliant, teams that achieve certain criteria of self-management receive a one-time bonus, a *team competency bonus,* which is paid to reward team members for learning new skills of teamwork and self-supervision and for demonstrating them successfully.[4]

Sutter General Hospital in Sacramento, California, avoided the issue of skill-based pay altogether. Sutter expected its employees to learn new roles and skills as part of their job requirement. For example, employees were cross-trained to perform a number of service and technical skills needed on a nursing unit but frequently performed by specialists. (See figure 13-1.) However, instead of rewarding their efforts with skill-based pay, Sutter offered its employees the reward of continued employment, a "carrot" that gets employee attention to an even greater extent than a pay adjustment.[5]

An organization that wants to implement a skill-based pay program should use the skills of either a consultant or a knowledgeable compensation professional. Although skill-based pay is not difficult to implement, it can become extremely expensive if done incorrectly.

Figure 13-1. Employee Tasks of a Patient Care Assistant before and after Multiskilling

Employee Tasks before Becoming Multiskilled	Employee Tasks after Becoming Multiskilled
• Taking vital signs • Documenting vital signs • Emptying bedpans	• Taking vital signs • Documenting vital signs • Emptying bedpans • Ambulating patients • Drawing blood • Performing EKGs • Cleaning patient room

Disadvantages of Skill-Based Pay

One disadvantage of skill-based pay is that it can place multiskilled employees at higher pay levels than they might have been in their component jobs, based on market surveys. Employment of a skilled compensation professional will help avoid an upward spiral of compensation expense. Another drawback to skill-based pay is that it may require implementation of a formal program of job rotation and competency certification to help ensure that employees retain new skill proficiency, which may encourage artificial or forced behavior on the job that neither is productive nor increases employee job satisfaction. Additionally, employees may have a job preference and dislike being rotated to perform other jobs. Rotation may be *required* in a skill-based pay program, whereas it can be allowed to occur (or not) more naturally if the team has become multiskilled for flexibility and is not forced into more job movement than is necessary. A third disadvantage to skill-based pay is that some employees may be more proficient in one skill than another and their performance in an area where they are less competent may diminish the quality of care.

People who are opposed to skill-based pay believe that an organization can achieve improved quality, productivity, and work force flexibility under their existing market-based pay systems, without the added payroll costs associated with skill-based pay. (See table 13-2.)

Broadbanding

Broadbanding is a pay system that reduces the number of distinct job classifications and pay grades within an organization. It frequently is used in conjunction with skill-based pay but can exist without the skill-based pay component. This compensation system blends well with an organization that has flattened its hierarchy and asked its employees to expand their skills horizontally as well as vertically. It produces job categories, or job titles,

Table 13-2. Regular versus Skill-Based Pay for Patient Care Assistant

Regular Pay System

Job Title	Hourly Pay
Housekeeping Aide I	$6.00
Food Service Assistant	6.00
Nursing Assistant	6.50
Patient Transport Technician	6.50
Patient Equipment Technician	6.50
EKG Technician	7.00
Phlebotomist	7.00
Respiratory Care Assistant	8.00

Skill-Based Pay System

Generalist Patient Care Assistant

Base Pay = $6.00 + $2.00 in increments = $8.00

Additional Skills and Increments

Basic Housekeeping, patient comfort	= $6.00
Bathes patient Transports patient Ambulates patient	+ $ .50
Performs EKGs	+ $ .50
Performs phlebotomy	+ $ .50
Performs spirometry	+ $ .50

in which there is a wider range and variety of job responsibility. It diminishes emphasis on job specialization and increases it on generalization and flexibility. (See figure 13-2.)

Advantages of Broadbanding

Broadbanding is a relatively new pay structure in the compensation field. It was created as a means of encouraging development of a more flexible and broadly skilled group of employees. In health care, past emphasis placed on specialization may have gone beyond what is practical and necessary to produce high-quality patient care. Broadbanding allows management to bring the pay system in line with the strategy of flattening the organization and broadening employee job responsibilities.[6] (See figure 13-3.) Additionally, broadbanding helps change career advancement emphasis from moving

Figure 13-2. Traditional versus Banded Pay Structure

Traditional Structure		Banded Structure	
Job Title	Pay Grade	Band	Job Title
Housekeeping Aide I	6	1	Patient Care Assistant
Lab Assistant	6		
Linen Assistant I	6		
Nursing Assistant I	7		
Patient Transportation Technician	7		
Patient Equipment Technician	7		
Nursing Assistant II	8		
Respiratory Care Assistant	8		
Phlebotomist	9		

Figure 13-3. Flattening the Organization and Broadbanding

Job Title	Pay Grade	Band
VP	18	12
Director	17, 16, 15	11
Assistant Director	14, 13	
Manager	13, 12, 11	Eliminated in flattening the organization
Supervisor	10, 9, 8	
Team Leader	9, 8, 7	10

Note: With broadbanding, the organization can reduce the number of management pay grades from eleven to two. In this example, the management positions and eight pay grades of supervisor, manager, and assistant director are eliminated. The responsibilities and tasks performed in those positions are transferred to teams and team leaders. Instead of having three separate team leader pay grades and three separate director pay grades, the roles and responsibilities are reflected in one pay grade that will be *broader* than an individual pay range. The skills of the employees occupying jobs in these broad pay ranges can be expanded.

vertically in the organization (becoming more highly specialized) to moving horizontally (expanding and broadening skills and knowledge).

Broadbanding has several advantages over traditional pay systems. For example:

- It reduces the red tape and bureaucracy of the typical pay grade and job classification system.
- It reduces the amount of time and effort that managers and others spend trying to revise job descriptions to justify upward movement in the pay grade system.
- It eliminates several pay grades and job titles, resulting in a simpler structure that is easier to manage, explain, and understand.

- It eliminates much of the bureaucracy and red tape of the typical job classification/job evaluation system.
- It can eliminate time lost in confusion or hard feelings as members of cross-functional teams learn and perform the skills of specialists in different pay grades. If the specialist were not in the same pay band, the employee who has learned to do a phlebotomy, for example, would expect to be paid at the specialist's rate of pay.

Health care organizations that are reorganizing and restructuring to meet the challenges of health care reform want to encourage employee flexibility. When a job category is reduced or eliminated, the employees in that job category could be laid off. An alternative is to provide training in new skills, move the employees laterally, and give them continued security at a time when job security is limited. A broadbanded pay system gives the organization flexibility to utilize employees differently as needs change.

Broadbanding can be implemented in a number of ways, each involving development of a clear strategy for employee utilization and an emphasis on employee growth and development. For example, broadbanding can be implemented within or across job families, for all jobs in the organization (including management), or simply for designated jobs within certain self-managed teams. Whatever implementation plan is undertaken, redesigning the pay and career development systems and restructuring jobs into broad bands requires the assistance of skilled compensation professionals. Although broadbanding is a simpler pay system, it is not simple to implement.

Disadvantages of Broadbanding

Employee and management reaction to broadbanding may not be enthusiastic. The boundaries that traditionally have been established by job specialization, job descriptions, and pay grades have provided a value system, without which employees will not have a clear method for assessing and comparing their worth. Also, as employees are banded together with others who formerly were in higher pay grades, their pay expectations may change. Employees may expect pay increases to put them on an equal footing with the highest-paid employees in their assigned pay band. When pay increases do not occur, employees may feel cheated.

• Pay System That Supports Individual Performance

The *merit pay* system (or *pay for performance*) rewards individual performance and is in opposition to the organizational strategy of self-managed work teams. Traditionally, it is considered by management and compensation professionals to be the "right way" to pay people, and is the most widely used compensation system in American industry. According to Lawler, a survey of the *Fortune 1000* found that 96 percent had merit pay.[7]

When an organization establishes a merit pay system, it sends a strong motivational message to its employees: "If you do more than your coworkers, or do your work better, you will receive a larger pay increase." Employees and managers alike respond to this message by changing and improving their work output, believing that their efforts will be appropriately rewarded at pay increase time. They believe "superior" performers deserve to be paid a "superior" rate of pay.

Merit pay also is widely used in the health care industry, although generally pay increases are based on a combination of market adjustment and merit. An employee doing "average" work may receive the market-adjusted pay increase only; an employee doing "good" work may receive the market-adjusted increase and a modest merit-based pay increase; and an employee doing "superior" work may receive a somewhat larger merit pay increase in addition to the market adjustment. With or without self-managed work teams, merit pay has not been that successful in health care for three primary reasons: cost, performance measurement, and employee dissatisfaction.

The first problem with merit pay—cost—refers to the expense involved in attracting and keeping qualified health care workers. In the recent past qualified health care workers were difficult to attract and keep, and health care organizations continually adjusted their pay systems upward in order to offer attractive and competitive salaries. With salary budgets growing at alarming rates merely to remain competitive, management can see little additional benefit to giving substantial merit pay increases on top of market increases. Thus, the pressure to remain competitive has led to an unfunded or underfunded merit pay program. The result is that superior-performing employees may receive little (if any) more than average performers. Thus, although the program may continue to exist on paper, it quickly loses its financial and motivational impact with employees.

The second problem with merit pay is that of basing it on performance measurement. Most health care employees provide some aspect of patient care and have interactions with many diverse human beings. They also work very interdependently. For example, the unit secretary cannot do his or her job if the nurse and lab technician do not do their jobs. Similarly, the pharmacist cannot do his or her job if the physician and nurse do not do their jobs. When something does not work the way it is supposed to, it is difficult to know whether the problem stems from poor employee performance or a foul-up in the system. When something works extremely well, generally it is because a number of people have worked together to provide that result. However, in this environment, measuring average, good, or superior performance by an individual employee is difficult if not impossible. Job performance evaluation systems do not work well in grading these degrees of performance.

The third problem with merit pay is that it can produce employee dissatisfaction. For example, some employees expect merit pay increases and do not receive them. Others receive them but are judged by their coworkers to have benefited from supervisor favoritism. In some cases, merit pay increases are not perceived to be large enough to differentiate between mediocre and superior performance. And an additional problem occurs when a supervisor who has not been responsive to an employee's request for information and approvals measures that employee poorly, when, in fact, the performance fault is the result of the supervisor's lack of action.

In a team environment, employees learn that their individual differences, knowledge, experiences, inputs, and perspectives can be combined to produce a better result than would have been produced by any one of them individually. Further, they learn to depend on each other in order to produce overall team performance. Because merit pay says that one employee is more valuable to the organization than another, employees would perceive concepts such as cooperation, collaboration, and consensus to be meaningless and teamwork to be a wasted effort.

• Conclusion

Currently, three pay systems contain design elements that support implementation of self-managed work teams—gainsharing, skill-based pay, and broadbanding. Gainsharing has been in existence for a long time and has proved to be a successful strategy for obtaining employee involvement and commitment to corporate goals. Although skill-based pay and broadbanding are newer pay systems than gainsharing and have not had as broad an application, they both contain elements that complement increased employee involvement, employee growth and development, and flattening of the organizational hierarchy.

The traditional system of merit pay works against the concept of teamwork. Instead, its precepts focus on individual performance. Despite the fact that merit pay has not been that successful in health care, managers and compensation professionals are reluctant to part with it because it has been so widely used.

Changing a pay system is a complex process and one that should not be attempted without serious deliberation. In many cases, it is advisable to seek the help of a compensation consultant or professional. To date, regardless of the extent of their experience with self-managed work teams, health care organizations have shown an unwillingness to adjust their pay systems to support the concept.

Organizations that have introduced the system alternatives of gainsharing, skill-based pay, and broadbanding have done so on a small and experimental scale. Little information is available on their success or failure.

Nonetheless, there is considerable agreement that traditional pay systems need to be modified to support the new high-involvement work systems exemplified by self-managed work teams. It seems clear that if a health care organization attempting to implement self-managed work teams retains its traditional merit pay system, both systems will likely fail.

References

1. Lawler, E., III. *The Ultimate Advantage: Creating the High-Involvement Organization.* San Francisco: Jossey-Bass Publishers, 1992, pp. 173–86.
2. Lawler, p. 160.
3. Skill-based pay: a status report. *Training,* Dec. 1992, p. 10.
4. Telephone interview with William B. Newkirk, coordinator of education and development, Alliant Health System, Louisville, KY, Aug. 13, 1993.
5. Telephone interview with Sylvia Swarner, nursing education, Sutter General Hospital, Sacramento, CA, Aug. 5, 1993.
6. LeBlanc, P. Pay-banding can help align pay with new organizational structures. *National Productivity Review* 11(3):317, Summer 1992.
7. Lawler, E., III. *Strategic Pay.* San Francisco: Jossey-Bass Publishers, 1990, p. 70.

Chapter 14

Reward and Recognition Systems

When an organization implements self-managed work teams, it needs to examine its reward and recognition systems to ensure that they support the team concept. For instance, rewards for individual achievement are definitively out of place in an organization trying to implement a team environment. If management wants employees to work together on teams, it should reward them as a team.

The use of rewards to change or motivate behavior has been a management practice for almost 100 years.[1] Rewards have proved to be an effective way of focusing both employee and manager attention on supporting new ways of doing business. In either a cash or noncash form, rewards also are given to recognize accomplishments, generate enthusiasm, and simply to say thank-you.

The practice of giving rewards and recognition has recently come under scrutiny. In his book *Punished by Rewards,* Kohn generates significant discussion among managers and consultants alike on the value of rewards.[2] He identifies some of the problems that arise when an organization uses rewards to motivate and recognize behavior. According to Kohn, the intrinsic reward of pleasure derived from performing a task well is superior to the extrinsic reward of being given a cash bonus for job performance. By focusing employee attention on extrinsic rewards, management is actually bribing employees to perform their work and diminishing the true pleasure they would otherwise derive from their work experience.

This chapter describes the different types of rewards that organizations use to motivate or change behavior, recognize achievement, generate enthusiasm, and say thank-you. It also discusses some of the drawbacks to and problems with the organization's reliance on rewards as motivators.

- **Cash Rewards**

Cash rewards come in the form of bonuses and incentives. Although cash is used extensively as a reward in industry, nonprofit health care organizations are hesitant to use it, viewing cash rewards as an added burden to their salary budget. Health care organizations also want to avoid tax law problems related to their nonprofit status. However, as long as they do not tie rewards to profits, ensure that income taxes are deducted from the rewards, and implement a cash award system with well-thought-out controls, these problems can be manageable.

For example, according to William Newkirk, coordinator of education and development with the Alliant Health System in Louisville, Kentucky, cash bonuses were used as incentives to encourage senior management to implement self-managed work teams in their reporting departments.[3] Prior to offering cash incentives, there had been little movement toward team implementation; however, after incentives had been offered, team implementation progressed rapidly.

In addition to offering cash incentives to senior management, the Alliant System offered cash bonuses to teams. Once a team was fully self-managed, it could apply for a one-time team cash bonus. If management found that the team had met all the necessary criteria, the bonus was awarded.

Memorial Mission Hospital in Asheville, North Carolina, offered similar incentives to its housekeeping teams.[4] The teams were expected to meet management-specified criteria regarding cleanliness, customer satisfaction, and attendance. They were evaluated monthly, at which time each team member was eligible for a cash bonus depending on how well the team as a whole performed against standards set by the organization.

Memorial Mission Hospital had a tiered bonus system. If the team achieved a certain level of performance, its members received a modest bonus; if it achieved a higher level of performance, the bonus was much larger. The bonus system has resulted not only in improvements in hospital cleanliness but also in employee behavior that management wanted to encourage (for example, improved attendance).[5]

In addition to offering goal-related bonuses, many health care organizations offer certification bonuses for skill and knowledge achievement. These bonuses represent a lump-sum payment for passing a certification examination in a clinical specialty area.

Any time that a cash bonus is promised to reward a specified future achievement, it is an *incentive*. It exists to prod or motivate a desired future performance. Often bonuses are given for suggestions, good attendance, longevity, productivity, holidays, or special achievements such as employee of the month and employee of the year. In addition, bonuses may be given employees for coming into work when not scheduled, accepting particularly difficult assignments, or working overtime or holiday hours.

- ## Noncash Rewards

Noncash rewards come in many forms. The most common are trinkets, food, "points for merchandise," and certificates, plaques, and trophies. In health care, trinkets, food, and certificates are used to a much greater extent than points for merchandise are.

Organizations can use noncash rewards to motivate employees as well as to recognize them for a job well done. Because trinkets and food generally have a smaller dollar value, they are not always treated with the formality of other awards. Perhaps because they are inexpensive and readily available, they are popular with self-managed work teams.

Trinkets

Teams may receive coffee mugs, T-shirts, ball caps, notebooks, pens or pencils, and pins and/or buttons. These rewards serve two purposes. First, because employees know that these are "gifts" for team participation, trinkets can both motivate and strengthen team membership. And second, because many employees believe that being part of a close-knit and recognizable group is the best reward they can receive from their membership on self-managed work teams, trinkets can be used to reinforce team identity.

Food

Health care organizations seem to use food more than any other noncash award. Departments or teams that perform particularly well may be rewarded with pizza parties, coffee and doughnuts or sweet rolls, platters of cookies, or special dinners. Often food is used to entice employees to come to meetings or to thank them for working during periods of heavy census.

It may be that the reason food is used as a bonus so often in health care is because it represents a hidden cost. Almost every health care organization has its own cafeteria, with some catering services. Food can be ordered internally and buried in the cafeteria or department budget.

Food is used primarily as a reward rather than an incentive. Generally, it is given as a postperformance surprise rather than a preachievement promise.

Points for Merchandise

The most frequent noncash incentive is the points-for-merchandise system. This system often exists as a tiered reward system. For example, employees are awarded certain minimum levels of points which allow them to select gifts out of a particular catalog. If they are awarded higher levels of points, they can select gifts out of a different catalog that have a greater dollar value. The organization can build as many tiers into this system as it chooses.

The drawback to the points-for-merchandise system is that it can be burdensome in terms of record keeping, documentation, training, and communication. Generally, however, the ordering and delivery of merchandise occur as transactions between employee and vendor. The health care organization does not order, receive, or distribute catalog gifts; it simply designates which employees can order from which catalogs.

Points for merchandise usually is an incentive reward system and has been used in industry to reward self-managed teams.[6] Its use is not prevalent in health care.

Certificates, Plaques, and Trophies

Certificates, plaques, and trophies are often associated with teams. Employees are awarded them for completing some or all of the training required for team participation. Many times, certificates are framed and displayed in a teamwork area, locker room, or lounge. The certificates themselves, or documentation of their receipt, also may be placed in employee personnel files. Certificates may be distributed by instructors at the end of a class or may be awarded during a ceremony marking the end or beginning of a phase of team development.

Generally, plaques and trophies are distributed at award ceremonies. These types of rewards denote permanence whereas other noncash rewards typically are perceived as temporary and consumable. Plaques frequently are given for achievements that take considerable time—for example, length of service, team of the year, greatest contribution to cost savings, most improvement in productivity, and so on.

Trophies are a sports tradition and generally are given to reward achievements that result from competition. In health care, trophies could be given to teams with the highest-level achievement, the best attendance, the most improvement, or the highest customer rating.

However, the practice of encouraging competition among self-managed teams can be problematic. When teams compete against each other for an award or recognition, they may lose sight of the overall benefit of their achievement to the organization. By trying to beat each other, they may actually create a situation in which the organization's overall performance suffers.

On the other hand, certificates, plaques, and trophies are rarely seen as incentives held out to entice employees to achieve. More often, they are given in recognition of an achievement, sometimes in advance of an anticipated future achievement.

Recognition

Recognition is used to motivate or manage employee behavior in much the same way that cash and noncash rewards are used. If employees behave in the preferred way, they receive recognition in the form of attention, praise, and positive feedback. If employees do not behave in the approved manner, they may receive negative feedback and/or disciplinary action.

Recognition is the reward system used by most organizations when they first implement self-managed work teams. Recognition events may involve the taking of photographs, presentation ceremonies or banquets, display walls, and speech giving. Recognition also may be used to reward teams that are celebrating anniversaries or that have reached certain milestones.

Recognition may be given more privately, for example, when a senior manager praises the team or an individual team member. Generally, praise is an effective recognition device. It is especially effective when it comes from either the senior level of the organization or the customer, when it relates to the work, and when it is specific and sincere.[7]

One aspect of this reward system that employees really seem to enjoy is recognition of team identity using team names, colors, shirts, slogans, and logos. At Memorial Mission Hospital, the housekeeping teams mentioned earlier in the book selected team names such as Mission Explorers; Have Mop, Will Travel; Spirit of the Night; and Sixth-Floor Sharpies. Each team has a vision statement that reflects its values and aspirations. Many of the teams have printed tent cards that they leave in the rooms or areas they clean. The tent cards contain their team names and team vision or slogan.

- ## Development of a Reward Program

Management should involve the employees in the development of team rewards, incentives, and recognition. Employee involvement is key to the self-managed team concept and should be incorporated in the development of the reward system as well. When employees are involved in determining the form that rewards and recognition will take, they are more likely to see them as components of the overall compensation and team system, rather than as performance bribes.

In addition to employees, compensation and accounting personnel need to be included in defining the policies and procedures that apply to the organization's reward and recognition system. Compensation specialists can help in the design of the system to ensure that the desired behaviors are the ones the rewards encourage. They also can help in the establishment of clear measures and criteria for rewards and recognition. Accounting personnel can help ensure that Internal Revenue guidelines are incorporated in the reward system's design, administration, and record keeping.

Two critical components of reward systems are measurement and feedback. Employees must believe that they are able to affect and control the results that are measured. If their ability to achieve awards is beyond their control, regardless of effort or quality of performance, the incentive or reward program will not achieve the desired results. Instead, it will demotivate and demoralize employees.

Regardless of when formal rewards are given, employees need regular feedback about their performance and progress. Whenever possible, feedback mechanisms should be incorporated in the employees' actual work. In this way, employees can measure how they are performing against the standard. If employees cannot get feedback directly from their work, they should receive it daily, weekly, or monthly from management. Feedback that only occurs quarterly or annually will have little lasting impact on employee behavior.

Another component of the reward plan that should be considered at the development stage is its duration. If possible, the plan should be designed with a start and end date. No matter how well incentives are conceived, they seem to lose their impact over a period of time.

• Drawbacks to the Reward System

Self-managed team implementation does not necessarily have to include a reward system component. If teams are well designed, they will bring a level of satisfaction to employees that cannot be brought by rewards or recognition. As mentioned earlier, the intrinsic reward that employees get from being able to control their work, make decisions, and expand their knowledge and influence makes serving on a self-managed work team reward in itself. Employees on well-designed teams do not need to be bribed with incentives or other rewards to stimulate their interest and enthusiasm or to obtain their commitment.

In fact, sometimes rewards can send the wrong message. For example, the fact that the organization has to give rewards to do the work could be interpreted to mean that the work is so tedious, boring, and dirty that no one would do it without a bribe. On the other hand, the organization could be saying that it has to move quickly from one set of behaviors to another and knows that the quickest way to gain the attention of its many different types of employees is through rewards and incentives.

Additionally, reward systems do not always produce the desired results. They may motivate employees to work only to get the reward and then to slack off once they have received it. In some cases, rewards can create a competitive situation in which a few employees win, many employees lose, and in the end both the organization and its customers lose. This could be particularly harmful in health care. Inadvertently, the team could end up compromising the quality of patient care in its scramble to earn the reward for achieving cost reduction and productivity goals.

The trouble with rewards is that they do not alter the way employees really feel about the work they do; instead, they only create temporary changes in the way employees behave. When the rewards are gone or no longer are meaningful, employees can easily revert to behavior they either prefer or feel is more natural. "[Rewards] do not generally alter the attitudes and emotional commitments that underlie our behaviors."[8] Thus, they may change what we do but not how we think.

• Conclusion

A reward system can be an important component of the self-managed team implementation plan. It can establish rewards and incentives that will help to focus employee attention on the new way of working and to generate rapid compliance to a new set of behaviors. Organizations can use cash rewards, noncash rewards, and recognition programs to encourage and motivate team performance and to change team behavior. In health care, organizations have used incentive bonuses to encourage team implementation, as well as to reward both teams and individuals for achievements.

When implementing a reward system, it is important to involve the employees in its design. Professionals from the compensation and accounting fields also should be involved to ensure that the reward system will achieve the desired results. In addition, consideration should be given to establishing start and end dates for reward plans because they do not always have a lasting impact.

Although a reward system can be useful, it is not essential to team implementation. Many employees derive much satisfaction from simply being on a self-managed work team. They enjoy the opportunity offered by the team setting to learn, make decisions, and control aspects of their work environment. In this case, a reward system that recognizes team identity through team names, T-shirts, and slogans can enhance employee pleasure and satisfaction and provide all the encouragement employees need to do their best for the organization and for themselves.

References

1. Kohn, A. *Punished by Rewards: The Trouble with Gold Stars, Incentive Plans, A's, Praise, and Other Bribes.* Boston: Houghton Mifflin, 1993, p. 4.

2. Kohn, pp. 120-26.

3. Telephone interview with William B. Newkirk, coordinator of education and development, Alliant Health System, Louisville, KY, Aug. 13, 1993.

4. A proposal for self-managed work teams and incentive pay in the housekeeping department, prepared by the housekeeping department, Memorial Mission Hospital, Asheville, NC, Aug. 26, 1992.

5. Team performance records—1993, the housekeeping department, Memorial Mission Hospital, Asheville, NC.

6. Orsburn, J., Moran, L., Musslewhite, E., and Zenger, J. *Self-Directed Work Teams: The New American Challenge.* Homewood, IL: Business One Irwin, 1990, pp. 303-4.

7. Kohn, pp. 108-9.

8. Kohn, p. 41.

Part Five

Making Self-Managed Teams Work

Chapter 15

Readiness Assessment

The *readiness assessment* is a tool that the organization or any of its departments can use to determine how well it is positioned for the implementation of self-managed work teams. After administering the assessment, the organization may decide to delay its move toward self-management, implement it slowly, or move forward aggressively. Whether done by an individual department or organizationwide, conducting a readiness assessment before plunging into the implementation process can help avoid a time- and resource-consuming mistake.

This chapter outlines the components of a readiness assessment and describes how they work. It also discusses how and when a readiness assessment should be administered.

- ## Components of the Assessment

The readiness assessment consists of questions that will help management define which aspects of the organization's culture and practices will support employee involvement and participation. Additionally, it determines the degree to which current management opinion is accepting of greater employee participation, looks at resource availability, and helps highlight influences that will be brought to bear by external pressures and practices.

The questions of the readiness assessment are divided into four basic categories. These are:

- The internal environment
- Management readiness
- Resource availability
- The external environment

Each category has a bearing on whether the organization should implement self-managed work teams. See figure 15-1 for a sample self-managed teams readiness assessment.

Internal Environment

This category comprises two sections of questions—those dealing with organizational change and those concerning organizational culture. These sections evaluate the organization in terms of existing barriers to team implementation and current participative practices. They also help identify past events or experiences that might either impede or accelerate the organization's readiness to implement the change to self-management. Additionally, these sections draw attention to stressors or changes that may have an impact on the attention and resources that the organization can devote to self-management both now and in the future.

Management Readiness

This category of questions stands out as the most important determinant in the organization's decision to implement teams. If management does not support the change, resources will not be available, managers will not model the behaviors they want employees to exhibit, employees will not be allowed to participate in training, and the systems that need to change to support self-management will not be modified. In other words, team implementation will not succeed.

A number of factors may predispose managers against or for self-management. Some managers may not fully understand the concept of empowerment and consequently fear that it will lead to *no control* and an environment of complete chaos. Others, particularly those who are graduates of the command–control school of management (see chapter 6), may hold unswerving values and beliefs that inhibit their ability to share supervisory responsibilities such as decision making and problem solving. Still others may have had an unfortunate prior experience with heightened employee participation—for example, a suggestion system that was a total flop. On the other hand, many managers have had positive experiences with employee participation and have witnessed firsthand the benefits that teamwork can offer the organization. Other managers may support the concept simply because they understand it and believe the organization needs to find new ways of doing business.

Whatever the managers' experiences, values, and beliefs, it is important that they be understood and assessed in terms of their possible impact on the success of self-managed team implementation. The readiness assessment also can prove helpful in revealing where managers need to broaden their knowledge and experience. For example, it can suggest that providing

Figure 15-1. The Self-Managed Teams Readiness Assessment

This questionnaire has been developed to help determine the degree to which your organization is ready to implement self-management.

Instructions: Complete each question by circling the number of the answer that most closely reflects the situation within your organization, department, unit, or section. After answering all the questions, total the points on the answer sheet.

I. **Internal Environment** (71 possible points)

  A. *Organizational Change*

   1. How many changes that affect the whole organization have been implemented within the past three years?

      (1) None   (2) 1-2   (3) 3 or more

   2. To what degree do you see change as a normal part of doing business today?

      (1) Limited   (2) Moderate   (3) High

   3. How many organizationwide changes do you anticipate implementing in the next two years (other than self-management)?

      (1) None   (2) 3-5   (3) 1-2

   4. To what degree has change been accepted by management in the past?

      (1) Limited   (2) Moderate   (3) High

   5. To what degree has change been accepted by employees in the past?

      (1) Limited   (2) Moderate   (3) High

   6. To what degree has the organization been committed to change in the past?

      (1) Changes were abandoned early.
      (2) Changes were treated as fads, implemented, and quickly discarded.
      (3) Changes have received strong organizational commitment.

   7. Have there been any organizational structure changes within the past five years? (If no, skip question 8.)

      (1) No
      (2) Yes

   8. Did the organizational structure change include any of the following?

      (1) Increase in management layers or numbers
      (2) Addition of a total quality management or quality improvement department/function
      (3) Implementation of a matrix or product-oriented organizational structure
      (4) Flattening of the organizational hierarchy

   9. To what degree is the organization involved in planning for and implementing change organizationwide?

      (1) Only top management is involved.
      (2) Top management and a few selected others are involved.
      (3) All layers of management are involved.
      (4) Employees at all levels are involved.

(Continued on next page)

Figure 15-1. (Continued)

B. *Organizational Culture*

10. To what extent is your organization's culture participative?

    (1) Top-level managers make all the long-range, mid-range, and short-term decisions.
    (2) Mid-level managers make most of the short-term decisions.
    (3) Committees, task forces, cross-functional teams and focus groups solve problems, develop proposals, and provide input into decisions.
    (4) Employees are able to make decisions about their own work without higher levels of approval.

11. To what degree is management respected and trusted?

    (1) Employees believe that management will take advantage of them when given the opportunity.
    (2) There have been recent employee layoffs.
    (3) Management seems genuinely interested in employees, and has implemented improvements in the work environment within the past 12 months.
    (4) Employees and managers believe that they have the same goals and work together as a team to achieve them.

12. What is the organization's relationship with its labor union(s)?

    (1) There are frequent grievances and threats of strikes.
    (2) The union does not participate on any management committees or in any organizational decisions.
    (3) Management and the union have worked together in the past to implement positive changes in the work environment.
    (4) The union is seen as a partner with management.

13. To what degree would the employees be willing to work in teams?

    (1) Limited   (2) Moderate   (3) High

14. How important is the customer to the organization?

    (1) There are no consequences for disregarding customer needs and expectations.
    (2) Customer relations are handled by a few specially trained employees.
    (3) Strategic and operational planning are focused on meeting the needs of customers.
    (4) Employees see positive customer relations as their first priority and are empowered to take action to meet the needs of customers.

15. To what degree does your organization emphasize employee involvement?

    (1) Employees are not involved in decision making, problem solving, or planning for the future.
    (2) Employees serve on task forces, focus groups, and committees to provide input into decisions.
    (3) Employees routinely participate in the decision-making process, future planning, and problem solving.
    (4) Employees make the decisions, solve the problems, and plan for the future in areas that directly affect their own work.

16. To what extent does your organization emphasize employee training and development?

    (1) Employees participate in 4 or fewer hours of training a year.
    (2) Employees participate in 5 to 8 hours of training a year.
    (3) Employees participate in 9 to 12 hours of training a year.
    (4) Employees participate in more than 12 hours of training a year.

Figure 15-1. (Continued)

17. To what degree are the organizational rewards focused on individual rather than team performance?

    (1) The compensation system is based on individual merit.
    (2) Recognition programs and bonuses are available for individual but not team accomplishment.
    (3) The recognition system focuses on team accomplishment.
    (4) Compensation, rewards, and recognition are based, at least in part, on team effort.

18. To what extent has the organization embraced the concepts of total quality management?

    (1) The organization has not begun to implement total quality management.
    (2) Total quality management is implemented in a few areas of the organization.
    (3) Total quality management is implemented in the majority of the organization.
    (4) Total quality management concepts are practiced throughout the organization.

19. What is the ratio of managers to staff?

    (1) 1 manager for every 5 employees
    (2) 1 manager for every 10 employees
    (3) 1 manager for every 15 employees
    (4) 1 manager for every 20 employees or more

20. To what degree does the organization feel pressure to take drastic action to implement change?

    (1) The organization feels no need to change.
    (2) The organization believes that employee involvement is a fad that will fade away before it has to be dealt with.
    (3) The organization believes that change is necessary but is willing to let it happen in a piecemeal manner.
    (4) The organization believes it will not survive if it does not implement planned change now.

II. **Management Readiness** (15 possible points)

21. To what degree does top management function as a team?

    (1) Limited   (2) Moderate   (3) High

22. To what degree does management respect the talent and abilities of the employees?

    (1) Limited   (2) Moderate   (3) High

23. To what degree does management perceive the work of the organization to be interdependent?

    (1) Limited   (2) Moderate   (3) High

24. How willing is management to revise its role and share responsibility with employees?

    (1) Limited   (2) Moderate   (3) High

25. How willing is management to support the team concept with resources?

    (1) Limited   (2) Moderate   (3) High

(Continued on next page)

Figure 15-1. (Continued)

III. **Resource Availability** (15 possible points)

26. To what degree is training staff available within the organization?

    (1) Limited	(2) Moderate	(3) High

27. To what degree is meeting and/or training space available to teams?

    (1) Limited	(2) Moderate	(3) High

28. To what degree is information on customers and team performance available to share with staff?

    (1) Limited	(2) Moderate	(3) High

29. To what degree is the organization in a sound financial position?

    (1) Limited	(2) Moderate	(3) High

30. To what degree can time and money be made available for team member training?

    (1) Limited	(2) Moderate	(3) High

IV. **External Environment** (15 possible points)

31. To what degree does the board of directors endorse the concept of teams?

    (1) Limited	(2) Moderate	(3) High

32. To what degree will physicians be willing to work on and with teams?

    (1) Limited	(2) Moderate	(3) High

33. To what degree have area businesses implemented self-managed teams?

    (1) Limited	(2) Moderate	(3) High

34. To what degree are important suppliers interested in forming partnerships with the organization?

    (1) Limited	(2) Moderate	(3) High

35. To what degree are the employees exposed to team concepts through affiliations outside work?

    (1) Limited	(2) Moderate	(3) High

Scoring: Total the points of the numbers you circled as answers for each question. Review the comments in the category that your score places you.

76–116 points: The likelihood of teams succeeding in your organization is high. In fact, there may already be areas that are functioning as self-managed teams.

51–75 points: You are moving slowly toward increased employee involvement. It is possible to start implementing self-managed teams, but go slowly and use a pilot department.

35–50 points: Your organization is not ready for teams. Implement some intermediate opportunities for increased employee participation. Try the assessment again in a year.

managers with case study examples and encouraging them to make site visits will help demonstrate the value of self-management and begin the process of creating management readiness for change.

Resource Availability

This short section of the readiness assessment deals with resources in the areas of training, consulting, information provision, finances, and space and personnel. The results of this section let the organization know whether it can implement self-managed work teams slowly, rapidly, or not at all without stringent reallocation of funds.

External Environment

External environment refers to the environment surrounding the organization. It encompasses the region and the business community in which the organization is located, the board of directors, and the physicians (if the organization is a hospital). The external environment may be so conservative and restrictive that the concepts of employee empowerment and self-management simply do not exist outside the pages of business magazines and journals.

On the other hand, the community or region in which the health care organization is located may offer a number of examples of businesses in which self-managed teams are flourishing. Some members of the board of directors may even be in the process of implementing self-managed work teams in their private businesses. The board also may have on it managers who have considered and rejected the self-managed concept.

In hospitals, physicians have considerable influence over any change in which nurses and other health care professionals are directly involved. If the employees decide that they are opposed to self-management, they may be able to persuade physicians to side with them against management. On the other hand, if management is dragging its feet and appears to be unwilling to permit self-management to the extent that the employees desire, the employees may appeal to the physicians to become advocates of the change. Thus, the employees may have the potential to actually subvert the organizational chain of command in order to solicit support and endorsement for self-management.

• Administration of the Assessment

If the majority and the most influential members of top management are totally opposed to self-management, it would be better to postpone administration of the readiness assessment. The mere administration of this questionnaire is enough to develop the expectation among lower-level managers and employees that change is being considered and may be likely. Consequently, if the organization decides not to implement self-managed teams, even when the results point toward the concept's acceptance, it will have to deal with considerable unrest, discord, and unproductive behavior.

However, if top management appears to be receptive to the concept, the readiness assessment should be conducted. Often a management willingness to consider the concept comes from having learned about it through books, articles, and, if possible, site visits.

The readiness assessment has several uses. First, it can be administered to senior and middle management to determine organizational readiness. Second, it can be used as a discussion guide rather than a questionnaire. When it is used as a discussion guide, senior management walks through each category and performs its own assessment of organizational readiness, trying to build consensus on the answer that is correct for the organization. And third, the readiness assessment can be used by a group of employees or middle managers who wish to ascertain the roadblocks to self-management before proposing it for their departments.

The readiness assessment is helpful in identifying areas of strength, weakness, or resistance to self-management that need to be highlighted or addressed before implementation is attempted. Some of the questions on the assessment will require research; others can be answered based on the opinions of the respondents.

• Conclusion

The readiness assessment is a tool that the organization, as well as individual departments within the organization, can use to determine the extent to which it is ready to make the change to self-managed work teams. It contains questions that can be used to assess the organization's feelings about self-management in four important areas: the internal environment (organizational change and culture), management readiness, resource availability, and the external environment. If used early on, this tool can save the organization both time and money.

If it is known from the outset that key senior managers are against the self-management concept, administration of the readiness assessment should be postponed until these managers have the opportunity to learn more about it. However, if several top-level managers have expressed an interest in the concept, administration of the readiness assessment may provide the incentive for them to learn more about the concept and to explore the possibility of its implementation. Additionally, the readiness assessment can be used to identify specific roadblocks to team implementation.

Chapter 16
Change Management

When health care organizations are ready to implement self-managed work teams, they are looking at a change of immense proportions. In order to ensure a smooth and effective transition, the change to self-management must be managed carefully. Change management involves developing a vision of the changed organization, implementing that vision within the organization, and successfully managing the human reactions to the change brought about by the implementation process. Thus, making the vision reality requires a well-thought-out change strategy.

The degree of difficulty the organization will have in implementing change depends in large part on its history and culture. Some health care organizations have not changed appreciably since they were created 50 to 100 years ago. They may have renovated or built buildings and added or changed technology but not changed their structure, values, or work systems. For example, some health care organizations still resist the customer concept; others have yet to explore and implement TQM; and still others have not restructured to support their major products or services. Consequently, change within these organizations will be strongly resisted, and when it does occur, it will occur slowly and deliberately.

On the other hand, some health care organizations have created a culture that is open to change and will accept it enthusiastically. These organizations see themselves in the forefront of modern thinking in areas such as clinical practice, technology, organizational restructuring, customer and product focus, employee involvement, total quality management, patient-centered care, and so on. Their environments all but crackle with energy and movement, and promise the ready implementation of almost any change initiative.

The size of the organization also is an important factor to consider when undertaking a change initiative. For example, an organization of 100 employees all located in one building will implement the change to self-management within a relatively short time frame, whereas an organization of several thousand employees located at different physical sites will require more time and resources.

This chapter discusses some of the different barriers that health care organizations are likely to encounter as they make the change to self-management. It also describes two change strategies, one at the organizational level and one at the individual level, that the organization should consider as it attempts to manage the change process.

• Barriers to Change Management

There is only one real reason why an organization should go through the turmoil of implementing a major change—to ensure its future. If management does not see the change to self-managed work teams as necessary to help achieve efficiencies and levels of performance that will provide organizational longevity, the change should not be attempted. Thus, to want to break down the barriers to self-management and invest the time and effort required, the organization must view the change as a compelling business necessity.

Every organization has within it barriers to change. The most common barriers and those most likely to have the greatest impact on the change process are the organization's managers, supervisors, systems, and unions.

Managers

Organizations must rely on their managers to lead the change effort; however, surprisingly, even when managers see the necessity for change, they often are the ones who most resist it. The principal reason for their resistance is that, of all the groups within the organization, it is the managers who have the greatest investment in maintaining the status quo. They are the ones who created the top-down structure, having been taught that it represents *the* right and best way to manage an organization. Their lifetime of experience has been in top-down organizations. They are competent within this hierarchical structure and have received rewards based on their positions within it.

Supervisors

Supervisors make up another group that resists the change to self-management and thus presents a major barrier to team implementation. As supervisors learn more about self-managed work teams, they may begin to view their positions as redundant in an organizational structure that allows teams to perform supervisory responsibilities. Their resistance to the change stems from the need to maintain job security. It is difficult for supervisors to think about what might be best for the organization when they are faced with possible unemployment.

If the organization can assure supervisors that they will not be released from employment as a result of the change to self-managed work teams, the supervisors will prove to be a major help in the change process. They can be used to interpret the change to employees, handle questions as they arise, and reinforce the positive aspects of the change.

Organizational Systems

Every organization develops systems, policies, and procedures that enable it to do its work. These systems may be formal (documented in writing) and/or informal (based on the traditional way of doing things). Among the systems that must change when self-managed work teams are implemented are the ways that work flows, departments relate to each other, decisions are made, compensation is determined, communication occurs, planning and budgeting are done, and information is provided.

These systems were designed to support individual work and a hierarchy of management-level decision makers. When an organization moves in the direction of teams, the hierarchy loses its importance and the need for individual work is greatly diminished. Because systems define roles and methods for getting the work of the organization done, they will be a major barrier to the change to self-management if they are not modified.

Unions

Unions are another possible barrier to team implementation, principally because they frequently see its disadvantages before they see its advantages. Unions will identify the expanded job responsibilities of employees and no increase in pay as a disadvantage to their membership. Union leaders, like managers in health care, may be skeptical about empowerment. They may find it difficult to understand that increased responsibility brings increased job satisfaction. However, those unions that may have had experience in health care organizations that have not changed and have witnessed layoffs and shutdowns may see the advantages of innovation and be more receptive to the idea of self-managed work teams.

Traditionally, the role of the union is to listen to employees to get them what they want, which often is more involvement in decision making and a greater role in determining their own destiny. If employees perceive that self-management will provide them a better way of doing their work, unions will not oppose the change.

From this review of the barriers to change, it may seem daunting to undertake a change of the magnitude of self-managed teams. However, self-management has been implemented successfully in a number of organizations throughout the United States. The key to successful implementation lies in the effective management of the human reactions to change.

- **Change Management at the Organizational Level**

To manage change at the organizational level, several key elements of human reaction and interaction must be considered. These elements can help the organization overcome the barriers to change and can provide a strategy for incorporating the human reaction to change (from senior managers to supervisors to employees) into improved motivation for change. These key elements, discussed in more detail in the following subsections, are:

- Communicate the vision for the future.
- Describe the benefits of the change.
- Obtain management commitment.
- Appreciate the past.
- Provide time for human nature.
- Listen.
- Involve others.

To be effective at the organizational level, the change must be led by the chief executive officer (CEO) or some other member of senior management.

Communicate the Vision for the Future

As mentioned previously, senior management must perceive a clear business necessity for implementing a change as comprehensive as that of self-managed teams. The organization does not have to be in financial difficulty, but management must either anticipate problems or see the opportunity to greatly improve performance in order to justify subjecting the organization to the stress of a major change.

To develop a vision for the future, senior managers must meet to discuss the impact on the organization of changes that are occurring in the external environment and to work out a strategic response. Senior manager interaction and involvement are critical at this stage. If senior managers do not invest the necessary time and thought, they will not consider all the possible alternatives for and against the strategy. They will not develop a position and gain commitment to it.

The unions also should be involved at this stage. Union leadership needs to understand the risks that senior management perceives, the forces in the external environment that are creating turmoil, and the struggles that management has gone through to arrive at a strategy that will create the need for self-managed work teams. Additionally, it is important to give union leaders equal opportunity to participate in developing the vision before it is shared with employees. Besides flattering their egos, it will allow them to exert some level of control, to identify and eliminate potential senior management errors, and to develop their own commitment to the vision.

Once senior management and union leadership have assessed the situation, discussed the impact of the change, and explored alternatives, they will have agreed on a strategy and a vision they can both understand and support. It is at this point that mid-level management needs to be involved.

An effective method for involving middle managers is to hold a series of focus groups to discuss the vision and get their reactions to it. The focus groups give middle managers the opportunity to learn more about the vision, air their objections, and learn how its implementation can and cannot be modified.

Once middle managers are involved, the vision should be communicated extensively throughout the organization—at board meetings, senior management meetings, and meetings with business leaders, middle managers, and employees. It should be written about in employee newsletters and discussed at special events and on ceremonial occasions. Repetition over a relatively short period of time will help bring the vision to life. People within the organization will start adapting to the vision before it becomes reality.

When management begins to communicate the vision throughout the organization, it needs to invest time and thought into how the vision is worded. The vision will not be motivating if it is mundane and pragmatic. For example, the following approach is unlikely to rally much support:

> If we cut back on our management positions and implement self-managed teams, and if everyone works harder, I can see another 2 percent at the bottom line by this time next year.

Instead, the vision needs to be expressed on the levels of ideas, emotions, and beliefs. It must provide a dream for the future. Following is an example of a vision that could inspire all levels of the organization to climb on the bandwagon:

> I see great opportunities for our organization during this period of health care reform. We can help our entire community achieve better health at lower cost. At the same time, we can make changes that will benefit you. We can create a work environment in which you will have more control over your work and increased opportunities to try your own ideas. This will be an exciting period of change and I am looking forward to working through it with you.

Describe the Benefits of the Change

Another element of the organizational change strategy is that of developing an understanding of the benefits the change will bring. From the outset, employees and managers alike will want to know the benefits of the change in both business terms (how the change will help the organization) and personal terms (how the change will help them). It would be a mistake to think that employees are not interested in the business reasons for the change. Generally, they want to believe and want proof that the change is not merely a management whim. If they can believe that the organization will prosper because of the change or that the organization needs to make the change in order to survive, they will be much more likely to accept it.

Additionally, managers at all levels of the organization need to understand the benefits of the change so that they can discuss them with their employees. However, when discussing the change, managers will need to deal with aspects that cannot be described as beneficial. Most changes have a downside, and managers must be able to listen with empathy when employees express their perception of the negative side of the upcoming change. However, regardless of the downside, acceptance will come with time. Thus, repetition of the vision and its benefits should continue until everyone has heard them numerous times.

Obtain Management Commitment

As mentioned earlier, although managers may understand the benefits of the change, they may not always be committed to the vision. In order for the change process to move forward with the least disruption, management commitment must be obtained. It is relatively easy to categorize managers' reactions and commitment by observing their behavior and seeing where they fit on the management commitment quadrant (see figure 16-1).

The management commitment quadrant illustrates four responses to change. Expectations for management behavior should be very clear; otherwise, the behaviors in support of change will not be as uniform as senior management might expect. For example, if managers are expected to actively advocate the change, that expectation needs to be stated. Otherwise, some managers will say, "I suppose it's a good idea" and others will merely suggest that employees attend meetings and make up their own minds. The result of unclear expectations will be a much slower implementation of change as well as confusion among employees and managers alike.

Middle managers who fall into the quadrant "Let It Happen" are making a strong statement that they do not support the change. They tend to believe they are fulfilling their responsibility as leaders by doing nothing either in support of or against the change. In some cases, they may see the change as coming from the top and expect senior management to do all the work necessary to support it. In other cases, their apathy may be the result of a past experience in which they actively supported a senior management change that died an early death and now do not want to risk losing face with their employees when the new change fails. However, regardless of the reason for their cynicism, "Let It Happen" is not an acceptable management response.

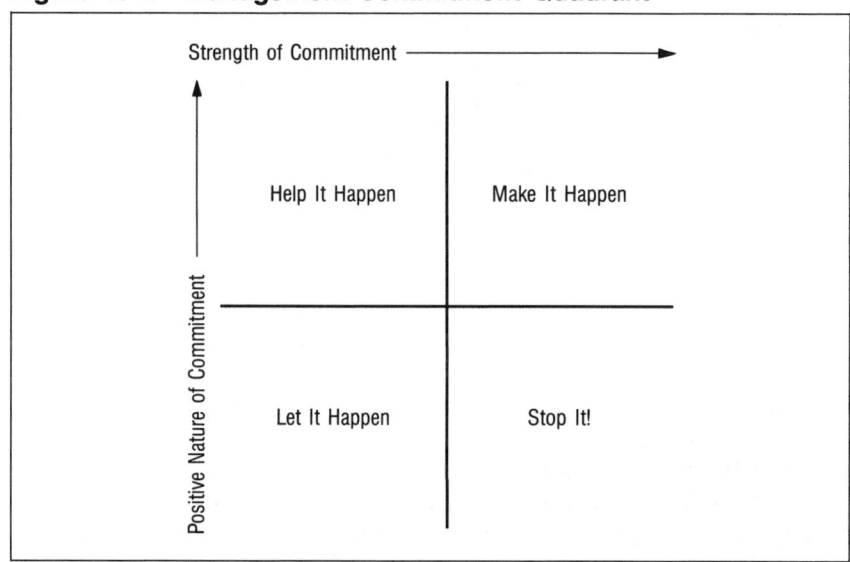

Figure 16-1. Management Commitment Quadrant

```
                  Strength of Commitment ──────────▶
                          ▲
                          │
          Help It Happen  │  Make It Happen
                          │
   ───────────────────────┼───────────────────────
                          │
          Let It Happen   │  Stop It!
                          │
   Positive Nature of Commitment
```

Managers who fall into the "Stop It!" quadrant are making a career-limiting move. They may find that they are not included in new organizational structures as managers or that dormant performance problems surface and become the justification for their discharge from employment. They may take the view that they are martyrs who must sacrifice themselves in order to draw attention to problems with the change, problems that no one else but they perceive. Some managers may be merely obstinate whereas others may be truly unable to see the benefits of the change. Regardless of their reason for working against the change, their actions must be stopped immediately. These managers should have expressed their concerns when they had an involvement opportunity, for example, during a management focus group meeting.

In addition, the employees working under these managers recognize their lack of active support as opposition to the change. They see their managers as apathetic and uncommitted.

Ideally, all managers will fall in the two quadrants "Help It Happen" and "Make It Happen." It is in these quadrants that enthusiasm, interest, and involvement are generated. These managers will fulfill their leadership role by providing an inspirational vision and helping lead the change to self-management.

Appreciate the Past

It is not unusual for employees to react to the future by clinging even more tightly to the past. When managers talk about the future, they have a tendency to forget the important accomplishments of the past. Although it is a mistake to get bogged down in the past, it is equally detrimental to a change effort to ignore past achievements. All employees, except those just hired, have memories of past successes within the organization. Some may have spent a lot of time and effort to produce policies and practices that will have to be modified when the change to self-management occurs. Others may have worked hard to be promoted to supervisor, only to have their hard-won position eliminated by the change.

The past has provided both good and bad experiences for employees and, when possible, should be evoked when communicating about the future. For example, communication might acknowledge how far the organization has come and recognize significant milestones, hurdles, and heroes of the past. Communication also should include reference to the present, describing the difficult situation the organization is facing before discussing the organization's aspirations for the future.

To refer to the past and present in a discussion of the future includes employees in the organization's transition. If communication of the change merely addresses the future, employees frequently are left feeling disconnected. It is more difficult for them to move forward. They need to be tied into the discussion by a reference to a period of the organization's history in which they have played a role.

Provide Time for Human Nature

Few employees are able to welcome all change with open arms. It is only human nature to resist change, especially when it is imposed by someone else. Whenever possible, change should be discussed long before it is put into practice. Employees faced with change often go through a sequence of reaction stages similar to the Kubler-Ross stages of death and dying (see figure 16-2). Following are four of these stages:

1. *Denial:* Employees really do not expect that change will ever occur or that it will ever affect them. They will not begin to accept the change as long as they are denying it. To help employees get through this stage, management needs to continue to repeat the message about the change, as well as to provide a timetable for it.
2. *Anger:* At this stage, employees tend to feel the change is unfair and unnecessary. They believe management is about to make its biggest mistake ever, and they are willing to express their anger to whomever will listen. At this stage, management needs to listen with empathy, and reiterate the reasons for and benefits of the change.
3. *Acceptance:* Denial and anger are followed by acceptance that change is inevitable. At this stage, many employees are beginning to understand why the change must be made, although they still may not necessarily

Change Management 203

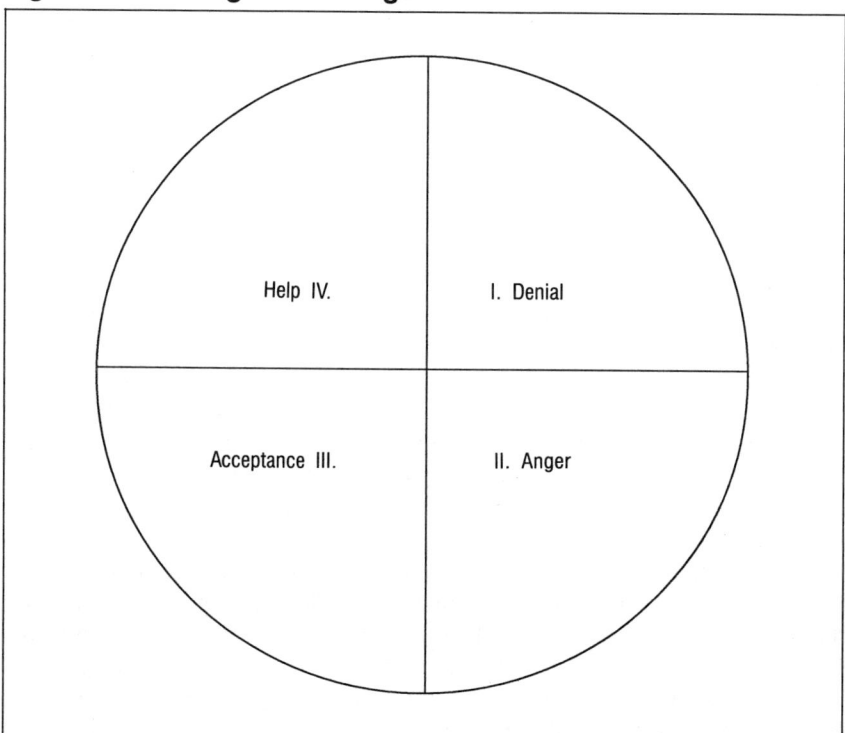

Figure 16-2. Stages of Change

```
          Help IV.  |  I. Denial
        ------------+-------------
       Acceptance III. | II. Anger
```

be happy about it. They have reached a level of comfort with the idea, and now may be seeking more information about the change and how it will affect them.

4. *Help:* At this stage, employees want to be involved in the change process. They may even identify ways to implement it to make it more effective.

Throughout all these stages, managers need to take certain actions to ensure a clean transition: They need to listen to the employees and provide them opportunities for involvement.

Listen

This element of managing change at the organizational level is extremely important. The respect that managers show for employees and their concerns reassures employees about the sincerity of management's commitment to their well-being. When managers can listen and express empathy, they are cementing the manager–employee relationship and showing employees that they are valued.

However, some managers make the mistake of trying to find justifications for the change that will counterbalance criticisms voiced by the employees. If managers were *really* listening, they would be able to incorporate employee criticism into means of modifying the change to make it work better. Employees are likely to see the change from a different perspective than managers and may be in a position to identify opportunities for improvement.

Involve Others

It is at this stage of change management that employees are given some control over the change and how it will affect them. When self-managed work teams are implemented, employees frequently are asked to participate on the design team for their area. The mere fact that there is a design team means that employees cannot reverse the organization's decision to implement teams; however, through their participation on the design team, employees can ensure that they have a say in how teams are structured within their work environment.

Moreover, employees who become involved in the change process have the opportunity to learn more about the benefits and complexities of the change, as well as about aspects of the change they may not have envisioned. The more they learn about the change, the less apprehensive they are. In this final element of change management, employees often begin to offer suggestions on how to make the change work, as well as to actively facilitate the process by performing needed tasks and talking to others.

• Change Management at the Individual Level

Change management also must occur at the individual level. Strategies that are effective at the organizational level have a different meaning and a different impact when they are implemented one-on-one between employee and supervisor. Frequently, supervisors know less about details of the change and more about individual employee reactions to it. Supervisors are the ones who have to deal with the cynicism that employees are unwilling to express to senior management. They have to deal with hundreds of questions concerning the impact of the change and to listen to sometimes bitter expressions of anger and betrayal that may never be voiced at the organizational level.

However, not all employees respond to change negatively. Some like change and immediately look at its positive aspects. Usually, these employees do not consume time and energy in a change management situation. The employees who do need time and attention fall into one of the following categories:

- Those who have lost status, power, or prestige. They may feel angry, resigned, or betrayed by the change.
- Those who view themselves as victims of a work world beyond their control. Feeling unable to do anything about the change, they lose whatever interest or enthusiasm they had in their work. They may feel angry or resigned.
- Those who feel confused and unsure. They see their world changing around them, and need reassurance and information to help them weather the change.

Employees Who Have Lost Status

When employees lose status, power, or authority in a change process, their top concern will be job security. They will want to know immediately whether the change will affect their employment, pay, and/or job title. They wonder what they will tell their spouse, family, or parents. They wonder how they will face their coworkers. Sometimes they see the change as a personal failure that perhaps they could have avoided.

Employee reaction might range from anger to sadness to no public reaction at all. Those who do not appear to react may be in a temporarily frozen emotional state. Regardless of the way they express their reactions, employees need time to adjust to the change, as well as the attention and respect of their supervisors and coworkers, to help them come through it in a positive manner.

Supervisors and managers, too, will find themselves in the position of having lost status, power, or authority as a result of the change to self-management. When they have lost in any of these important areas, the first thing they need from their own supervisor is reassurance that they have not lost even more (for example, their job). When providing reassurance, the supervisor should be as specific as possible. For example: "Beginning next Monday, at 9:00 a.m. you will be in training to become a team facilitator." The supervisor should not be wishy-washy and say: "I'm sure there will be something for you to do around here, I just don't know what it is."

Employees Who Are Victims

Employees who view themselves as victims of the change process are likely to become angry or sometimes withdrawn. Those who withdraw are the ones who are the most difficult to work with. They probably have reached a point in their careers at which they have experienced one too many changes. They no longer accept the argument that "this change will be good for you"; they no longer care.

Employees who have withdrawn do not talk about their feelings. They do not give supervisors the opportunity to listen with empathy or to discuss the benefits of the change. They silently go back to work. Some supervisors welcome this employee reaction because it requires less time and attention and is less emotional. However, employees who withdraw during a period of change are the same ones who stop offering ideas for improvement and stop doing the extra things that keep customers satisfied. These employees are likely to produce less work and work of lower quality. They are the organization's so-called walking wounded and become detrimental to overall organizational effectiveness and employee morale.

Supervisors attempting to deal with employees who have withdrawn first need to give them time and space — time for quiet reflection and contemplation and to observe how other employees are reacting to the change, and space to protect them from the well-meaning employees who are 100 percent sold on the change and who want to share their enthusiasm with everyone.

After an appropriate period, supervisors then need to talk to the employees in order to discover how they see the past, present, and future. Once supervisors really listen and discover what is happening in the change process that is causing the employees to withdraw, they may be able to help the employees move forward. For example, supervisors may find out that the employees fear they will be giving up something they value. As a result, the supervisors can help the employees identify benefits they might derive from the change as well as opportunities that might come their way to take control of their work environment.

By helping employees look toward the change instead of away from it, supervisors can start them on the path of acceptance. Eventually, employees may even help make the change work for their department or section.

Employees Who Are Confused

Employees in this group do not know how they fit in; they cannot imagine what their workday will be like in the new environment. They want to know specifics about how the change will affect them, what they will be doing differently tomorrow, how the work area will change, and so on. They have a lot of questions and want them all answered at once. The best help that supervisors can provide to employees who feel they have lost their footing is to give them as much information as they can. Once the employees build back the details of their life, they will regain their comfort. These employees are less concerned with what they will lose or gain; instead, they need to know what will replace those things that will no longer exist.

• Conclusion

Organizations must change in order to perpetuate themselves into the future. In some cases, change can energize the organization and open the door to new opportunities. In other cases, it can throw the organization into turmoil, regardless of how well managed the change process is.

Managing change is a complex undertaking. It involves looking at needs from both organizational and personal perspectives. Change at the organizational level encompasses changes in systems, structures, behaviors, and work styles. Change at the individual level involves dealing with human feelings, helping employees say good-bye to the past and find reasons to welcome the future. It is at this level that supervisors can play a particularly vital role in the change process, working one-on-one with employees and taking their individual fears and needs into consideration as they help them learn to accept the change.

When developing the strategy for change implementation, the leaders of the organization must consider barriers they are likely to encounter. It may come as a surprise to managers that they frequently are the greatest barrier to change within the organization. Supervisors, organizational systems, and unions also present major barriers to change.

There is no one best prescription for change management because every organizational culture is different. For example, some organizations are more conservative and slower to change than others. Some employees are more accepting of change than others. However, regardless of the variables, the one element that is key to successful change management is extensive communication. Implementing change within an organization is a daunting process that should not be undertaken without good reason. Justification for making the transition to self-managed work teams needs to be communicated throughout the organization so that employees at all levels can feel part of the process and understand the benefits to be reaped from a change that will so thoroughly disrupt their work lives.

Chapter 17

Unsuccessful Teams

Over the course of their existence, almost all teams will experience problems as a normal part of team development. It is expected that teams will have difficulties and that problem solving will be part of their growth and continuous improvement process. However, in almost every organization that implements self-managed work teams, at least one team will fail. Unsuccessful teams have gone beyond the "problems" stage. Team members no longer are willing or able to work together. Generally, the end result is that the team either disbands and reverts to its former nonteam organizational structure, or stays together but no longer can achieve its goals.

This chapter explores some of the common reasons why teams are unsuccessful. It also identifies specific warning signs and discusses corrective actions that can be taken.

• Reasons for Team Failure

Self-managed work teams fail for a number of reasons. The causes of failure can be internal as well as external. Following are the most common reasons for team failure:

- Sabotage from within
- Insufficient training
- Insufficient time to accomplish management functions
- Failure to have regular team meetings
- Failure to have challenging goals and expectations
- No feedback on team performance
- No team leader
- Management refusal to let the team be self-managed

Although there is no guarantee that a team will not fail, being aware of the warning signs can help the organization anticipate the need for intervention and avert permanent damage to the team.

Sabotage from Within

One of the most insidious reasons for team failure is sabotage from within. This can happen when one or more team members deliberately set out to undermine or destroy the team for personal reasons. For example, they may attempt to make team performance fall below an acceptable level because they object to being "forced" to participate on the team. Or they may start a smear campaign against the team leader because they are vehemently opposed to his or her appointment. Whatever their motivation for sabotaging the team, disgruntled employees have the potential to undermine the trust that team members have for each other, their team leader, and the organization at large.

Employees who are required to participate on teams either participate willingly or resist participation. In an ideal situation, those who resist participation eventually leave the team or become active supporters of it. The problem occurs when, for whatever reason, a resistor remains on the team and tries to destroy it. This is the individual most likely to engage in sabotage.

Warning Signs

Sabotage is difficult to recognize. Unless team facilitators are very close to their team members and observe them continuously, they may not be able to identify the destructive behavior or its source until damage has already been done. Warning signs that sabotage may be afoot include a personality conflict between a team member and the team leader, an unwillingness on the part of one team member to give another team member a second chance, or continuous failure to achieve team goals, regardless of the "apparent" efforts of all team members.

Corrective Action

One way to try to identify a saboteur on the team is for the team facilitator to meet one-on-one with all team members to ask if they can help clarify what the problem is and how it might be resolved. This approach may result in one team member feeling free to speak up about actions being taken by another to undermine the team.

Another way to approach the problem of sabotage from within is to rotate team members off the team in order to change the group dynamics and diminish the power or control that the disgruntled employee has over the other team members. During that individual's absence, another team member may choose to enlighten the team leader or team facilitator, or team performance may improve enough to warrant making a permanent change in team membership.

Insufficient Training

At Hartford Memorial Hospital in Hartford, Wisconsin, one team was temporarily unsuccessful because it had not received appropriate preparation and training to assume self-management. Because the team—a nursing unit—was functioning very well as a *group* of employees, it was assumed that the transition to becoming a self-managed work team would not immediately require additional education.[1] As a result, the team floundered and was unable to function effectively. It would have failed completely without the application of needed training and skill development.

Another incident occurred at Memorial Mission Hospital in Asheville, North Carolina, when the cardiology department was transformed into a self-managed work team. The team eventually disbanded because neither team members nor management had the skills, knowledge, or training to make the team a success.

Initially, teams need training to learn why the new concept is being implemented, what the new structure and role changes will be, and what their performance expectations are. They then need to learn interpersonal skills, as well as new work skills (if they are expected to perform additional tasks) and management skills. At the beginning, the team will devote a great deal of time to training. As the team matures, training will still be needed for growth and development but will not be needed to establish team processes and skills for performing the basic functions of teams. No matter how willing or adept employees are at their jobs, they are not equipped to be a self-managed work team without training both at the outset and during the developmental stage.

Warning Signs

A number of signs indicate when training is needed. Following are some common examples:

- Team members do not know what the team purpose, goals, and performance expectations are.
- Team members do not know how to make decisions as a group.
- Team members do not know how to perform their assigned functions.
- Team members are confused about their roles on the team.
- Training records for frequency and recency of training reveal that training is not regularly scheduled and does not occur regularly.

Corrective Action

Each team should have an education plan and a skills checklist, and should receive training in a systematic manner according to a training implementation schedule. When the team has achieved a skill on the checklist, it should be marked off. Team training should not be sacrificed or postponed indefinitely because of work priorities or the team will never be able to function effectively.

Insufficient Time to Accomplish Management Functions

According to reports from the Alliant Health System in Louisville, Kentucky,[2] and Memorial Mission Hospital in Asheville, North Carolina, some of their teams disbanded because team members had no time to perform their management functions. When a self-managed work team is formed, generally the supervisor position and the 40 hours of work a week that went with it are eliminated. The responsibilities of record keeping, reporting, goal monitoring, financial management, meeting attendance, performance review, and so on are then assigned to the team members and their leader. In most instances, teams are not given staff or full-time equivalents (FTEs) to perform the management functions they have been assigned, nor are they given additional time to hold or attend meetings.

Initially, teams are excited at the opportunity to be self-managed and involved in management work. The prospect means that they will be learning new skills and working with new information. However, as they perform management functions, team members have less time to do the work of the department. Eventually, they are faced with a choice: Take care of the patients or complete the reports. Some employees start taking management work home at night to get it done. Others let the management work go, hoping that eventually they will have time to do it.

When time does not miraculously appear, performance expectations and deadlines are not met. When taking work home becomes a burden, team members lose their enthusiasm for self-management and ask to return to the former organizational structure with a designated supervisor position. Thus, the designated supervisor can take back the management duties with the team's blessing.

Warning Signs

One warning sign of this type of failure is that teams will not perform their management functions either well or on time, nor will they show signs of trying to improve. Another warning sign is that team members may begin to express their frustration with the amount of time that management work takes and voice complaints about being understaffed. Overtime may increase, and they may begin to question the value of self-management.

Corrective Action

One action that can be taken to correct this situation is to evaluate the amount of time that management work takes and provide the team with the additional staff or FTEs to accomplish it. For example, at Hartford Memorial Hospital, each team is allowed .5 FTEs for management work.[3] In nonpatient care areas of the organization, there is a greater ability to prioritize and adjust schedules so that management work can be done during regular work hours. In nursing units, particularly critical care units, there is less flexibility. Nursing teams may have the greatest need for a staffing allocation for management functions.

In patient care areas where staff are not so consumed with direct patient care duties, there may be no need to allocate additional staff time to management functions. Whatever the situation, it is important to closely monitor the work of the team and its staff and to be realistic about the time the staff needs to accomplish its management work.

Failure to Have Regular Team Meetings

One critical difference between employees working in a group and those working as a team is the work they do *together*. Employees working in the same department and seeing each other as they perform their individual functions may feel like a team; but until they actually develop goals, make decisions, and solve problems together, they are not functioning as a team.

Team members need to know and trust each other. Team rapport evolves as members meet with each other and work together on assignments. Employees who rarely see each other often become distanced, which can lead to a lack of trust and eventually to unsuccessful team performance.

When employees become comfortable with each other, commitment increases as well as trust. Regular meetings give team members the feeling of being "in this together." They learn each other's values and "hot buttons," and they improve their ability to work together efficiently and effectively.

Warning Signs

A number of behaviors signal that team members have not been meeting regularly or working together often enough. For example:

- Distrust grows among team members.
- Team members do not support each other. For example, they are unwilling to swap shifts or days off.
- Team members do not feel comfortable either asking each other for help or offering help.
- Team members apparently do not know each other. They are unable to predict their coworkers' reactions and perspectives.

Corrective Action

The most effective approach to this problem is to develop a meeting schedule and stick to it. Team members need to be provided with opportunities to work, solve problems, and make decisions together.

Failure to Have Challenging Goals and Expectations

Sometimes organizations get on the self-managed team bandwagon and implement teams without setting clear and challenging business goals for the teams to accomplish. For example, it is not uncommon for a group of employees or managers to want to implement a team in order to improve employee morale. If a team is formed solely for this reason, it is doomed to fail.

Employees working together on a team need to understand that the team was formed for an important business reason and that their efforts can accomplish an important business objective. Although enhancing work relationships is important, this sole justification for team implementation does not inspire the imagination, creativity, and commitment that learning new skills and achieving valued business goals do. Eventually, a team without challenging business goals will lose the interest and commitment of its members. Boredom and job dissatisfaction will set in, team performance will diminish, and turnover within the team may occur.

Warning Signs

Following are some of the behaviors that signal that the team lacks clear and challenging goals:

- Team members argue among themselves for no apparent reason.
- Attendance starts to drop off.
- Team members often express frustration or boredom.
- Team members begin to request transfers off the team.

Corrective Action

The most effective corrective action is to pull the team together to set new or revised goals and performance expectations. If these new goals require new employee skills and additional learning, the improvement in team performance and morale will be even greater. Although initially some team members may express dismay when given a new and challenging assignment, generally they will prefer the challenge over doing the same old thing, having no goals, and continuing a boring existence.

No Feedback on Team Performance

Self-managed work teams need feedback from their work, their customers, and the organization. Without it, team members start to question the value of their effort and commitment. Their questioning eventually will affect their performance and, if unaddressed, could cause the team to fail.

Teams that believe they are working on something important and worthwhile will devote the time and energy necessary to get the job done. However, teams that believe their work is not important or goes unnoticed will stop performing. Teams judge the value of what they are doing by the attention it receives. The more attention or feedback team members receive, the more important they perceive their work to be.

Warning Signs

Teams suffering from little or no feedback show some of the following behaviors:

- Team performance is inconsistent. It may be high one week and low the next.
- The team leader or team facilitator may notice a slow but steady decline in both performance and effort.
- Team members are no longer willing to sacrifice to accomplish goals, for example, to work overtime or take on additional assignments.
- Team members begin to demonstrate disruptive or negative attention-getting behaviors. For example, they may argue among themselves or with other teams, begin making errors, or become withdrawn or aloof.

Corrective Action

The most appropriate action to deal with this problem is to start a systematic and sustainable feedback process. The team leader or team facilitator may meet with the team to identify when and how team members would like to receive feedback. If possible, the team's work should be redesigned so that team members can get direct feedback from customers. Another benefit of work redesign is that feedback mechanisms can be incorporated in the work so that performance is immediately discernible to the employee doing the work.

It also is important to develop a system for reporting team progress on goals to the organization and for the organization to provide feedback to the team. Feedback from the organization should occur at least quarterly.

No Team Leader

The team leader's job is to direct and redirect the team's attention to performance expectations. He or she emphasizes team goals and helps team members organize to accomplish them. The team leader also ensures that members understand their role and have the resources and information to fulfill their function.

When a team either loses a leader or has no leader designated, it is at a disadvantage. Attention to goals starts to disintegrate, and team members lose their dedication and commitment. The team becomes unfocused and inefficient, and begins to wander from agreed-to standards.

Some teams will try to persuade management that they do not need a leader. They are convinced that a democracy with no designated leader will work well for them, and are reluctant to designate one of their members to take on a position that will distinguish him or her from the rest of the team. Members of these teams tend to be more concerned with relationships within the team than with systems and methods for getting work done. No matter how hard the team tries to work without a leader, it cannot succeed and eventually will flounder.

Warning Signs

Following are warning signs that a team without a leader is beginning to fail:

- There are frequent and unproductive discussions within the team about what work needs to be done and whose job it is.
- Team members begin to disenfranchise themselves from the team, spending work time with people from other teams or requesting transfers off the team.
- The team is missing deadlines, not completing reports, or meeting without agendas.

The team without a leader is missing someone in the oversight role. It no longer has a central individual whose responsibility is to pull all the pieces together to ensure that work is done according to schedule and to established standards and procedures.

Corrective Action

The action to be taken in this situation is simple. Management needs to designate and train a team leader.

Management Refusal to Let the Team Be Self-Managed

Once the team has been developed and trained and knows its functions and performance expectations, management needs to let the team do its work. Too often, because self-management is such a new concept to managers, they fail to relinquish their control over and involvement in the team's daily work and decision making. The result is that team members feel angry, confused, and manipulated.

Warning Signs

One clear indication of a team response to management interference may be found in the looks of anger and frustration that team members show when management is present in their work area. Another indication is that of the team's failure to take initiative. Team members may shift from being highly motivated about their work to being lackadaisical. They may continue to refer problems and questions to management. In short, they do not display signs of self-management.

Corrective Action

The most appropriate corrective action to take in this case is to clearly reinforce management's new role as coach or guide, rather than as decision maker and problem solver. If managers are appealed to for answers, they need to help team members arrive at the answers themselves by asking questions and referring team members to the tools at their disposal to obtain the information they need.

• Conclusion

Teams are unsuccessful for a number of reasons. Some fail because one or more of their members want them to fail and try to sabotage them from within. Others fail because team members were insufficiently trained or not given sufficient time to complete their management functions. Still others fail because other demands within their work environment take priority. For example, members of these teams can lose touch because meetings had to be postponed to care for patients or complete other assigned tasks.

Management plays a major role in team success. Teams may become successful because of appropriate management actions and support—and unsuccessful without them. Managers can create a situation in which failure will occur if they do not provide the team with challenging goals and expectations, do not give feedback to the team, or fail to designate a team leader. Additionally, management can cause team failure by not letting the team be self-managed.

Teams exhibit early warning signs of problems. An alert team facilitator can identify the warning signs and help the team, organization, or management implement action to correct a problem before it becomes too disruptive. The team facilitator's role is critical in this regard. Team members often are too close to what is going on within their team to be able to recognize symptoms of problems, and managers usually are too far removed from the team to detect subtle changes in team behavior. Thus, the team facilitators are the critical link between management expectations and team performance.

References

1. Telephone interview with Loretta Klassen, vice president of patient care, Hartford Memorial Hospital, Hartford, WI, Jan. 12, 1994.
2. Telephone interview with William B. Newkirk, coordinator of education and development, Alliant Health System, Louisville, KY, Aug. 13, 1993.
3. Telephone interview with Loretta Klassen.

Chapter 18

Team Improvement Strategies

When organizations choose self-management as a philosophy and set up a team structure to implement that philosophy, they also must make the commitment to help their teams succeed. Although, as mentioned in chapter 4, teams go through stages in which their performance fluctuates, all good teams possess certain basic characteristics. To help their teams succeed and improve, organizations must ensure that the teams understand these basic characteristics, have the support they need to incorporate these characteristics in their systems, and have access to assessment tools that will enable them to become even better teams.

When a team is performing well, the temptation is to leave it alone and hope that it will maintain its "good" performance level on its own. However, this strategy can set the team up for eventual failure. Teams need to be encouraged and even required to strive for continuous improvement. They need to work on increasing their knowledge and improving both individual and team performance. Without persistent emphasis on performance and improvement, good teams will not only not get better, they will start to decline.

This chapter describes the characteristics of good teams and some strategies for team improvement. It also provides tools that teams and team members can use to assess their current performance and set goals for improvement.

• Characteristics of Good Teams

Good teams possess certain characteristics that provide the foundation for success and growth. These are:

- Clear, valuable, and challenging goals
- Clear roles

- Shared leadership
- Support and feedback
- Formal systems
- Respect for team member differences
- Authority to make change

Following are descriptions of each of these characteristics and an explanation of why each is essential to self-managed work teams.

Clear, Valuable, and Challenging Goals

Teams exist to accomplish the work of the organization. Key to their success is development of a goal system. Goals help teams define what they need to accomplish, when they need to accomplish it, and how they fit in with the overall direction of the organization. In short, a goal system provides teams with a focus. Teams that do well believe their goals are important and understand the value of their goals to the organization.

If the team has information about the organization's needs, strategic plan, and customer expectations, it can establish goals that are valuable and worthwhile. Every team member needs to be involved in developing the team's goals. And once goals are developed, every team member needs to be committed to them and willing to devote time and energy to accomplishing them.

Goals need to be clear and specific so that team members have no question about what is expected of them. In addition, goals should be challenging. A team will lose energy and its commitment to performance if it either is given or takes on goals that will not stretch the minds and skills of its members.

Finally, the team must have goals that it can accomplish. If a team commits to a goal but has neither the resources nor the authority to obtain the resources to accomplish it, the goal is meaningless. The goal is likewise meaningless if the team commits to it but has no authority to make the changes necessary to accomplish it. When for reasons beyond its control the team is unable to accomplish a goal, team members become demoralized, discouraged, and lose their will to succeed.

When management approves goals for the team, it needs to evaluate each goal using certain basic criteria. These criteria include:

- Does the goal fit with the organization's overall strategic direction?
- Is the goal important to the organization?
- Does the goal fit with this team's role within the organization?
- Will the organization support the team's goal by providing the resources necessary to accomplish it?
- Will the goal challenge the knowledge, skill, and creativity of the team?
- Does the team have authority to make changes to accomplish the goal?

If the team's goals do not meet these criteria, the team's direction is wrong and it may end up doing the wrong thing in the right way, which is neither productive nor satisfying.

Clear Roles

Each team has a role in the organization and is part of the overall structure that has been established to accomplish the work of the organization. Within the team, each team member has a specific role or roles. These roles give team members the ability to accomplish their work because they define who does what. Employees who are assigned to teams have many questions about how they are supposed to function and what they are supposed to do. In general, employees on teams play a larger role than they have played before and are confused about boundaries, job duties, roles, and responsibilities.

Role clarification gives team members needed guidance and instruction. It helps them understand the expectations their coworkers have of them and helps clarify how the work of individual members fits in with that of the entire team. A useful tool in role clarification is the process flow diagram. (See figure 18-1.) The process flow diagram clearly shows who is responsible for what assignment, and identifies gaps (where work is unassigned) and overlaps (where work is duplicated). If the work of the team can be outlined with a process flow diagram, role clarification will be relatively easy to accomplish.

It is critical to team efficiency and effectiveness that each team member understand his or her assignment. Clear roles can help eliminate bickering, chaos, and confusion. They give structure to the team so that it can accomplish its work without stumbling.

Shared Leadership

Self-managed work teams depend philosophically and pragmatically on shared leadership. If the team leader or some other member of the team starts to assume an authoritarian or dictatorial role, an important part of the team's strength is lost. The team no longer has the benefit of its members' collective wisdom and experience. Moreover, it no longer has their commitment.

Whether team leadership is permanently assigned, rotated, or dispersed, it needs to be structured in a way that requires it to be shared. No one team member should be in a position of such power that he or she can take action contrary to team consensus or intimidate and coerce other team members. Decision making for the team must be a team responsibility, not an individual responsibility.

Support and Feedback

The organization has a responsibility to provide information, resources, and feedback to each team that it establishes. Often teams can become islands

Figure 18-1. Process Flow Diagram for Role Clarification

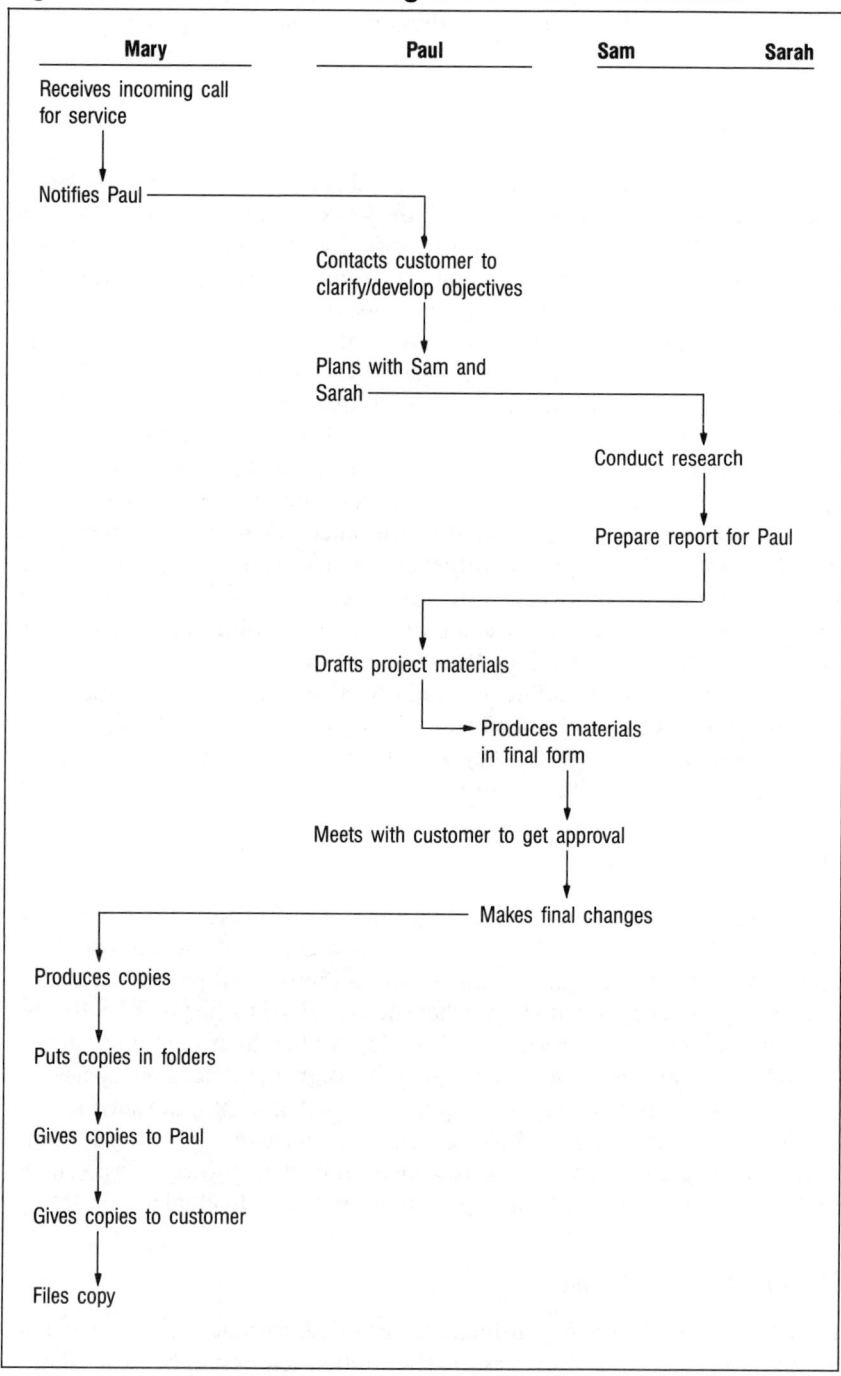

Mary	Paul	Sam	Sarah
Receives incoming call for service			
↓			
Notifies Paul ——→ Contacts customer to clarify/develop objectives		
	↓		
	Plans with Sam and Sarah ————————→ Conduct research	
		↓	
		Prepare report for Paul	
	Drafts project materials ←———————	
	↓		
	└→ Produces materials in final form		
	↓		
	Meets with customer to get approval		
	↓		
	Makes final changes ←———		
Produces copies ←—————————————————			
↓			
Puts copies in folders			
↓			
Gives copies to Paul			
↓			
Gives copies to customer			
↓			
Files copy			

without access to the rest of the organization. To remain part of the picture, they need to be informed of what is currently happening in the organization and what is being planned for the future. They also need to know whether their actions and activities are meeting the organization's requirements for timeliness, quality, quantity, and cost. With regular information, they will be able to adjust their priorities and practices to better meet the organization's needs.

Teams also need information from their customers. They need to know their customers' performance requirements and quality expectations. They also need to know what their customers' goals for the future are so that they can adapt and change their services to meet those future needs.

Additionally, teams need support and feedback from within their own ranks. They must be able to count on member loyalty and commitment. Teams that are cohesive will be more creative, take more risks, and experience more dramatic improvements in performance. Problems within the team will be more easily addressed and performance levels will improve. When team members support the team, they feel free to bring problems to the team, enabling solutions to be implemented before grudges and animosity develop.

Formal Systems

The best teams establish formal systems for dealing with decision making, problem solving, communication, conflict resolution, record keeping, and reporting. Although the necessity of formal systems might not seem as obvious for small teams, once a problem occurs, or something that should have been communicated was not, the need becomes clear. Little time is needed to establish formal team systems and they are used on a daily basis. They help improve team functioning, eliminate ambiguity, and improve efficiency.

Respect for Team Member Differences

Team members rarely think alike or have the same values, backgrounds, education, and experiences. In a sense, team member differences are healthy. For example, teams whose members share characteristics that are too similar will have difficulty achieving high levels of creativity or reaching the best alternative solutions to complex problems. However, team member differences frequently can lead to conflict that will prevent a team from moving forward. The teams that are most effective have learned how to value, work with, and balance member differences so that the team and organization benefit from the energy they create.

Authority to Make Changes

Authority to act and implement change is critical to the success of high-performance teams. Teams that have to propose, wait for approvals, modify recommendations, resubmit, and wait again will move slowly, carefully, and ineffectively forward. Team members will feel neither control over outcomes nor responsibility for them. The sense of ownership that gives self-managed work teams the edge over other team structures will be missing. Team members will feel that they are doing other people's work and achieving other people's results.

• Team Improvement

To make a good team better requires time, interest, commitment, and the willingness to invest in assessment, development, and recognition. Good teams can become complacent. Team members can become bored, disruptive, and eventually create a situation in which performance suffers. For teams to do well, and continue to do well, they must be constantly challenged.

Many teams are so busy doing their work, and many organizations are so committed to seeing that the work is done, they fail to recognize the value of reflection and evaluation. No team is perfect. Every team needs time and permission to work on its own improvement.

The easiest way to begin an improvement effort is to perform an assessment. Assessment tools are useful in helping teams and team members identify areas for improvement. Assessments can stimulate discussion and overcome inertia.

In effect, the complete assessment is a four-stage process. The stages include:

1. Team assessment
2. Self-assessment
3. Improvement goals
4. Recognition of accomplishments

(In addition to the team assessment and self-assessment, the team could seek evaluation from its customers, facilitator, and managers.)

Team Assessment

The team assessment enables teams to evaluate their performance in various areas by assigning points to statements grouped into the following sections: goals, communication, working together, leadership, and meetings. (See figure 18-2.) The assessment should be administered to the entire team at once. Each section can be scored separately so that the team can identify the section that needs the most improvement. (See figure 18-3, p. 227.) Then each question within that section can be reviewed to determine consensus on specific areas to target for improvement.

Figure 18-2. Team Assessment

This assessment was developed to help teams identify areas for improvement. Complete the assessment by rating each item according to the legend below. After completing the entire assessment, total your score, section by section, and fill in the answers on the separate score sheet (see figure 18-3). Identify the section with the greatest opportunity for improvement. Focus on the problem areas in that section first, before beginning improvements in other sections.

Legend: 5 = Almost always   2 = Occasionally
         4 = Frequently   1 = Almost never
         3 = Sometimes   NA = Not applicable

Goals (40 possible points)

_____ 1. Our goals are in writing.
_____ 2. Our goals are clear and specific.
_____ 3. Our work assignments are in writing.
_____ 4. Our roles are clear.
_____ 5. We assign time frames for accomplishing goals.
_____ 6. Our goals support the strategic direction of the organization.
_____ 7. We follow up to ensure that goals are accomplished.
_____ 8. We recognize our accomplishments and celebrate them.

_____ Total

Communication (50 possible points)

_____ 1. We are comfortable asking for what we want from others.
_____ 2. We are polite, courteous, and friendly to each other.
_____ 3. We communicate effectively during stressful situations.
_____ 4. We confront issues.
_____ 5. We are specific and work focused, not personal, when we express our needs.
_____ 6. We initiate communication to solve problems.
_____ 7. There is an environment of openness and trust.
_____ 8. We listen and try to understand the other person's point of view.
_____ 9. We do not engage in gossip.
_____ 10. We respect confidentiality.

_____ Total

Working Together (60 possible points)

_____ 1. We value differences on the team.
_____ 2. We maintain each other's self-esteem.
_____ 3. We demonstrate sensitivity to each other's feelings, problems, and needs.
_____ 4. We use a good problem-solving method.
_____ 5. We use a good decision-making method.
_____ 6. We have the necessary skills to function effectively.
_____ 7. Training is readily available.
_____ 8. We evaluate our effectiveness regularly.
_____ 9. We make improvements in the way we function.
_____ 10. We welcome new employees to our team.
_____ 11. We have a good orientation process.
_____ 12. We have the information we need to be effective.

_____ Total

(Continued on next page)

Figure 18-2. (Continued)

Leadership (60 possible points)

_____ 1. We have a clear vision of where we are going.
_____ 2. We each share the responsibilities of leadership.
_____ 3. Our leader is visible and available.
_____ 4. Coaching is effective.
_____ 5. Our leader expresses enthusiasm and commitment.
_____ 6. Our leader encourages everyone's participation.
_____ 7. Our leader invites feedback on his or her performance.
_____ 8. Our leader provides specific feedback on our work.
_____ 9. Our leader acts as a role model for the team.
_____ 10. Our leader is committed to customer satisfaction.
_____ 11. Our leader models a commitment to quality.
_____ 12. Our leader involves us with other teams when our work will affect theirs.
_____ Total

Meetings (45 possible points)

_____ 1. Our meetings start on time.
_____ 2. We have an agenda.
_____ 3. We accomplish our purpose before we adjourn.
_____ 4. We come to meetings prepared.
_____ 5. We avoid unrelated discussion.
_____ 6. Everyone participates in our meetings.
_____ 7. We document our meetings.
_____ 8. We have regular, informative meetings.
_____ 9. We end our meetings on time.
_____ Total

Self-Assessment

The self-assessment is divided into the same sections as the team assessment and can be used as a follow-up to evaluate individual team member performance. (See figure 18-4, p. 228.) Individuals use it to assess the degree to which they are contributing to the problem identified in the team assessment. Once the assessment has been completed, it is scored the same way as the team assessment. (See figure 18-5, p. 230.) The self-assessment also can be used as a self-evaluation during performance review or any time team members want to evaluate their performance.

Improvement Goals

Once the team has completed the team assessment and self-assessments, the areas identified for improvement need to be translated into improvement goals. These improvement goals must then be managed just as any other goals are, with action plans, task assignments, and completion deadlines.

Figure 18-3. Team Assessment Score Sheet

Instructions: Total your score for each section on the team assessment and transfer those numbers to this score sheet. Figure the percentage for each section. Any section below 50 percent is in strong need of improvement. A rating of 80 percent or above is very positive. (A 3 or less for any individual question indicates an area for improvement.)

Goals

Total: _____
Possible: __40__
Percent: _____ (Divide total by possible; multiply by 100.)

Communication

Total: _____
Possible: __50__
Percent: _____ (Divide total by possible; multiply by 100.)

Working Together

Total: _____
Possible: __60__
Percent: _____ (Divide total by possible; multiply by 100.)

Leadership

Total: _____
Possible: __60__
Percent: _____ (Divide total by possible; multiply by 100.)

Meetings

Total: _____
Possible: __45__
Percent: _____ (Divide total by possible; multiply by 100.)

Grand Total (Add totals from all sections.)

Grand Total: _____
Possible: __255__
Percent: _____ (Divide total by possible; multiply by 100.)

Figure 18-4. Self-Assessment

This assessment was developed to help team members identify areas for improvement. Complete the assessment by rating each item according to the legend below. After completing the entire assessment, total your score, section by section, and fill in the answers on the separate score sheet (see figure 18-5). Identify the section with the greatest opportunity for improvement. Focus on the problem areas in that section first, before beginning improvements in other sections.

Legend: 5 = Almost always   2 = Occasionally
           4 = Frequently   1 = Almost never
           3 = Sometimes   NA = Not applicable

Goals (30 possible points)

As a team member, how often do I:
- _____ 1. Ask questions to clarify goals
- _____ 2. Ask questions to clarify roles
- _____ 3. Accomplish my work within established time frames
- _____ 4. Volunteer to help others accomplish their work
- _____ 5. Follow up to make sure my goals are accomplished
- _____ 6. Take initiative to create a team celebration event

_____ Total

Communication (45 possible points)

As a team member, how often do I:
- _____ 1. Ask for help
- _____ 2. Behave in a polite, courteous, and friendly manner
- _____ 3. Communicate honestly and sincerely
- _____ 4. Listen and try to understand the other person's point of view
- _____ 5. Confront issues
- _____ 6. Admit my own mistakes
- _____ 7. Provide specific feedback to my coworkers on the team
- _____ 8. Demonstrate trust and openness in my communications
- _____ 9. Refuse to talk about a team member who is not present

_____ Total

Working Together (60 possible points)

As a team member, how often do I:
- _____ 1. Value differences that exist among my team members
- _____ 2. Maintain the self-esteem of my team members
- _____ 3. Demonstrate sensitivity to team member feelings, problems, and needs
- _____ 4. Use the team problem-solving model
- _____ 5. Devote time and energy to increasing my knowledge and skills
- _____ 6. Project a positive attitude about the team
- _____ 7. Offer suggestions and ideas
- _____ 8. Make improvements in the way I work
- _____ 9. Identify opportunities for team performance improvement
- _____ 10. Make new team members feel comfortable, valued, and part of the team
- _____ 11. Share my knowledge and skill with my team
- _____ 12. Share information with my team

_____ Total

Figure 18-4. (Continued)

Leadership (55 possible points)

As a team member, how often do I:
- _____ 1. Ask questions to clarify the team vision
- _____ 2. Give feedback to the team leader on his or her own performance
- _____ 3. Give feedback to other team members on their performance
- _____ 4. Encourage input from quiet team members
- _____ 5. Make sure that some team members do not dominate the team
- _____ 6. Make sure that the whole team is involved in decisions
- _____ 7. Take responsibility for encouraging team members
- _____ 8. Act as a role model for the team
- _____ 9. Make sure customer needs are addressed
- _____ 10. Involve others outside the team in areas that will affect them
- _____ 11. Focus on quality

_____ Total

Meetings (30 possible points)

As a team member, how often do I:
- _____ 1. Arrive at meetings on time
- _____ 2. Come to meetings prepared
- _____ 3. Stick to the agenda
- _____ 4. Avoid unrelated discussion
- _____ 5. Avoid side conversations
- _____ 6. Offer input, ideas, and information

_____ Total

In health care organizations, planning and goal setting are undeveloped skill areas at the employee level. When employees form teams, they rarely have knowledge or skill in these areas.

When a team completes its assessment, it is likely that it will identify making "goals clear and specific" as an opportunity for improvement. This will also be an area for individual development. See table 18-1 for sample improvement goals.

Recognition of Accomplishments

Once the team has achieved its improvement goals, team members should take time to celebrate their accomplishment. Whether the goal involved changes to be made by individuals or the team as a whole, the team is affected by the efforts and changes and will benefit from them. Taking time to celebrate helps build team morale and team spirit. It also can make a work situation fun and rewarding.

In most health care organizations, team celebrations involve food. Whether the team plans to go out together or have a pizza party, cookout, or dessert at work, employees enjoy the lightened atmosphere of fun that celebrations bring. Celebrations are a time to give credit for a job well done

Figure 18-5. Self-Assessment Score Sheet

Instructions: Total your score for each section of the self-assessment and transfer those totals to this score sheet. Figure the percentage for each section. Any section below 50 percent is in strong need of improvement. A rating of 80 percent or above is very positive. (A 3 or less for any individual item indicates an area for improvement.)

Goals

Total: _____

Possible: __30__

Percent: _____ (Divide total by possible; multiply by 100.)

Communication

Total: _____

Possible: __45__

Percent: _____ (Divide total by possible; multiply by 100.)

Working Together

Total: _____

Possible: __60__

Percent: _____ (Divide total by possible; multiply by 100.)

Leadership

Total: _____

Possible: __55__

Percent: _____ (Divide total by possible; multiply by 100.)

Meetings

Total: _____

Possible: __30__

Percent: _____ (Divide total by possible; multiply by 100.)

Grand Total (Add totals from all sections.)

Grand Total: _____

Possible: __220__

Percent: _____ (Divide total by possible; multiply by 100.)

Table 18-1. Sample of Improvement Goals

What	Who	When
1. Obtain training on goal writing and planning.	Entire team	May
2. Write clear specific goals with deadlines for the next quarter.	Entire team	May
3. Assess the quality of the goals and revise as necessary.	Entire team and facilitator	June
4. Develop an implementation plan for each goal.	As assigned	June
5. Implement the plans for July, August, and September.	As assigned	July
6. Report on goal progress and barriers.	As assigned	At weekly meetings
7. Evaluate goal clarity and follow-up.	Entire team	October
8. Reflect on new knowledge and skill.	Entire team	October

and to stop for a moment and enjoy the feeling of success. Teams can invite management-level people to their celebrations, their facilitators or others who are a part of the larger health care team.

• Conclusion

Good teams possess seven basic characteristics: clear, valuable, and challenging goals; clear roles; shared leadership; support and feedback; formal systems; respect for team member differences; and authority to act. These characteristics need to be incorporated into all team structures so that teams have built-in tools they can use to evaluate performance.

To make a good team better requires an investment of time and the opportunity for development. Good teams need access to team and self-evaluation tools, as well as the organization's permission and support to spend time on assessment and improvement activities. Team improvement requires the same level of commitment and structure found in any goal accomplishment strategy. Once a team has achieved its improvement goal or goals, it should give itself time to celebrate. Celebrations help improve team morale and build team spirit.

If left on their own, even good teams can lose momentum. They need attention from the organization and they need to be continually challenged to grow and develop for themselves and for the organization they serve.

Additional Books of Interest

The Health Care Organizational Survey System
by Donald N. Lombardi, Ph.D.

Everything you need to know to

- **create and conduct an employee survey** (including a sample survey questionnaire)
- **analyze the results** (with survey analysis guides)
- **build action plans** (through sample action plans and case studies)

Catalog No. E99-088175 (must be included when ordering)
1994. 200 pages, 18 figures, 4 appendixes.
$50.00 (AHA members, $40.00)

Managing the Mosaic™: Addressing Workforce Diversity and Managing Institutional Change in Health Care
by Trisha A. Svehla and Glen C. Crosier

A pioneering guide to the management of workforce diversity in health care, *Managing the Mosaic*™ presents new techniques to help today's manager utilize fully the skills of employees from all cultural and ethnic backgrounds. The book describes management/staff development processes, recruitment and retention mechanisms, quality improvement strategies, and models for building effective survey instruments, focus groups, and training sessions to identify and address workforce diversity issues.

Catalog No. E99-088170 (must be included when ordering)
1994. 234 pages, 10 figures, 7 tables.
$47.50 (AHA members, $38.00)

**To order, call TOLL FREE
1-800-AHA-2626**